INNA

BETWEEN TWO WORLDS

Surviving Stalin's Russia and Hitler's Germany

A Memoir by Inna Grinfeldt Zimmermann

Translated from the Russian

By

Elizaveta Farafonova

ISBN – 978-0-578-29124-6 (print)
ISBN - 978-0-578-29362-2 (eBook)

Credits
Book interior design by Watercress Press
San Antonio, Texas, 2022
Original Cover by Watercress Press

Published by Epsilon Books, 2022

Printed in the United States of America by Ingram Spark and distributed by Ingram.

Dedication

Inna with Parents – Circa 1930

"Dedicated with love to all Russian people living in foreign lands who have lost their homeland and heritage, old and new emigrants alike."

Inna Grinfeldt Zimmermann

Contents

Introduction - You Can Never Go Home Again....1

Chapter 1 – A Day to Remember....3

Chapter 2 – Feast to Famine....15

Chapter 3 – You Dare Not Lie!....27

Chapter 4 – Light in the Black Market....31

Chapter 5 – The Shrouded Wagon and the Samovar....35

Chapter 6 – Unexpected Guests....44

Chapter 7 – Cured and Uncured....49

Chapter 8 – Cleaned Out....54

Chapter 9 – Vadim Moralevski Comes Calling....59

Chapter 10 – Ride of the Black Horse....62

Chapter 11 – Departure....72

Chapter 12 – Anapa....81

Chapter 13 – My Cousins....91

Chapter 14 – My First Secret....99

Chapter 15 – Renunciation and Indoctrination....107

Chapter 16 – Spring Returns....117

Chapter 17 – How I Became Independent....124

Chapter 18 – My Old-New Home....130

Chapter 19 – The Invisible Bridge....140

Chapter 20 – The Prophecy of the White Dove....151

Chapter 21 – The Witches' Den....157

Chapter 22 – In the Heart of Mother Russia....162

Chapter 23 – Released 171
Chapter 24 – Catherine the Great's Castle 178
Chapter 25 – Quiet Before the Storm 185
Chapter 27 – Return to Krasnodar 198
Chapter 28 – First Contact 204
Chapter 29 - Occupation 210
Chapter 30 - Rescued 215
Chapter 31 – Into the Storm 220
Chapter 32 – In the Clutches of the Demon 226
Chapter 33 – My Only Love Sprung from My Only Hate 232
Chapter 34 – Stopover in Vienna 238
Chapter 35 - I Become a German 244
Chapter 36 – Sent Away 248
Chapter 37 – Minamama and the Visitor 255
Chapter 38 – The War Ends and a New Struggle Begins 262
Chapter 39 – Over the Final Mountain 271
Epilogue 279
Afterword 282

I'm a traitor.
A traitor to my land, a traitor to the party, and a traitor to my past.
I gave up all that I knew to be true to myself.
Because most importantly...
I'm a survivor.
This is my story...

Introduction - You Can Never Go Home Again...

What shall I do? Where shall I go? Where will I find my place under the sun? Who will embrace and comfort me in this difficult moment? With whom shall I share my sadness and joy?

I am so lonely, and the world is so vast!

Everywhere people scurry about like ants on an anthill. Everywhere I meet sad and happy, young and old, strange faces. But none of them care about me.

My soul is tormented by longing for the past, for the lost things that can never be recovered. Several times I've tried to escape this nightmarish loneliness. I looked for a confidante and held out my hand to him, wanting to give my heart and soul for just a little of his attention.

I wanted to feel happy and loved. But it was impossible!

One day I thought I had found my salvation in the aura of this dark-eyed stranger, and I decided to give him everything I had. He willingly took my heart, but all he gave me in return was suffering. Having been brought up in a different way of life, he did not understand my aspirations. And having fallen on hard times following the war, he could not continue to love me, leaving a deep trace of unfulfilled hopes in my soul.

Longing dragged me back to the place, my Russian Motherland, where my soul was first formed in poverty and the harsh struggle for life. Where, for the first time, I learned what tears and sorrow were and tasted the sweetness of young love.

How far my fate has taken me from you, my beloved Motherland! You, a wide and distant Soviet nation, covered with the curses of your thousands of children thrown overboard. You, soaked in the sweat, blood, and tears of millions. You, glorified in song by your fearless patriots and self-sacrificing heroes. You, dear Russian land!

Why do you torment my soul? Why have you shut the door to so many thousands of your children, who dare not fathom that their path may again be directed home to you?

How I wish I could see my relatives and acquaintances again, find my mother, and cling to her bosom! They all remained behind, in our homeland.

But I carry a "heavy guilt" on my shoulders, and no one from my homeland can or will extend an open hand or vindicate me.

Am I really to blame? Or is it fate alone? It was not of my own free will that she, my Motherland, seized me and threw me into the boiling abyss of “wickedness.” She spared no one and tried to destroy me as well. But I, grasping at everything that rushed past, always made it to the surface again.

I won this nightmarish struggle, I am alive! Behind me lies a harsh youth, and ahead a foggy uncertainty!

And only the memories of the past and the awareness of the righteousness of the struggle I lived through give me the strength to live and fight on.

These memories and this awareness I now share with you...

Chapter 1 – A Day to Remember

The Soviet Union was a new land with a bright future – so we were told. It was October 1930. Just a decade prior, not long before my birth, the 1917 Revolution and five-year civil war that followed had wiped away the last Czar and centuries of imperial rule and ushered in Lenin and the creeping totalitarianism of Stalin. This was the land, caught between past and present, in which I came of age.

I was 8 years old at the time, and aside from the hushed whispers of my parents and stoic grandmother, "Babushka" Nadieshda, I had no clue that my family, outwardly supportive of Communism, feared this new Russian empire, and that a dark and foreboding shadow of suspicion hung over us all.

My family had been displaced by the Soviet Revolution, and for a time lived in poverty and had to conceal their identity and noble lineage, as they had supported the Czar and sympathized with the anti-Communist White Russian Army during the civil war. Despite that, through my father's steadfast diligence in attaining his professorship, we now enjoyed a modest middle-class existence, and even had the means to hire a maid.

My father, Vladimir Grinfeldt, was the son of the illustrious Cossack General Alexander Grinfeldt, who died fighting the Germans for Czar and Empire in the First World War, just one year before Russia's capitulation and descent into chaos. Having lost his own father so early in life, and having his world turned upside-down by the ensuing tumult, my father had grown into a cautious, unassuming intellectual – a mathematics professor at the local university who cared very much for his students - but kept largely to himself. A handsome man of medium height and slight, almost frail stature, his sparkling dark eyes betrayed a hidden anxiety. Yet when he looked at me, his only child, they were filled with love.

My paternal grandmother, Nadieshda, descended from the once-proud Sankovski family. Her uncle, Peter Sankovski, had long been mayor of Poltava, a proud Ukrainian town in the heart of Cossack-country. Now gray and lacking its former luster, the downtown was still adorned with museums, statues, parks and university buildings. Aside from a few faded photos, and stories of Peter the Great's great victory over the Swedes at a nearby battlefield two centuries before, the past before 1917 was to be forgotten and shunned. As I was to find out later, for good reason.

Babushka Nadya, once among the most eligible young women of Poltava, was, like the city she grew up in, a weathered and worn time capsule, with many secrets, tragedies and treasures locked away in the depths of her proud old soul. The wartime death of her beloved husband Alexander, coupled with the family's misfortunes following the Soviet Revolution, shattered her life in two successive blows. Yet somehow, she lived on, and doted on me to no end.

But the past was the past, and today was a new day: It was my mother Zinaida's birthday to be precise. In contrast to my father, with his quiet demeanor, she was bold and outgoing. Her dark, intense, almond-shaped eyes shone with passion and emotion. Unlike my father's family, which was weighed-down by the unseen burden of the past, her life was rooted firmly in the present and she beamed with vitality. Her long dark locks of hair, supple skin and dainty nose and mouth had made her the object of my father's attention – and that of many others as well.

Also, unlike my father, whose family *(with their highly un-Russian "Grinfeldt" surname)* traced their roots back to a mythical Nordic-Germanic ancestor named "Karl" - Mother was a proud Ukrainian from the large Pigurenko family, and a nearby village still bore the family name. Her family lineage reflected the centuries of Greek, Armenian and Turkish influence on the Black Sea region, from which they originally hailed – as did her dark, enchanting Mediterranean features.

As the only child of the house, I was certainly not neglected, but I wasn't coddled, either. My parents were loving and firm at once. Although I did not take advantage of my situation, I also did not shy away from reveling at being the apple of my parents' eye.

That morning, I awoke to "Inna, hurry and get up!" My father stood next to my bed, with a bright smile on his face. The October sun shone mildly through the window, as if wishing to conjure summer one final time.

I rubbed my eyes, hopped out of bed, and began to put on the dress that our family maid, Motya, had set out for me. "We need to look our best today. Your great-aunt and uncle are coming soon," Motya said, peeking in through the door.

Once I had finished getting ready, my father took me by the hand and led me outside. Autumn had settled gently over our garden, which still sported its emerald green lawn covered in golden leaves and bright fall flowers. The air was crisp and the morning dew dampened the ground. The garden beds were all neat and well-cared for, and in one, chrysanthemums were in full bloom. "Look daddy! Mama's favorites...let's take these." My father carefully cut several blossoms, and soon I was holding mother's birthday bouquet.

I ran into the house bursting with joy, and tiptoed through the hall to my parent's bedroom, quietly opening the door. Mama sat at her dressing table, the mirror reflecting her face and large, expressive eyes, which shone with happiness. The room looked particularly festive that day, as everywhere on the mahogany side-tables, window-sills, and even on the floor, father had placed vases with the roses, lilies and cloves he knew she loved. I slipped into the room unnoticed and tenderly kissed her hand good morning.

Joyfully she placed me on her lap and caressed my hair. "Up so early to surprise your mother, my love?"

"Yes, mommy. Happy birthday!" I said in as festive a voice as I could muster, holding out the flowers. "Oh, what beautiful chrysanthemums!" she replied with delight. "Go and have Motya put them in a vase on the piano in the study." I had no desire to leave her side, and pressed myself close to her chest. "You're so beautiful today, mommy!"

Mother laughed, "Ah, what are you saying..." But she was, without question, a very beautiful woman, and everyone in our home loved and adored her. Alone Babushka Nadya, who now entered the room, did not think well of mother's always bubbly, jovial spirit. "The time for parties and celebrations is over and done with," she would often say to father. "Never forget that we live in a very different Russia today and be careful what you say and do."

Father would try to soothe Babushka, telling her: "Only God knows what the future holds, but as long as I still can, I want to make my wife happy." Babushka would leave these conversations with a look of consternation and retreat to her nook, quietly sighing to herself as she looked out the window, trying to make sense of it all. As she left my mother's room that special day, I followed her out and began, with my childish intuition, to feel the gloom Babushka could not conceal.

"Babushka, why are you so sad on mama's birthday?" I asked as we entered her small quarters.

"Oh!" She replied, feeling compelled to smile, "It's not so bad, my dear, now go outside and play."

As I closed the door behind me, I heard her sigh her all too familiar sigh, and whisper cryptically under her breath:

"This oppression will never end...we will never escape. How many people have these brutes murdered already...?"

I poked my head back through the door and asked, "Babushka, what are brutes? Are those the bad boys who steal the birds' nests after they've spent so much time building them?"

"Yes, yes, sweetheart." she answered with a reassuring voice, wiping a tear from her eye. "But go now...and don't think of it again." I walked slowly out to the garden. It must not be very nice to be old, I thought. I wondered why Babushka couldn't just be happy like mother.

The time passed slowly that morning as we waited for the guests to arrive. None of the adults paid me much attention. Even Motya, who was normally busy fretting over me, had disappeared amidst the bustling activity.

My Great Uncle Nika and Aunt Masha arrived by train from Kharkov mid-morning and I greeted them at the front door. Nikolai Grinfeldt was the younger brother of my grandfather, General Alexander, and had attended the Poltava military academy like his older brother before him. His career was no less outstanding, as he had been decorated for bravery during both the 1905 War with Japan and the First World War and wounded twice in combat before joining the anti-communist resistance in Ukraine as a Colonel during the Civil War. Of course, I knew none of that, and that is how my family wanted things.

I didn't know it at the time, but our family's martial past was no longer a mark of honor, but a potential death sentence. Somehow, Nika had survived the First World War, revolution and civil war and managed to conceal his past for over a decade. He even had a modest job as a local railroad inspector. His wife Masha had lost her first husband, though we never knew what had happened to him, and never spoke of it. They were married in their 50s and seemed always happy together.

That day the adults had a lot to discuss and seemed to be perturbed by something. I overheard Uncle Nika say with concern in his voice: "Yes indeed, they could still take us all away..."

I didn't understand what this "take us all away..." meant.

"Listen, we don't need to live in fear," My father said reassuringly. "Nobody here really knows our past that well, and I've worked hard over the last few years to gain tenure and my students all appreciate me. I even know the local chief of police and invited him to join us today." The room went silent for a moment.

With consternation in his voice, Uncle Nika replied with a Russian saying: "If you want to walk in the dark forest, you've got to be able to howl with the wolves."

I asked my Grandmother if he meant the wolf from Little Red Riding Hood.

"Please!" Babushka interrupted "Be careful what you say. Inna doesn't need to hear this."

Towards evening, Babushka called me into her small room. She had dressed up and was wearing a black velvet dress embroidered with silk trim. Her gray hair was combed back in waves. On her ring finger was a large, red stone that she only wore on very special occasions. She looked me over carefully, combed my long, thick hair and straightened my bow. "We are going to go out to greet all our guests" she said. "Don't forget to do as your told, you're a big girl now." We went together to the study, all decorated for the party. By now the room was filled with people, and all rose to greet Babushka and shook my hand. I smiled and curtsied for each guest.

"What a pretty, well-behaved young lass." said one of the ladies quietly. "She seems too well-bred for the times we're living in..."

"Yes – that isn't valued these days!" came a reply. I heard the comments about good behavior not being valued but didn't find them off-putting in the least. Instead, I relished being the center of attention with a sort of childish pride.

Full of joy, I approached my mother, who, with her beautiful ivory-colored silk dress and a beautiful long necklace of pink pearls, looked just as I imagined a beautiful lady from out of a fairy tale. Many of the guests knew my mother possessed a warm and melodic voice. Soon they were saying, "Zinaida Yosifovna! Sing something for us!"

She sat down at the piano with a smile and began to sing:

"They faded long ago
The Chrysanthemums in the garden
But love yet lives
In my heart aching...
But love still lives
In my heart aching"

The ladies applauded my mother's soulful rendition, and the gentleman kissed her hand. My father stood next to her beaming proudly and looked out across the room warmly at our guests.

"And now the little lady should sing something!" said my Aunt Masha, and everyone seconded her request. At first, I anxiously began to accompany mother in song, but soon forgot my nerves, and was able to sing the final verses clearly and concisely.

"Bravo, she will be a great performer one day!" came the praise from my Uncle Nika.

"If God wills it," My mother added.

With that, Babushka arose from her chair, warmly addressing the guests: "May I bid you all to please take your seats for dinner." Each gentleman offered a lady his arm.

My Uncle jokingly offered me his arm, "Little Lady, would you like to be my date?" "But of course, dear Sir!" I replied in earnest, taking his arm. We joined the procession of guests and made our way to the dining room, in which a large table consisting of smaller tables pushed together had been prepared.

I was to remember that table for the rest of my life. It would be the last time I would see so many beautiful decorations and dishes in my parents' house. And none in attendance could know in that hour what a storm was approaching and how quickly our lives would change.

The guests ate and drank merrily. Toasts were made accompanied by small speeches. Although I was young, I tried to hold my own in conversation with the adults.

Soon, Babushka walked sternly over to my side: "Inna, it's time for your nap." she said dryly.

I looked sorrowfully at mother.

"Let her stay a little longer." Said Uncle Nika.

My mother nodded approvingly. I was overjoyed that, for once, I didn't have to do what Babushka said. I was even able to sip some of the sweet wine, as the glasses and bottles were emptied one after the other. The guests' mood rose as jokes and laughter gave way to singing.

Someone shouted: "Up with the birthday girl!" The men sprang from their seats, and in the next moment I could see them lifting my mother on her chair high above my head and beginning to sing as they carried her along the long dining table.

"Me too, please!" I called out, delighted. No sooner had I spoken than I was lifted into the air as well. In that moment of sheer joy, there came a harsh, jarring knocking at the front door. Everyone stopped and turned towards the thumping. The smiles and jokes ceased abruptly.

I was disappointed to find myself sitting in my chair on the ground again. But in a split second, that disappointment evaporated into sheer terror. Several pistol shots rang out in the main hall. The study door was thrown open, and the petrified guests were confronted by several militia men in yellow-green uniforms who took up positions on either side of the door. A man in a neater uniform, with a pistol in his right hand, strode in with large, heavy steps and turned to my father.

"Thank you for the invitation, professor!" the chief said slowly and harshly. "It appears you've already dined quite extravagantly without me." He looked around the room, his eyes burning with hostility. Everyone was frozen, still unable to move. He turned to my mother: "And you, one of the capitalists who wear pearls, eh?!" he said with a contemptuous snarl.

And before my mother could make so much as a sound, he tore at the beautiful pearl necklace she was wearing. The pearls clattered like so many beads onto the hardwood floor and scattered everywhere. My mother, frozen by the shock, started back and fainted as the guests screamed in horror.

My father caught her as she fell, shouting "Zina, my God, my dear, are you alright?" He turned quickly to Babushka: "Mother! Water!!" Then turning to the chief, his supposed-friend, my usually meek father burst out in a rage: "Out of my house you wretch!" "Seize him!" came the reply.

In this surreal chaos, I could peripherally feel someone grab me and carry me away to my room. They deposited me hastily into my bed, half-dressed, without so much as turning on a light, and no one paid any attention to my fearful, sorrowful cries. After a few minutes, Babushka rushed into the room, cradling something in her hands.

"They're searching the house top-to-bottom." She whispered. "If they find this, we're lost! Hide this in your bed." And with that she wedged something hard and rectangular under my pillow. "Pretend to be asleep!" she pleaded. "Maybe then they'll leave your bed alone." She hurried away, leaving me alone again. Out of irresistible curiosity, I reached to see what she had left behind. From under my pillow, I clasped a small metal box with a key. I turned the key, slowly propped open the lid, and saw several blazing golden coins glowing inside. What beautiful, shiny treasure I thought. I quietly took the coins out and hid them in the pleats of my skirt. I could hear how they clinked together, almost jingling like bright little bells. When I suddenly heard heavy footsteps approaching my room, I crawled back into bed and pretended to be asleep, pressing my hand firmly over the little bulge in my skirt to conceal the coins.

The doors of my room were flung open. Out of the corner of my eye, I saw a couple of militiamen stumble in and, without so much as noticing me, begin to rifle hurriedly through my room. They threw all the books and toys from every shelf and closet and cursed loudly, as if they couldn't find what they were looking for.

With horror I could see how one of the men grabbed my favorite doll, Alice. He briefly examined her, then threw my pretty little baby, her head made of Japanese porcelain, violently to the ground. Her head shattered into countless shards and her beautiful sleepy eyes fell out and rolled around on the floor. The fear inside me now grew so intense that I could no longer remain still.

With the golden treasure still pressed against my hip, I jumped to the floor and hurried awkwardly, almost with a limp, through the open door. The men tearing my room apart either didn't notice or care to halt my escape.

"Mommy! Mommy! Where are you!" I cried loudly and hurried towards my parents' bedroom. With this, I was confronted with an additional horror: Our home was being torn apart. In every room, furniture, books, clothing and everything else had been overturned, scattered and strewn everywhere. Dishes and mirrors were shattered, and pictures torn off the walls. For a brief moment, I'm not sure how long, I stood as if fastened to the floor trying to process what was going on.

In my parents normally tidy bedroom, everything had been turned upside-down. Birthday flowers mixed with the shattered remnants of vases and perfume bottles littered the ground. Feathers from torn-up pillows and blankets still fluttered in the air. In the far corner of the room, I could see mother sitting in her dressing table chair with a hot water bottle on her head, as if in a surreal daze. Motya stood next to her.

Babushka stood at the window and looked silently out into the night. She didn't so much as turn around as I rushed into the room. Only her shoulders began to sag and shudder, as she heard my frightened voice:

"Mommy, Mommy! What's going on!?" My mother opened her eyes. In one hand, I could see her clutching a round, shiny locket with fancy engraving, which she quickly clapped-shut and shoved in a drawer. She just stared at me, momentarily unable to speak. Then she started, first quietly, then ever-louder, to sob:

"My poor, poor child! Our papa is gone! Those people took him away! What will become of us now??"

At some point, the men had left just as abruptly as they'd appeared and taken my father with them. The guests had also long-since disappeared. The fear in my heart at this unthinkable news became unbearable. My hands dropped to my side in total defeat and dismay, and I threw myself into my mother's arms. The coins that I had been holding against my hip in my skirt the entire time now fell in a clanging, clattering cascade and rolled into every corner of the room.

Babushka wheeled-around, her eyes drawn immediately to the gold scattered across the floor. For a few moments, she didn't know whether to cry-out or marvel in silence: These bright, untarnished golden rubles, stamped on the front with the head of the last Czar, Nicholas II, and on the reverse with the heraldry and symbols of Eternal Russia, seemed to her the last, unblemished remnant of an impossibly distant past where hope, honor, truth and God had once existed.

She hurried over and hugged me tightly. "Oh child, my beloved child! Did you take all of the money out of the metal case?" As I nodded yes, she also began to cry. "You're our guardian angel! Those plunderers will never find the money! We're saved!" She kissed me and then fell to her knees. "Dear God in heaven! Lord be praised a thousand times!"

Broken and exhausted, she sat in one of the few chairs which had not been tossed over. In that moment, Babushka suddenly appeared much smaller to me. Her entire strength and power, gained through a harsh life of self-discipline, seemed to have been drained from her that evening. She now appeared to simply be a tired old woman.

My mother laid me down next to herself in bed. "Sleep, my dear, please just go to sleep now, it is very late!" She said to me gently. I found some tiny semblance of warmth and peace again and pressed myself closely to her side. Exhausted by the experiences of that dark day, I feel into a restless sleep.

Chapter 2 – Feast to Famine

The days that followed brought many changes that before would have seemed unfathomable and inexplicable. The entire house was engulfed in chaos. Nobody paid me any attention. There were no meals on the table, and nobody seemed to care how I spent my day or how I was dressed. Many strange people came to our house and looked at the rooms. Others hauled away various pieces of furniture on carts, large and small.

I observed this all with a sort of childish curiosity, and even tried, at times, to speak to these random people, but most simply ignored me.

"What are you looking for?" I asked a strange lady who walked through our glass doors and poked around.

"I want to look at the room." She replied.

"What room?"

"The one that's for rent." She said.

I didn't understand what that meant.

"Just a moment, I'll call my grandmother over." And with that I disappeared into the main hallway. "Babushka, Babushka!" I called through the house, but nobody replied. After a long search, I found all three women, Babushka, mother and Motya, upstairs in the drying room, looking as if they had something to conceal. As they heard my approaching steps, they seemed terrified.

Motya whispered "It's just Inna."

"Thank God" replied Babushka. She turned and said quietly: "Did anyone see you come up here?"

"I don't think so, but there is a woman downstairs who wants to look at a room."

"Another one?" mumbled Babushka gruffly. "It seems as if these people are reveling in our misfortune."

With that, she went down the wooden ladder and to the glass doors. "What do you want here, my dear?" She asked sternly.

"I just wanted a room."

"Please, we aren't renting any rooms." Came Babushka's abrupt reply as she closed and locked the door in the woman's face.

"You'll rent it yet, you'll see, you old aristocrat!" growled the strange woman before leaving.

"Babushka, which room did that lady want?" I asked, having keenly eavesdropped on the entire scene. "One of our nice rooms, my child! Our house doesn't belong to us anymore. It used to be our house, but they've seized it."

"Seized it? What does that mean?"

"They took it away!"

"But...why did they take our house away?"

"I can't explain it to you right now, you're still too little."

With that, Babushka wanted to leave me, but I clung to her and whined: "Babushka, I'm so hungry!"

Everything that I saw and heard was at once so terrible and oppressive to me, that I didn't know exactly what was wrong, and I began to cry bitter tears. Babushka took me by the hand to the kitchen and gave me a small glass of cold milk, pressed a piece of bread into my hand and left me alone with my humble meal.

How often I had heard her say: "If only you would eat something without us having to force you, you never seem hungry. Seems like you'd be happy If we didn't call you to dinner the entire day."

But today, I thought, she was no longer pleased to see me asking for something to eat. Before I would always need to be prompted to finish my meals and try some of the well-prepared dishes. Now I couldn't find much of anything, just stale bread and milk. How times had changed, I thought to myself. Despite all that,

I contentedly finished crunching my bread. This little meal went remarkably quickly, and then I went looking for the adults again.

This time, I found them in what had once been our elegant study. They had hurriedly brought in beds, pictures, carpets and dishes and were still busily at work. Everything was arranged in a big circle, and the once elegant room now looked like a hoarder's closet.

"You are getting this cubby up here for your toys, Inna," said Babushka, pointing to a small black box high on a shelf. "Go over to your room and grab your nicest things, but don't take too much, we all need enough room here in our new space." I obeyed and went to my former room. I hesitantly looked my toys over and couldn't decide what I most wanted to keep.

Distracted by my own indecision, I started to play with my doll house, and completely forgot what Babushka had asked me to do. I soon sank completely into my childish daydreams.

And soon the day turned to evening, and Babushka called for me: "Come dear, I'll get your toys and bring them over to your cubby later."

"Oh Babushka" I complained. "I want to keep all my things. Please don't let them take my room!"

"If only I could sweetheart," she said as she led me away from that once secure little space of my childhood to our new home, which she with mother and Motya had since neatly arranged.

From then on, our former study would serve as our bedroom, dining room, kitchen and living room. The adults had gathered all the necessities together. And although the room was now tidy, it had lost every bit of the elegance that once defined it, and now seemed somehow dingy.

And that's how things were. This was our new reality! After a few days, Babushka left us and went to live with Uncle Nika and

Aunt Masha in Kharkov. Motya found a new job elsewhere. My mother and I were left to fend for ourselves in our new "home."

Our former rooms had all been rented to complete strangers. Each to an entire family. Like the others, we had to pay rent for a single room. Our home, though reduced to this solitary space, still looked quite nice when compared to the others in the house. None of the new residents had furniture as nice as what remained of ours. In some people's rooms there were just a couple of iron bed frames, an unpainted table and a few chairs or a stool. Not every family had a closet, and most hung their clothing on nails hastily driven into the wall or simply threw them haphazardly into a shoddy wooden crate.

Inna Grinfeldt and her mother, Zinaida Josefna Pigurenko Grinfeldt, taken in Poltava in 1926

Aside from these basics, each family possessed a small "Primus" kerosene stove that smoked and stank terribly. The gorgeous light carpets that once adorned the floor soon grew soiled and sooted. The pretty parquet was left to deteriorate. It was mopped over and left damp, and soon took on a dirty gray color. Our once stately house came to look gray and spooky, as if haunted by the times. As a child, I quickly adapted to the new conditions. My mother, by contrast, suffered terribly through this harsh transformation, and could barely find the strength to work. I saw her time and again with tears in her eyes and felt deeply sorry for her.

I would often hug her and say, “Mommy, dear mommy, please don’t cry!”

“It’s so hard not to cry,” she replied. “The hardest part is that we don’t have your papa anymore,” she added with downcast eyes. Then my heart started to ache as well. I felt great sympathy for her and wished I could do something to cheer her up.

“Can I do something to help you mommy?” I asked gently. “I want so much to help.”

“Yes, child, go to the market and just buy the basics we need to get by.”

Soon I counted shopping, fetching water, cleaning up our room and heating the oven to my daily chores. I did everything my mother asked without talking back. My days were full and passed quickly. Now and again a short, ugly man visited us. Mother locked the doors behind him, and there always followed the same conversation:

“Good evening Zinaida Yosifovna!” He began.

“Good evening Isak Adamovich! You really can’t give me more than 50 rubles per gold coin? Isn’t that too low a price? Prices for food keep rising at the market by the hour!”

“If 50 rubles seem like too few for you, you can keep your gold coins, until they take them away!” The little man turned abruptly and started towards the doors.

Mother hurried after him: “Wait, Isak, stay! Here are the gold pieces.” She pressed a few coins into his hand and received the promised banknotes in return.

“You should be happy, that I’m exchanging these at all, it’s dangerous!” Said the little man and disappeared stealthily through the front doors.

“How lucky that you saved those coins for us!” She sobbed. “Otherwise, we’d have starved by now. But don’t tell anyone about it. Otherwise those people will come for me too, just like your poor father!"

"I'm not that stupid, mother." I answered resolutely, feeling quite grown for my nine years.

One day, however, my mother said: "Inna, I have to tell you something important." She sat on the edge of her bed and pulled me close to her.

"Listen, our money is running out. I have to find work. What do you think?"

"Work? What type of work?"

"I don't know yet myself. Maybe in an office or factory."

"And what will I do when you are gone the entire day?" "Won't you be able to do any work around our house for the other families, mommy?" I replied, as I felt a pang of fear.

"Housework is so poorly paid, we can't live from that. Let's try to figure something else out."

"We can sew and mend clothing." I suggested.

"You have to learn how to do that first Inna. Perhaps I could learn how to sew and tailor."

Mother sat still for a few more minutes in silence. She then retrieved the few remaining gold coins from the cabinet and counted them. "It may be just enough to get us through until I learn how to sew. You are right, my child, you are still too small for me to leave you alone all day."

With that my mother learned to sew and tailor. From that day forth, all of the housework fell upon my childish shoulders. It wasn't easy, because in addition to these daily chores, I was still attending school and being taught by mother to play piano. There was certainly no time for me to play with the other children in the house. Yet, despite this difficult life, I was still somehow able to be a child.

At night as I lay in my little bed, I would create a more beautiful world in my childish imagination. I imagined how wonderful it would be if I had a magic wand. I would return our home to its former glory, just as it had been before. How happy my poor mother would be. Maybe this is all a bad dream, I thought. Maybe when I wake up tomorrow, things will be as they once were. With that thought I would often fall asleep, but the next morning everything was just as gray as the day before.

One day, however, my mother's first customers arrived. They were very satisfied with the quality and tasteful work of a skilled tailor. Mother proudly tabulated and collected her first payment. "We are going to make it through, Inna." She assured me with renewed confidence. "And papa won't have to worry about us."

"When will daddy finally come home?" I asked with a heavy heart.

"I don't know, dear. We'll wait for him." She replied as she gave me a heartfelt hug. And in those moments, I loved her all the more.

Despite all of my mother's efforts, our lives grew more-and-more difficult. We became cogs in a giant, industrial machine that didn't tolerate private property or contentment, and forced people to work under the slogan: "He who does not work does not eat!"

Anyone who had lived more-or-less decently up to that time and owned some land, or a workshop or store, had their lives permanently turned upside-down. Collectivization began in earnest. Private property was confiscated and placed into the possession of the state. Only the poor had nothing to lose because there was nothing to take away from them. Heretofore middle and upper-class people were thrown out of their homes onto the street. The men in these families were usually imprisoned or exiled to hard labor in Siberia or the Urals. No one cared about their wives and children. Those who could, somehow adapted, while others were condemned to starvation.

Orphanages were set up for homeless children, where they were raised as obedient slaves to government ideas. In the villages, land and livestock were taken from the peasants and they were forced onto a collective farm known as a "Kholkoz," where they had to work for the state. "*The land belongs to the people!*" was written in all the newspapers. Priests were expelled, churches were closed, and atheism was preached everywhere. I remember in school learning the following poem from a newspaper:

Christ's resurrection is an invention of the pope.
In the priests we place no faith, nor for miracles do we hope.
And tempted we will never be, by the kulich bread.
But proudly we'll march with our brigade, to sow spring fields instead.
Religion has enslaved us, with its many lies.
We know, yes we know, that the kulaks want to rise.
The Bolshevik Spring will be Red without holy feasts.
The collective building of our land is abhorrent to the priests!
Our common field we'll sow and till,
To our wrathful enemies' spite!
So that blossom with a godless will,
Our collective sowing might!

But what did all this godless collectivization lead to? Ordered onto a collective farm, a peasant who had one or two cows would slaughter them and sell the meat at the market. They logically reasoned, "Why should I give my cow to the collective farm for nothing? I'd rather slaughter it and get some money for the meat."

In the winter of 1931-32, huge quantities of corned beef appeared on the market, practically given away and sold for next-to-nothing. In the spring of 1932, however, the vast fields of Ukraine were left largely unplowed: There were not enough tractors yet, and the cattle had been slaughtered in vast numbers.

The fall and winter of 1932-33 brought with it an indescribable famine. Food disappeared from the market, and bread rations were reduced to 50 grams a day. People, having no reserves, were starving to death like flies. In addition, right in the middle of winter, there was a massive typhus epidemic, and the death rate rose even further. In almost every family someone died of typhoid fever. Orphanages were overflowing with orphans.

Many other foods could not be purchased legally - or were altogether impossible to find. Prices rose to unaffordable levels. People were rummaging through garbage pits looking for potato peels and bones. Bandits and thieves appeared everywhere, stealing everything in sight.

I can still remember it well: I went to the market every day and normally bought a liter of milk for breakfast for 5 rubles, then two small measures of barley, around 200 grams, for 8 rubles, an onion for 1 ruble and a bushel of wood for 5 rubles. I purchased lunch from an inn. This typically consisted of borscht, and a small piece of meat or some barley gruel. That cost 10 rubles. Mother worked late into the night sewing and mending clothes just to scrape together enough money for this meager fare. She looked tired and drawn and eventually became so skinny that I began to fear for her health when I looked at her.

Still, despite this mass starvation, the Soviet administrators "did not lose heart" in their efforts to squeeze every last drop of gold and silver from the populace. In our town there was, remarkably, a place where everything seemed to be available. It was an oasis of food in a starving desert. Through the windows of this store, known as a “Torgsin”, an abundance of sausage, butter and ham, bread, sweets and even fruit were on display. “GOLD AND SILVER ONLY” was written in large letters near the entrance. I remember with horror how a man, swollen with hunger, stood for hours in front of one of the shop windows and collapsed in death throes.

This remarkable store did not belong to some wealthy merchant or greedy, opportunistic capitalist. After all, no such people were left. This store belonged to the state. I often found myself standing with many other hungry children in front of those windows, dreaming that I had the gold and silver to buy the wonderful things just on the other side of the glass panes. I often dreamed I could, just once, get my hands on a big sandwich covered in butter.

“Mommy, don’t you have any more gold or silver?” I asked one day as I returned from shopping.

“No, dear, we used it up.”

Not long thereafter, I carefully examined the holy pictures hanging in the corner of our room. In the Eastern Orthodox Church, these pictures of holy figures are central to the religious life of the people who possess them and are known as “icons.”

After reflecting for some time, I asked: “Mommy, aren’t the clothes of the saints made of silver? Oh, how I’d like a piece of bread.”

I knew that for my mother the icons were sacred and feared she would fly into a rage at my impudence. Having earlier been religious as a small child, I had long since given up believing in God and the prophets and praying to them. From my first school days, I had been raised and taught to reject religion. My teacher would often tell us aspiring “Pioneers” – the new communist children’s organization:

"The wealthy invented their precious God to deceive the workers! An ignorant superstition. The Popes are nothing but abominable scoundrels who steal from the poor."

I came to believe my teacher and thought how old-fashioned my mother was to kneel and pray before the icons every evening.

I even tried to teach my mother what I'd learned, but she simply started to cry bitterly and said: "That's why everything has gotten so bad: No one believes in or fears God anymore!" From that point on, I never bothered her while she was praying. But when I pointed out the silver engraving on the icons and begged for bread mother was, to my great surprise, not furious. She quietly fetched a chair and took down the images.

She gingerly plucked the silver from the clothing of the saints, kissed them remorsefully, and hung them back in their place. "Here, go buy some bread dear." She said quietly and handed me a bit of the silver. Then she looked up at the icons and sobbed. "Our Lord God is so very poor today, because people have grown so evil!" she said. She looked at Mother Mary and the Baby Jesus and added: "Holy Mother, forgive us and forgive me!" and made the sign of the cross.

I also looked up at the icons. Mother Mary's face appeared shrouded in sorrow. And somehow, I imagined, in my minds-eye, a tear running down the cheek of the holy child. I looked over with wide eyes as another icon began to blacken and burn from the inside-out, fire spreading gradually from the heart of the saint, slowly melting the worn lacquer surface with a smokeless crimson flame that obscured his face. At once, an inexplicable wave of emotion took hold of me. I raised my hand and solemnly made a sign of the cross. With silent amazement and revulsion, the obedient, atheist Pioneer in me reviled this completely unexpected outburst of piety. I couldn't help but think how I was betraying the words of my teacher, so oft repeated: "It's all superstition. There is no God."

I looked up again at Mother Mary. Her face was calm as before. The holy child was no longer crying. The saint was serious and cold, his engraving untouched by flame. Everything was as before, yet everything had changed. For me, the now Godless youth, the icons had become something soulless and foreign, part of a long-forgotten past.

Chapter 3 – You Dare Not Lie!

Each day when I went to school, my mother would give me 40 kopeks for a bowl of borscht that we children received during our lunch break. At first, I used the money to buy my soup. But I soon came upon the idea to spend my lunch money for something else, if I saved enough. For a long time, I had wanted a small, shatter-proof doll to replace the one I'd lost that fateful day. I even planned to use the remnants of mother's sewing work to make her clothing.

I had mentioned my wish to mother, but she had come out firmly against it: "You are already much too old, Inna, to play with a doll like that. You can use your free time for something more useful, and besides, we don't have the money for it!"

Mother certainly had not considered that, by forbidding it, my desire for a doll only burned more intensely. Day after day, I sat and watched hungrily as the other children enjoyed their soup. I was often so hungry that I wanted to take out the money, but my desire for the doll was so strong that I even overcame my hunger. Finally, after a couple weeks I held the adorable little doll, barely larger than my hand. She had blue eyes and was completely naked, poor thing! Gently I pressed this object of my affection to my chest and forgot all the sacrifices I had made to get her. I was so happy!

"I will call you 'Alice' after my favorite porcelain doll, and I promise to sew you many beautiful clothes." I whispered in her ear as I took her home. The closer I got to my home, however, the less joy I took in my newly purchased little doll. I could hear my conscience: "This is wrong! You defied your mother and bought the doll! Throw her away so no one will know how selfish and disobedient you are! Throw her away!"

I looked at little Alice, and a maternal feeling arose inside me. "No, I love you, little Alice, I can't throw you away! But what will we do, when mother sees you?" I slowed down and finally stopped in my tracks.

"Shame on you, throw the doll away." My conscience repeated more clearly than before.

"No, no, I want to keep her," came the reply.

But the difficult part became: How? In this moment of guilty agitation, a thought came to me: It's simple. I'll just tell mother I found the doll.

"It's a lie!" my conscience sternly warned: "You dare not lie."

"But what good is it to throw her away? Mother won't notice I'm lying." I stubbornly replied to my battered conscience. "After all, she hadn't seen how I'd bought the doll..." After these entreaties my conscience fell silent and I quickly resumed my walk home, the doll in hand and my school pack on my back.

"Mommy look, I found a doll." I said calmly, entering our room.

Mother put aside her work and observed me and the new little baby in my hand. "Found her?" she said leaning forward "Where did you find her?"

I wasn't prepared for that question and started to stutter: "On my way hu...home from school. I tripped on a stone...and then, uh, I suddenly saw her lying there in the gutter."

"And where was this, Inna?" She asked sternly. Her face grew pale and her eyes flared with anger.

My fear grew, but I didn't want to give up the fight and answered curtly: "By the drug store mommy!"

"It's been raining outside, Inna. You couldn't have found a dry doll in the gutter."

Mother was not so easily convinced as I had imagined. I could tell that she wanted to catch me in the lie and put me to shame. That made me very bitter. I remembered how many sacrifices I had put up with and retorted: "I found the doll – in the gutter! Maybe someone had just lost her – and that's why she was still dry."

My mother's patience seemed to be at an end.

"Where did you get the doll? Tell me the truth!" she demanded. But I stuck by my story. Mother got up out of her chair, took me firmly by the hand and led me down to the basement. She got out the box where father's clothing was stored, took out a belt, and started to whip me.

"You want to tell me the truth now? You dare not lie to me!"

"I'm not lying!" I shrieked.

"Oh really?" She grabbed me by my pigtails and threw me to the floor. I screamed and tried to defend myself from the blows. Mother, however, was strong. Very strong. She held me fast with one hand and with the other belted me across my back and bottom.

"You want to tell the truth now? NO??" She lashed me even harder. I hated her terribly in that moment. But she only grew more furious at my insolence, pulling my pigtails so hard that it knocked the breath out of me. I pleaded with her, still refusing to admit my lie. Mother understood that she wouldn't be able to get it out of me by force, and finally let go. Broken and exhausted, I went back up to our room and started in on my homework. Tears streamed down my face. I thought about what had happened and it made me even more upset.

"You did wrong and earned that beating," I could hear my conscience return. But by that point I no longer had the courage to ask my mother, who didn't so much as look at me for the rest of the day, to forgive me. That evening she cooked the usual meal, sat down on the table, and started to eat without me. I couldn't stand to see this, so I took my doll and went over to her.

"Mommy, I want to tell you everything now." I began quietly and seriously.

Mother looked at me kindly, her demeanor once again soft. Then, without raising my eyes, I told her how I had saved the money she had given me for lunch to buy the doll. Mother remained silent for a moment. Then she embraced me and gave me a kiss.

"See Inna, you are a grown girl. I didn't realize that you would still want such a childish toy. You must have wanted that doll enough that you were willing to go hungry for quite some time. Why did you need to lie to me about it?"

"I was scared."

"Of what?"

"That you'd be mad at me."

"But weren't you afraid that lying would make me mad?"

"I thought you wouldn't notice!"

"You're not such a little girl anymore, but believe this, a mother notices immediately when her child is lying."

I felt truly ashamed.

"Mother, please forgive me." I said, deeply moved by everything. "I'll never do it again."

"Good. And I promise to never punish you so long as you tell me the truth, whatever it may be. When you can admit your own mistakes, you will be free of blame. But woe to you if you ever dare lie to me again!"

"I'll never lie again!"

"That's good. Now I'm going to give you a few nice pieces of fabric so you can make a dress for your new doll."

My heart began to warm. My mother loved and cared for me so much, why did I fear her? That evening, we sat together peacefully at the dinner table. Mother sewed a pretty little dress for Alice and showed me how it was done. Then she went back to work, and began to mend her customers' clothing. I was overjoyed that we had made amends.

Chapter 4 – Light in the Black Market

Not long after this episode with lying, mother and I sat together working furiously mending clothing. Suddenly, someone tapped loudly on our window. I jumped and ran to the door. Mother followed and, as I opened it, cried out in surprise. Outside stood a pale, emaciated man, dirty and unshaven. His clothing was torn and hung awkwardly around his body. He didn't have shoes, just some rags tied around his feet.

"Vladimir! My poor, dear husband!" Mother finally let out between joy and agony.

"Papa!" I cried, as I finally recognized him.

"Zina!" He replied with a weak voice – I can't even hug you. I have to take off these rags first. We were covered in vermin.

Mother quickly sent me to fetch water. When I came back with my two buckets, father was lying in bed. Mother looked very sad.

"Daddy is very sick." She warned me. "He can barely stand on two feet."

The next morning, I had to go for a doctor. Father hadn't been able to sleep the entire night and had tossed and turned with a fever all night.

"Typhus!" came the doctor's verdict. After a few hours, an ambulance came and took him away. Mother had ceased crying. Only her eyes seemed to have grown larger, and her face looked more tired and full of concern.

What followed was a very difficult time for us. We had no wood or coal. But every day it got colder, and soon a deep snow covered the ground. We sat in our room dressed in winter jackets and boots and froze. Mother began to cough, and soon after father was taken to the hospital, she also could no longer get out of bed and had a high fever.

"Pneumonia!" ruled the doctor.

I was at the end of my wits.

Mother called me over, handed me 40 rubles and said: "This is the last of our money Inna. Buy some barley and a big bushel of wood at the market. If a miracle doesn't happen, I'll have to go to the hospital tomorrow and you to the orphanage."

I was terrified by the entire situation. I'd already heard many times how the adults had said there was so little to eat at the hospital that very few seriously ill patients ever made it out. But to avoid upsetting mother, I bravely held back my tears. I walked slowly away from her and cried bitterly. I wanted to stop time, so that tomorrow would never come. I raised my eyes and suddenly saw a strange man. He was neatly dressed, smiled, and gave me a small cookie made of cornmeal, known as a "corn cookie" in Russia.

I thanked him and stuck it in my coat pocket. "I'll save it for mommy." I thought.

"Why aren't you eating it? Don't you like cookies?" Asked the man.

"I do! But my mother is so ill." I replied. For some reason, I trusted this friendly man and told him about all my worries.

"Poor kid." Said the man and patted me on the head. "It's so difficult to help people out here, there is so much misery everywhere. But you know what? Come with me, I'll get you a few cookies."

"Where can you get them?"

"In the cantina of the store I work in." He said.

"What do they cost?"

"Four rubles per kilo. Do you have money?"

"Yes. Please, please buy two kilos for me, I'll pay for it." I said eagerly.

"Gladly dear, if it will help you."

The burden on my heart began to lighten a little. The thought of owning two kilos of cookies was very appealing. "We can live from them for a couple days, and if things work out, maybe mother won't have to go to the hospital." I thought to myself.

I gladly followed the man. "What's your name?" He asked.

"Inna Vladimirovna."

"My name is Comrade Pokrovski. If anyone in the cantina asks who you are with, just tell them that I am your uncle, ok?"

"Ok, Uncle Pokrovski."

"Uncle Vanya!" he corrected and led me through the courtyard of the building at which he worked to the cantina.

"You can go buy it yourself, dear, I have to go to work now, goodbye!"

"Thank you and goodbye, Uncle Vanya!" I went into the cantina and purchased two kilos of the cookies that could normally only be bought by employees. My pockets now stuffed with gingerbread treasure, I departed merrily for the market to buy the wood mother had requested.

"How happy mother will be when I bring her these cookies. If only we always had the money to buy them in that cantina. We wouldn't always have to starve."

Suddenly, a fantastic idea flashed across my mind. It was such a good idea that I had to stop and consider it for a moment – then took off running as quickly as I could. I had often seen how women had hawked cookies at the market just like mine - two for a ruble. "If I just imitate them, I'll earn a lot of money." I thought.

No sooner said than done! At the market there were throngs of hungry people looking for something to eat.

I grabbed a few cookies from my pocket and thrust them in the air: "Cookies, fresh cookies!" I shouted, imitating the other traders. "Two for a ruble!"

Soon I was surrounded by a throng of people resembling hungry wolves. Each held out money and waved it in front of my face, almost as if they wanted to force it upon me.

"Give me two, I'll give you 2 rubles! I'll give you more...!" I heard from all directions. In just minutes, my cookies were gone, and the pack of hungry people abruptly dispersed to chase whatever else they could find to eat that day. I was left standing alone, staring down at my quivering hands, grasping a heaping, sweaty wad of wrinkled banknotes. I anxiously counted the money,

"Five, ten, twenty, fifty...one-hundred-twenty-four rubles!"

I hurried to buy milk, barley, oatmeal, a piece of bread and a big bundle of wood that I could barely carry. I stuffed the money that was left over into my pockets. Slowly, but very happily, I made the trek home. When mother saw all I had bought, she seemed horrified:

"Inna, what did you steal to get this?"

"No, mom, don't worry, I didn't steal. I just sold a batch of cookies at the market. I want to buy you nice things like this every day." I enthusiastically told her how I had come upon the gingerbread and promised to do it again. Mother laughed for the first time after countless dark days.

"You really are a wonderful girl." She said. "And this Comrade Pokrovski, our savior, was sent to us by God."

"By God?" I thought with my usual skepticism, but deep down I had also imagined this as some sort of divine intervention.

As I made a fire to cook the oatmeal, I knew what I had to do. I gave a portion to mother and took the other half and put on my jacket.

"I'm taking it to Papa at the hospital." I said. "Otherwise he'll die of hunger on us."

Mother feebly nodded her approval and smiled.

Chapter 5 – The Shrouded Wagon and the Samovar

One night I dreamed of a huge bowl of sweet porridge sitting in front of me on our table. I wanted to grab the bowl, but it always slid further and further towards the edge of the table until, "boom!" the bowl fell to the floor and broke into a thousand pieces. Then suddenly everything went dark.

The clock struck six: "Time to wake up!" I rubbed my eyes and looked around.

For a few moments I sat and reflected on my dream. What did it mean? A longing that would never be fulfilled? The overwhelming hunger I felt seemed to confirm that interpretation and reminded me of the coming day's business. It was still dark outside, but I couldn't go back to sleep. The big market and all the hungry people were waiting. I hurriedly made a fire, set things out for my sick mother who was still asleep, and left our room. Outside a sharp, harsh wind whistled against my face, resisting my every step. My old, thin jacket provided little protection from the cold. Both hunger and cold prompted me to quicken my steps, and soon I came to the hospital, where my father lay fighting for his life with typhus. I stood for a few moments looking at the second story window where his room was.

"Hopefully he'll get well soon!" I thought.

Mother, delirious with fever, would often call for him. I tried to soothe her and told her that father was doing better and would soon be well. In reality, he was still in critical condition.

When I asked at the hospital how he was doing, the nurses always replied dryly: "Not any better."

The kind doctor, however, gave me hope that my father would make it through, thanks to his strong heart.

"Main thing." He implored me "is that you see to it that your father gets something extra to eat every day. The food here is bad and offers little sustenance to the seriously ill."

I knew exactly what my mission was: I had to feed my family and get both of my parents back on their feet. Standing there thinking about it all, I had momentarily gotten lost in my thoughts.

"Get! Hoa – Get!" I suddenly heard someone shout very close to me. I raised my eyes and noticed that the hospital gate had opened, and two large, fully loaded liter wagons pulled by horses had ridden out and were about to pass me. The wagons were covered snuggly with a cloth tarp.

"What could be under that thick cloth?" I thought. "If only I could see..."

I followed the last wagon a few steps with an insatiable childish curiosity to see what was inside – I carefully began to lift the heavy tarp and bent forward to peek underneath. In that moment, the cart hit a pothole and jolted. Something rubbery struck me sharply on the nose. I raised my head, and to my horror, I could see a stiff, blue, human hand sticking out from underneath the cloth. Someone grabbed me firmly by the arm and yanked me to the side. Startled, I quickly looked up over my shoulder...

"Scared – are yah – nosey? They're all dead and won't harm a hair on your head." Boomed a large man with a long, black beard, laughing and holding me fast. "You're going with me to the police, no one is allowed to see this! Why are your sticking your nose into something that's none of your business? What are you doing up this early wandering around on the street?"

"Mister, mister, please let me go!" I began to plead. "My father is here at the hospital, my mother's sick at home in bed. I have to take care of them both by myself. If you take me away, they'll both die!"

"Fine then, fine then." He said with a kind voice. "Run away, and let this be a warning: Don't tell anyone what you've seen! You hear?"

"Yes Sir!" I wanted to leave, but what I'd seen had so overwhelmed me that I had to ask another question: "Where are you taking all these poor people?"

"You are a curious one – to the cemetery of course!"

"With no coffin?"

"What do you think kid, that we can afford a state funeral for each of these poor devils? They don't even have any relatives. We don't even know what some of their names are."

"How awful." I said. "So, tell me mister, when someone dies who still has relatives, then they get a coffin at least?"

"Yes – if their relatives are willing to pay for it! But now leave me with your questions, you curious little cat, otherwise I'll really have to haul you off to the police!" The black bearded man again made as if he wanted to take me by the arm, but I pulled away and took off.

Horrified, I thought back to the cold, dead hand, and was filled with fear and dread. I felt as if someone was approaching me with muffled footsteps, following me, tapping me on the back, tapping me with that cold, dead, blue hand. As I reached the market later than usual and saw the many familiar faces, I breathed a little easier. I opened my bag, got out the corn cookies that I'd purchased just as the previous day and, in no time, sold them all.

My nights after this terrifying experience, however, became very long and filled with anxiety. I often dreamed that my father had died and was being loaded onto the wagon with the other corpses without a coffin. I would wake up covered in sweat and couldn't go back to sleep for hours. One day I told my mother about my dreams, but didn't tell her what had happened to me in front of the hospital.

My mother was oddly happy about my dream: "The fact that you saw your father dead is a good sign!" She explained. "He will recover from his illness and live a long life!"

Mother was very superstitious, as are most Ukrainians and Russians, and placed much significance on the interpretation of dreams. When someone dies in a dream it means that he or she will live a long life. And so it was: Mother's prediction came true. Father soon overcame the worst phase of his illness and was no longer in grave danger. Even mother's health improved, and she slowly began to work again. Her face had grown even more pale during her illness, but now she again looked relaxed and supple, as if the usual strain had been wrung out of her. My poor mother had, so it seemed to me, regained hope for a better life.

After a few more weeks, father did actually come home from the hospital. He was still so weak that, at first, he had to learn to walk again like a small child. His skin was sallow and so transparent that you could see the blood running through his veins. The main thing, though, was that he was home again and on the mend. And my parents got along quite well in the beginning. I continued to support them in that I bought and sold the corn cookies. They often called me their guardian angel and even admitted that they wouldn't have survived without me.

But one day my father said: "Our daughter has to stop with this peddling. I'm going to find a new job."

Unfortunately, he couldn't go back to the university and teach. He was counted among those old intellectuals who had become disposable in this new era and were considered to be a "traitorous element" no longer to be trusted to educate the youth.

Several weeks passed before father found work as a bookkeeper at a shoe factory. Such work was, of course, depressing for a former university professor. And father only earned a small salary of 200 rubles a month, with which he couldn't even support himself, not to mention an entire family. As a result, my dear mother had to take on even more work to keep us afloat.

As summer arrived, fruits and vegetables appeared again at the market, which modestly eased the famine, although bread rations remained small and prices high. My parents, now busy making ends meet, had little time to dedicate to raising me. Rarely did anyone ask if my homework had been done, whether I'd eaten anything, or if my clothes were in order. I had to take care of myself.

There was one thing, however, my mother always looked after: My piano lessons. If I neglected that, she would have been very disappointed.

"Inna" she said "you are talented and have to practice. When you are grown and want to leave home, I won't be able to give you any money. So at least learn to play the piano from your mother and take that with you."

To avoid making my mother's health worse, I practiced more diligently, even though I had no real desire to do so. Oh yes, had I known then how often I would come to need this art, I would have practiced even more... Our family's extreme hardships had other side-effects that brought my parents into conflict. Father, who would come home evenings tired from work, was often confronted by a big mess. Bits of cloth and twine lay strewn across the floor, the table was rarely clean, and dinner rarely prepared.

"Zina, what is there to eat? I'm so hungry..." He began.

"What am I supposed to give you? Other than stale bread there is nothing! Please cook some tea for yourself." Replied mother, who still sat hastily sewing.

Father fired-up the kerosene cooker and put the water kettle on. He stood a while sadly next to it, then sat on a stool and took off has worn-out shoes.

"My socks are totally torn up again!" He complained, turning to mother.

"Then take a needle and mend them!" She answered testily.

"Mending socks? Is that a man's work?"

"So it's a woman's job to care for the family and earn enough money? Other men at least make the effort to support their family. Their wives have time to look after the household."

"Where am I supposed to earn a better salary? I work all day long!"

"And me, does it look like I spend the whole day dancing and having fun? Why don't you look for a better-paying job?"

"You know full well, Zina, that there isn't one out there."

"Isn't out there?" Said mother: "Or why don't you just say that you don't want to make the effort for us. If nothing else, go out and make money on the black market. The other men are doing it and have earned a fortune. And they take wonderful care of their wives and children. Just look at Isak Adamovich!"

"Please don't tell me about that man. Should I also make money by swindling people and being dishonest?"

"Dishonest. Swindle. What profound words!" my mother mocked. "But leaving your family to starve is honest and upstanding? Just admit you don't want to get your hands dirty, you old aristocrat!"

My father put his hand over my mother's mouth: "Be quiet you lunatic, the neighbors are going to hear!" He said, overcome by anger.

"And me?" mother went on shrilly "I work day and night and take care of you, and you dare to call me a lunatic!?"

At the end of her nerves, mother threw on her jacket and left the room. I ran after her with tears streaming: "Mommy, don't leave, come back and drink some tea with us."

"I can't stand the shamelessness of your father any longer!" she replied and shook me off. Sadly, I watched as she stormed off. My father sat down silently at the table and buried his head in his hands. I turned off the fire under the water that had been left boiling for some time now and prepared the tea.

"What a life we have my daughter!" sobbed my father sorrowfully. "Learn everything you can in life so that you'll be able to make it through without so much hardship. Then you won't have to suffer as much as me."

"Poor father. Suffering?" I asked skeptically with a hint of irony in my voice – and added: "If my family were in trouble, I wouldn't hesitate to trade on the black market!"

"It's not so simple for people like us. Perhaps you'll understand that one day and think differently of your father."

One day, however, father came home earlier and happier than usual. Mother, who always sat at work sewing, looked at him with surprise.

"Zina" he said kindly "I got us two tickets to the theater and was hoping you'd like to go."

"To the theater? This evening? Of course I'd enjoy that. But what should I wear?"

"Something ordinary. These days it's not so important, people go to the opera without dressing up."

Mother sobbed: "Oh yes, earlier one would always wear the finest things!" With that, she went to the closet and took a dark skirt and paired it with a simple white blouse. She covered her head with a silk cloth and looked questioningly at father.

"Right!" He complimented: "You look like the wife of a worker!"

I watched this scene carefully and was happy that my parents were on good terms again.

"Inna" They said, as they made ready to leave: "We won't be home until midnight. Go to bed on time and don't wait up for us." Then they set out, stopped for a moment and waved up to me as I watched from the window. Then father offered mother his arm. I stood for a while watching as they left. How happy I would be to see them always getting on so well. And what could I do to ensure that they would be this way from now on?

I looked around the room. Things were a mess as usual. "I'll tidy everything up." I thought suddenly. "After that I'll go to bed, pretend to sleep, and see what my parents have to say about it." I liked the thought and set about organizing and cleaning. After I had set everything in order, I took a white linen cloth from the closet and used it to cover the table. It made me happy that our house finally looked truly cozy.

"I'll cook some tea and set a beautiful table for my parents." I thought. To my disappointment there wasn't a drop of kerosene to found in the house, and I couldn't use the stove to cook water. Too bad, no tea after all. Then I remembered an old samovar I'd uncovered earlier under a pile of clutter in the closet.

"What luck!" I thought: "If I use the samovar, I won't need kerosene! And I can use the wooden coals mother uses to heat the water to iron clothes."

I rummaged around and pulled out the impressive but outmoded contraption. By then it had long been dark outside and was only half an hour to midnight. I took the samovar outside, removed the lid and filled the spacious pot with water. I then made a strong fire in the pipe that ran through the middle.

I was excited and hoped everything would be ready on time. I returned to our room to finish setting the table and noticed the quickly moving hands of the clock on the wall. I ran back outside to the yard to bring the piping hot samovar inside, as the water was now boiling and bubbling. In my excitement, I had forgotten, that, as was customary, I had placed a long pipe on top of the samovar to intensify the fire. And then it happened... I smacked the pipe with my arm and tipped the entire pot over. The boiling water poured out across the ground and over my feet, and a searing pain engulfed me, as if I was melting into the ground.

"Help me!" I screamed with a piercing howl. Neighbors looked out from their windows in horror. Someone ran out to me, picked me up, and carried me to our room.

With that mother also came running. "What happened, Inna?? My God, what's happened?!" She looked at me in a state of total shock.

"My fee...e...eet!" I could only sputter between my cries and screams.

"She was burned by the boiling samovar!" the neighbors said.

Mother gingerly took off my shoes and socks. I saw my burned feet, now just a red mass. The skin was completely gone. A doctor was called to the house. I stammered to tell him that I had been trying to make my parents happy, and how it had happened.

Mother turned to father, spitting with a hot rage: "It's all your fault! If you hadn't bought us those stupid tickets, and gotten a real job instead!"

Bitter and disgusted, father replied: "Curse this life!"

Oh - how those awful words hurt me all the more in the midst of my physical agony.

My parents' brief glimpse of happiness was dispelled as quickly as it had come.

Chapter 6 – Unexpected Guests

My painfully burned feet banished me for several weeks to a hospital bed. How slowly and monotonously the days passed! Few friends and relatives visited to see how I was doing. Just a nurse looked in on me each day and treated my wounds with an ointment and coated them with a Sulphur powder. It didn't seem to help much, because a hardened crust had formed and underneath, things looked bad. My feet hurt so much that I couldn't turn over in bed without help from my mother or the nurse.

One day as I lay in my own bed, finally home from the hospital, I heard bright voices behind my window:

"Here's the house! She must live here!" Knocks came at the door and in the next moment my bed was surrounded by the boys and girls from my class. How immensely happy I suddenly was.

"How are you? Good to see you..." I heard them speaking over each other. "Look here, we collected these things for you!" And they handed me a large package.

"Open it!" Everyone shouted. I hastily opened the package. Various toys, books and candies were inside.

"That's from me! ... And that's from me! We bought the sweets together!" They all shouted. They told me all the news from school and asked if I would be coming back soon.

"I don't know how much longer my feet will need to heal." I said sadly. "I wish I could go with you now."

The kids looked around our home.

"You have a big room. And what nice furniture." They said. "There's even a piano! And what a tall mirror."

"And comrades, look!" a girl shouted as she pointed to mother's holy images: "There are icons hanging over there in the corner!"

“Really?!” The others said in amazement. The faces of my visitors suddenly lost their childish spontaneity and kindness.

“Wait Inna, are you a really a true Pioneer?” asked my table-mate Vera excitedly.

“Yes!”

“Don’t you know that Pioneers are supposed to fight against the church and so-called God?”

“Yes – of course! I tried to tell my mother, but she didn’t really listen.”

“Didn’t really listen? But it isn’t ok for a Pioneer to allow icons in her home!” The rest said, almost in unison.

My mother now interrupted the conversation: “This isn’t your home. It’s mine.” She said sternly. “Inna has nothing to say about it. She has only to listen to me.”

“We are going to tell our teacher at school!” Came the defiant reply from Vera.

Mother leaned to one side, considered the situation, and decided to tread carefully: “You don’t need to tell the teacher, I wanted to take the icons down anyway and just didn’t get around to it.”

This occurrence darkened my mood and the conversation with my classmates grew stifled and awkward. Soon my young compatriots left. Mother sat speechless with her work. She had finally been forced to recognize that it would be difficult, if not impossible, to go against the tide of this new era, and that she had to yield to this new reality. And the new generation, sparing nothing, not even those things nearest and dearest to the heart, broke and destroyed everything old.

So the holy icons were taken down for good and lay a long time on top of the shelf. I also rarely ever saw my mother pray again. If she did, she did so secretly. Like many other adults, she feared that her child, who was being subjected to Soviet indoctrination, might betray her. The insurmountable barrier between us, which at that time existed in almost every cultured family between the old and the new generation, was only growing larger.

I rarely saw my father during my convalescence. He now regularly came home very late in the evening, well after I had gone to sleep, and left early the next morning. When I asked why father was never really home, mother told me that he had too much to do at the office and had to work overtime. Mother often left me home alone all evening and went to see a movie or spend time with friends.

"I can't stand being at home anymore! I still want something from this life!" She told me one day when I pleaded with her not to leave me alone. And soon enough she brought home a handsome, youthful looking man. She was so jovial and exuberant, in a mood that I hadn't seen for many years. Her dark eyes sparkled brilliantly, and her face looked much younger than usual.

"This is Uncle Moralevski!" she said, introducing me so to this stranger. "He wants to learn to play the piano. But first we are going to have a cup of tea...Vadim!" mother turned to my newly minted uncle, and he didn't refuse. The two spoke and laughed together, but never got around to playing the piano.

"It's already ten, I have to go Zina!" Uncle Moralevski finally said.

Mother put on her jacket. "I'm going to accompany your uncle a bit." She explained. "If your father comes home in the meantime, tell him I'll be back soon."

As they both left the room, I floundered in my own confused feelings. Although this uncle was very handsome, there was something I didn't like about him that I didn't quite understand. I even felt jealous somehow. "What would papa say if he knew that mother was speaking so merrily with this uncle?" I wondered.

But when Papa came home, I didn't say anything of it. He looked so stressed and worried, that I just couldn't bring myself to tell him. He seemed somehow foreign to me that day, perhaps because he hadn't been around much and had done so little to care for me. But when he noticed that mother had left, he sat down on the side of my bed and stroked my hair with his large hand.

"How are you doing my dear?" He asked kindly. "Do your feet still hurt?"

"Yes Daddy!" I replied and sat shyly up next to him. "Why do you always come home so late?"

"I have lots and lots of work, sweetie!" And your mother and I don't get along so well anymore." He said thoughtfully.

I was silent and looked at my father observantly. He was unkempt and unshaven. His clothing looked worn out. His movements were slow and awkward.

"*My father doesn't look handsome anymore!*" I thought to myself. "*But that Uncle Moralevski certainly does.*"

"Father!" I began to lecture. "Why don't you take better care of your appearances?" If I were you, I'd wear a nice collared white shirt and a dark blue tie, along with a nice suit. And your beard doesn't look good either!"

"White shirt...blue tie...nice suit...where do you expect me to get that?" asked papa and looked at me with surprise. "What brings you to these thoughts, anyway?"

"I don't know. I just thought that you would look more handsome then."

"Look more handsome?" father laughed: "It's not so important for me, my dear!"

"Yes, it is!"

"Why?"

I wanted to tell father all about that evening and the dandy Uncle Moralevski, but it wasn't to be. Mother walked into the room. Suddenly, it was as if a cold chill had descended upon the room. An imaginary wall seemed to spring up between the three of us. My parents didn't even greet one another.

"It's very late Inna, you need to go to sleep." Mother said.

Then she quickly undressed and disappeared under her blanket. Soon thereafter the light in the room was extinguished.

I couldn't fall asleep for a long time. In my mind's eye I could see Uncle Moralevski: Young, handsome, and well-groomed: And next to him I saw my father, who looked so run-down and wretched. I imagined how good it would be if my mother could laugh and talk with my father as she did with this uncle. I wanted to plead with her to start treating my father lovingly again.

Fate would take another path. That night I was particularly hot lying there in bed. My lips and throat were dry and I became so thirsty that I had to wake mother up.

She brought me a glass of water and felt my forehead: "Our daughter has a fever!" She said in shock: "The thermometer is reading over 100 degrees!"

Mother looked carefully at my feet, still badly swollen. "Vladimir! Please call for the doctor, quickly!" She said as she shook him awake.

My illness had grown much worse after the difficult and oppressive experiences of that evening. That same night an ambulance arrived and took me back to the hospital. My feet hurt so badly that I couldn't think about anything else. Only the next morning was I finally able to fall asleep, exhausted by all that had passed.

Chapter 7 – Cured and Uncured

At ten o'clock the next morning, I was awakened by the nurse, washed up and helped to comb my hair and tidy up my bed.

"The doctor will see you soon." She said hurriedly.

I looked around at my new environs. It was a large hall. Ten iron bedframes stood in two rows, and each was occupied with a different patient of every age who now eyed me curiously. Most were talkative and immediately asked what was the matter with me. From listening to them I found out that the people in this hall were only there because they were awaiting an operation. That insight caused me to panic.

"It's not so bad!" said the lady next to me – who had a broken femur and lain there with an open wound for half a year in the hospital. This all concerned me a great deal, and I started to cry for my mother. The doors swung open and a friendly, older gentleman in a white smock stepped in.

"Who is crying like that - and what for? He asked me kindly.

"I want to go home! I don't want to have an operation!" I said in a muffled sob.

He called the nurse and asked her what my condition was. Then he examined my feet.

"It's not going to be a major operation, sweetheart, we just need to remove the crust so your skin can breathe, I'll do the operation myself and promise that you will be healthy again soon. Ok?"

"Is it going to hurt a lot?" I asked with dread.

"You won't even notice, don't be afraid and trust me." He patted me gently on the hair. Then he said something in Latin to the nurse, bade the patients farewell and left the hall.

The nurse turned and said: "You're lucky that Doctor Tarschiz is treating you personally. He's the best doctor in the hospital."

Shortly thereafter, two nurses took me in a wheelchair to the operating room, laid me down on an elevated operating table and restrained my hands and feet.

Doctor Tarschiz held my hand, comforted me and told me how he had a daughter my age at home. Then he put a white cloth cover over my face and something with an unpleasant gaseous sweet-sour odor seeped into my eyes, nose and mouth. I felt like I was suffocating and gasped for air. I could only vaguely hear the kind doctor reaching for his implements and my senses began to blur.

Then everything went dark...

The operation went well and my feet soon began to heal. In a few days the pain had noticeably subsided. The doctor visited me daily to dress the wound. He changed it with such care that it barely hurt anymore. I nonetheless grumbled loudly to garner sympathy from the other patients.

"Your mother told me you are musical, Inna." Said Doctor Tarschiz one day. "Would you like to sing us a little song?"

"Gladly!" I agreed and immediately began to sing a Ukrainian folk song. Everyone liked it, and the fatherly doctor began to call me his "little nightingale."

Soon I began to feel quite at ease in the hospital. My parents took turns visiting me almost daily and always brought new newspapers and books, from which I read aloud to my roommates.

"Today there's something really nice in the newspaper, a New Year's surprise!" said my father one day, handing me the "Harvest" newspaper.

After he left, I read the other patients an article proclaiming that, in 1935, rationing of bread would be suspended and it would become available for purchase without restriction. The price for a kilo of white bread would be fixed at 5 rubles and dark bread at 3 rubles.

"Finally! What good news!" The patients cried, listening with glowing enthusiasm. "Life will finally be better, and people will finally be free of the constant fear of starvation!"

None of these poor people had greater expectations from life. "If we just have enough bread, we'll be happy." They had all been humbled by the constant misery and distress of years gone by. The hopes and ambitions of this once proud people never stretched far beyond a loaf of bread in our brave new world. Everyone was excited by the good news, and even my mother was lively and laughed happily when she visited.

"Life is going to get easier for us my child. You see to it that you get well and come home soon." She said kindly.

In the new year, it finally came to pass: My feet had healed and I was able to stand up. At first slowly and carefully, then with more confidence. Soon I was able to move around the hospital hall and walk again without assistance. After a moving farewell from Doctor Tarschiz, the nurses and my fellow patients, I left the hospital happy and full of life. When I went back to school for the first time, my classmates celebrated me like a hero. I had to repeatedly tell how I had burned my feet and had to be operated on in the hospital.

"And the icons, did your mother remove them?" Asked my classmates.

"Yes, of course, that same day you visited." I confirmed.

"Then we want to play with you again!" came the reply from my table-mate Vera.

It didn't take long to realize that I had fallen behind and found it difficult to keep up. I was by now in the sixth grade where each subject was taught by a different teacher. I went home anxious each afternoon and sat for hours struggling with my homework, often with little success.

Uncle Moralevski, who had become a regular guest at my home, came to my aid. He explained everything I was struggling with and helped me make up everything I had failed.

"Vadim, you are a true friend!" mother often said to him. "What would I do with Inna if I didn't have you?"

I also genuinely found Uncle Vadim to be a true friend and was always happy to see him visit. My father, on the other hand, rarely saw me after I came home from the hospital. There were times when I didn't see him for days at a time. When he did come home, mother never bothered to ask him where he had been.

My parents usually exchanged the following words:

"It's your pay day today, isn't it?" began my mother. "Did you bring us any money?"

"No...I don't have any money!"

"Where is the money you earn, Vladimir?"

"Do I always have to calculate it out for you? I have to pay the bills, I used some of the money to pay the taxes and some more to pay the rent. Then there was so little left that it barely covers the cost of my cigarettes."

"So....! Then tell me why I even have a man in the house? That I work and care for?"

"What am I supposed to do?" Father said with a heavy heart.

"Leave! You should leave and get out of my sight!" Mother shouted, losing all composure.

"Where should I go? Everyone is foreign to me. I've often tried to leave and couldn't. I'm always being drawn back home." He said downcast and downtrodden.

Mother was not assuaged in the least by these excuses: "You are always drawn back home?" She asked scornfully...Just because you always assume that I'll take care of you."

"Enough of this hypocrisy, I'm telling you for the last time Vladimir: If you don't make a much greater effort to at least provide for yourself and our daughter, that I'm going to end it, you hear? End it for good!"

After such exchanges, mother usually got dressed up and left the house. Father, plagued by hunger, would search through the house for something to eat, but usually find nothing. Mother locked everything up and took the key with her. Seeing that broke my heart. I couldn't stand to see how my once wealthy, well-cared for father was so hungry and chain smoked one cigarette after the other just to calm his nerves.

One evening I led him to the basement and showed him where mother stashed the ham and other food. Father was very happy, took a big piece, and went with me back upstairs. There was a light burning in the room. We opened that door. Mother turned and looked at us, horrified. Next to her, tall and handsome, stood Vadim Moralevski.

"Uncle Vadim!" I said.

Something suddenly fell to the ground behind me with a thud.

I looked around and saw the large piece of uncured ham lying in the doorway. Father had disappeared...

Chapter 8 – Cleaned Out

Mother had come to love her chosen profession of tailoring. Her work was of such high quality and good taste that she soon earned a reputation as one of the best tailors in Poltava. She had a keen sense of fashion, sketched her own designs, and could transform outdated garments and simple scraps of cloth into a stylish masterpiece. It made her particularly happy when customers raved about her work and recommended her to others.

She began to earn more and was even able to afford a maid. But since there was no labor office, and help-wanted ads were not allowed in newspapers, mother had to ask around among her customers and friends to find someone. Finally, we found a young country girl from a nearby village named Nyurka who said she could arrive each morning and work until evening.

Nyurka seemed very reliable, and mother soon taught her to do all of the household chores, which she took on with great diligence. From then on, our home was always clean and well looked after. There were regular meals, the dishes were always done, and the clothes ironed and put away. Mother also looked better and well-cared for. She sewed the finest things for herself and came to be admired and envied by all our acquaintances. She slowly grew more content with her lot in life, fought less with my father, and when he did turn up from time-to-time, no longer demanded money.

Father, however, made no effort to make himself more attractive to his elegant wife. Next to her, he looked poor and unkempt. And mother kept her money to herself and didn't give father a single ruble for his needs.

"I've earned everything with my own two hands, you could do it too, if you only made the effort." She would often say to him. He didn't have the energy, however, to make the leap to a new profession, and still sat day-after-day in his old office job.

Uncle Moralevski had also stopped visiting for quite some time. He had been transferred to another city where he'd received a position as the director of a small factory. Father was naturally happy about that and was, for quite a while, at peace, until one day something incomprehensible occurred. As always, I came home that evening from school, relaxed and singing a song with a spring in my step. I was shocked to find the house completely transformed.

The song I was singing stuck in my throat as I looked across our home. Here again, as on that fateful day the chief of police had arrested father, total chaos reigned. The dressers, closets and cupboards were all open and empty. The silk quilt and tablecloth were gone. Clothes lay strewn across the floor.

Neither Nyurka nor mother were present.

Only now did I notice that the doors that led to our home were unlocked. That struck me as very odd and troubling.

"What is going on???" I asked myself in astonishment and waited for something to happen, but nothing happened and nobody appeared to explain this sinister situation. I decided to look around and ask the neighbors. I hadn't gone far, when I saw mother approaching with two militia men. One of the men led a large German shepherd by his side.

"What happened?" I called, and ran into my mother's arms.

"We've been robbed! Someone robbed us of everything we own in broad daylight!" she cried.

I felt totally defeated. I knew how much work and effort mother had put forth to bring our lives to this point. Had all of her sacrifices and privations really been for naught? Could she find the courage to start all over again?

The militia men inspected our home. One sat at the table and noted the damages. The other, with the police dog in tow, soon left the room and began to retrace the steps of the thieves. The militia man at the table shook his head sadly and relayed to us that there was little hope that the perpetrators would ever be apprehended, as this was likely the work of an organized crew of thieves. Mother recounted her day to the man, how everything had gone, that she went into town around noon to go shopping, leaving behind our maid Nyurka. When she returned, the doors were all unlocked, Nyurka was gone, and the room had been completely ransacked.

"What did your maid look like?" the militia man asked, squinting his eyes.

Mother described her appearance.

"Aha!" He said: "we've been searching for her for quite some time! A notorious thief!"

"Oh God, my God!" said mother in exasperation. She seemed so decent and honest and always made an effort to be punctual and do things the way I wanted.

"That was always her greatest strength, those innocent eyes of hers, but she's a career criminal!"

"And she had such good references!" Mother added. "Certainly all fake! Oh my God, all the long, heard years I worked through the night!"

The militia man tried to console mother and promised to do everything necessary to restore what had been lost. Then he bid us farewell and left us alone. As usual, father came home very late that evening.

Mother ran out to meet him: "Vladimir! We were robbed! All my things are gone. What should I do now?"

"Robbed? Why?" Wearily he looked in silence at the room, sat down on a chair, and slowly began to untie his shoes.

Mother looked at him questioningly.

"Well – what do you think about it all Vladimir?" she said impatiently.

"When something falls off the wagon, you won't profit from it." He answered with a Russian saying.

Mother became angry: "I think that deep down you're happy that this misfortune fell upon me!"

"It was you who never wanted me to mind your affairs. And you kept things locked away from me anyway, always afraid that I might take something that belonged to you. I've already made my peace a long time ago with the fact that nothing here belongs to me anymore."

"But you lived here, ate my bread, slept upon my bed linens, and now you say I locked everything away from you?"

"It wasn't always right what you did Zina! When you are married to a person, you shouldn't always count who owes who what. After all, I used to earn more and always did everything for you. I never told you: The money all belongs to me. Maybe this is you being punished for your actions." Father concluded somberly.

But for my mother that was too much. Burning with fury, she sprang out of her chair, smacked the table and cried hot tears:

"Another man would have comforted his wife in this difficult hour, but here you are casting blame! You're even happy at this chance to finally humiliate me!" Her face alternated between flush red and pale white. She looked so terrible now, as if she wanted to attack him.

A terrible fear rose in me and I tried to calm them. "Mother! Dear mother!" I called out: "The militia man promised that they would find our things and catch that thief. Then we might even get everything back!"

Mother was beyond the point of my being able to calm her down and renewed her furious attack: “Get out of my house, you callous swine! I never want to hear from you again!” With those words, mother piled together all of father’s few remaining possessions in a bundle and threw them out the door. In the dead silence that followed, someone knocked violently on the wall. It was a neighbor who was bothered by all the commotion.

Father rose: “Alright, I agree we should separate” he said darkly: “There is no more life for us here.” Then he lifted his eyes, looked at me tenderly and gently caressed my hair. “Farewell my child! I’ll never come back!”

Slowly, with heavy steps he went to the door, opened it hesitantly, as if he might reconsider, and then disappeared into the darkness of the hall.

“Poor father!” I sobbed from the bottom of my heart.

Mother looked at me with sadness and uncertainty, but after a moment, said: “It’s better like this Inna, think about the hard times we have ahead of us that we will get through more easily without your father...”

Chapter 9 – Vadim Moralevski Comes Calling

One evening after several days marked by silence, mother livened up and declared: "I'm going to write your Uncle Moralevski and ask him to come and give us his advice and assistance. You go to bed now, Inna, it's gotten late."

Although I didn't have anything against Uncle Moralevski, who had always been kind to me, I wasn't particularly fond of my mother's stated intentions.

"We may not even like Uncle Moralevski anymore, why don't you wait a while mother! At least until we've recovered our things and our room isn't so empty." I implored.

"Vadim," she countered, "is a true and dear friend. He'll certainly stand by us in our hour of need and lend us a hand. Especially since your father just abandoned us."

"But it was you who sent father away!" I couldn't let her comment go unchallenged.

"Uncle Moralevski doesn't need to know about any of that. At some point the situation with your father had to finally be resolved. And anyway, what do you think of Uncle Vadim?"

"I don't know, Mother...I think he's too young for you..."

"Too young? That doesn't hurt anything" she responded. "Main thing is, he really likes me. How often he told me, if I were only single, there is no other woman he would want." Mother's words came as an unpleasant surprise. I always noticed that Uncle Moralevski enjoyed visiting us, but he had always been dignified and reserved.

"No." I thought. *Vadim as mother's husband?* Deep down, I couldn't accept the idea. Mother, however, couldn't be dissuaded. She wrote him a letter and waited impatiently for a reply.

In the days of waiting that followed, she was so scattered and childish that I could only cringe whenever I looked at her. Her hair was always undone, her blouse unbuttoned, and her shoes never polished. She barely ate and didn't sew a stitch for her customers.

"Hopefully he'll come soon" she said increasingly as time passed. And finally, somewhat to my surprise and dismay, that day came. One bright Sunday morning, Vadim Moralevski appeared, tall, young and handsome as always.

"I got your message, Zina. It upset me to read about the terrible things that have happened." He said.

"Now that you've come, everything will be fine Vadim." Answered mother, as she approached and sought to embrace him.

He, however, stepped away and went to the table. "Ah...we need to discuss things Zinaida." Shouldn't Inna go outside first?"

Mother seemed caught off guard. "She won't bother us, she can stay here, it's ok." I was naturally extremely curious to hear what would follow and was only too delighted to stay.

"I really like you Zina" Vadim began, his voice filling with enthusiasm. "I really appreciate you, you're a good, intelligent woman." It was always a pleasure for me to visit and spend time with you."

"I knew it, dear Vadim. But until now, my husband was in our way."

"Yes, of course, and we always paid attention not to cross any lines that we might come to regret later."

"I always appreciated that about you my love, you never lost your head." Then mother added with a profound tone: "But today...today I am free and we no longer need to hold back."

"What do you mean Zina? You wrote me that you were in serious trouble, and I'm happy to help you out. Here are 500 rubles to get you through for now." He laid the money on the table.

Mother looked at him with a surprised look in her eyes: "What's this money?" She asked skeptically.

"I think you'll need it Zina." He said firmly and stood up. "I've got to go now, please write me if you need more. I'll help if I can."

"Go?? You want to go, Vadim?" Mother said, in total astonishment. "I...I thought" she said as her eyes choked with tears.

"We haven't seen each other in a long time Zina." He began hesitantly, as if he knew that mother expected more: "I never really thought you'd be willing to sacrifice everything to be with me...so after I left town for my new job, I found another woman and married."

Mother could only stare, totally appalled, into the distance. Then she let out a shrill cry and collapsed in a fit back into her chair. Vadim left in great haste. My poor mother sat motionless in her chair a long time. I dared not speak a word. Finally, she stood up, went silently over to where her long-neglected work lay, and took up her needle and thread and began to sew. It was the first time I had ever seen her work on a Sunday.

"Maybe there really is no God?! So many things have gone wrong...one-after-another, how could he allow it?" She muttered to herself darkly. Outside, ominous clouds rolled in and it started to rain. I looked up to where the icons had sat atop the cabinet and noticed they had disappeared. Mother's dark reaction had left me somewhat bewildered. After all, her friend had at least given her 500 rubles, enough to get us through the days ahead, and that was important. In my childish naivety, I couldn't comprehend why her mood was so irreconcilably dark...

Sad and confused, I asked: "Mommy: Why do you think everything went wrong?"

Her hands trembled as she sewed, but no answer came...

Chapter 10 – Ride of the Black Horse

One day my mother called me over. She was holding a round, shiny locket.

"Gold?" I marveled. "Where did you get that?"

"Open it up and look inside." She replied, handing it to me.

It seemed somehow familiar. Hastily I pried it open. "How beautiful..." I was delighted at what I found inside. Two photos with two young, fresh, smiling faces peered back at me: One each of my mother and father shortly before they married.

"You were so lovely back then Mommy, and Papa too!"

"Yes, back then we were still young and happy together." Mother reflected nostalgically: "Your father gave it to me as a present for our engagement."

"And why haven't you shown me this before?"

"On that terrible day that everything was stolen, I hid it. Despite our dire situation, there was no way that I was going to let it go, which is why I never told you about it before now."

"And you never will give it away mother." I pleaded.

"Of course not, because one day I am going to pass it on to you when you leave home."

"Leave home? I'm always going to stay with you. Do you really believe that I would ever leave you alone?"

"I know you won't leave me alone. But I wanted to show you where I hide it, in case something happens to me and I have to leave, just so you know."

The thought of being left alone in the world without her made me suddenly anxious: "What are you talking about? Why would you think you'd have to leave? I'll go wherever you go."

"It's fine, don't worry dearest. I also want us to always be together." She said reassuringly and led me to the attic to the hiding place.

Afterwards, we came back down to our room. Mother looked perturbed, as if she were holding something in. We sat down, clasped her hands together, and looked up at me: "Inna – I had a dream last night..." Her face grew pale. "In my dream, I was riding a black horse and wearing a long black dress. Around my neck I had a heavy chain necklace with a large cross over my chest. The wind was whipping and the horse kept galloping faster and faster...faster and faster until I could see a cliff approaching..." She put one hand over her head and partially obscured her eyes. "Right before we reached the cliff...right before we galloped over the edge...I saw a furious bolt of white lightning...it felt like the horse was flying out of control...and...then...I woke up..."

She paused for several seconds, which seemed like an eternity. I could see she was in a cold sweat: "Inna. I'm sorry...I'm sorry...I had to tell...I had to tell you so you'd understand...and not think mommy..." She paused again, this time more briefly: "That's the reason I decided to finally show you the medallion I've been hiding away all this time."

"So, this was all just a dream?" I said, relieved that nothing bad had actually happened. In that time of real, daily struggle to fend off starvation, agonizing over a scary fantasy seemed absurd. I knew mother liked to interpret dreams, but I'd never heard of a premonition, and couldn't comprehend why this upset her so. In my own childishly naïve, straight-forward way, I said: "Dreams aren't real mommy, don't be silly, it's just your imagination."

For a brief moment, I felt like I was the grown up comforting the child, and it gave me an odd sense of satisfaction and pride. This was amplified by the fact that I'd overcome my own nightmares about father dying, which reinforced my belief that I knew better.

But why didn't Mother know better?

"I hope you're right Inna." Mother said, sobbing anxiously. "But dreams aren't always imaginary, sometimes they're a sign...a sign from heaven."

"*What outdated nonsense.*" I thought to myself incredulously, feeling that, thanks to my teachers, I was wiser than mother with her religious superstition. Despite my exasperation, I said nothing further.

Always busy with my own affairs, I hadn't really noticed how much mother's face had changed since father left. Her eyes seemed to flicker with an unsteady light, her movements were increasingly disjointed, and she often sat quietly brooding for hours on end. For me, life as a 13-year-old had so many new things to offer and was filled with beauty. The school year had come to a close. I finished the eighth grade with good grades and would enter the ninth as one of the top students in my class.

Summer drew me outside into nature. I made a point to finish my housework early in the morning so that I could spend the day exploring forests and walking along the murky Vorskla river that ran along the eastern edge of town with my classmates. I had always loved the outdoors, and spent hours wandering through the prairies and woods, and took a keen interest in the great variety of plant and animal life and enjoyed listening to the birds singing.

Along the riverbank, I would search for the abundant black crabs, turning them over and amusing myself at how they flailed about. But I never did anything to harm a living creature. Every time I would examine one, I would see to it that I placed it back where I had found it and let it go.

In the heat of the day, you could always find me in the water. I was a good swimmer and often fetched water lilies from the middle of the river to take home to mother. One evening as I was returning home with a lily bouquet, Mother unexpectedly came out to meet me with a happy look on her face and handed me what looked like a postcard. Surprised, I read from the officially typed telegram that Nyurka had been arrested: "Your stolen items have been almost entirely accounted for and are being stored at the police station. We ask that you retrieve them as soon as possible."

"What wonderful news!" I said.

Mother seemed suddenly agitated. "Yes...but I can't get the dream with the black horse out of my mind..."

"But Mommy, how could you spoil such wonderful news with that nonsense?"

"You're probably right, I shouldn't let it bother me, but I can't seem to forget it..."

"I think you have too much time to sit around and think about it." I finally interjected. "Wouldn't you like to take a nice long walk with me by the river for once?"

She hesitated, and said: "Yes...yes, I think that would be good. Tomorrow after we pick our things up at the police station, we'll go for that walk."

"And do you happen to know where your father is staying?" Mother said, surprising me. "Now that we're getting all our things back, he can finally come back home..."

I was delighted to no end at those words. "I'll go first thing tomorrow to his office and call on him." I promised enthusiastically.

"You do that, my child. He is probably not doing so well himself." She said, sounding as if a weight had been lifted from her heart.

Oh, how Mother seemed to have changed, I thought. Happily, I exclaimed: "Everything is going to be alright when Papa returns, you'll see, Mommy!"

"You're right, and I'm going to start to share everything I earn with him." She pledged with a quiet, shaky voice.

The next day we had a lot planned. Mother put on a white dress, fixed her hair and prepared breakfast. I cleaned our room and got dressed up nicely in my dark blue sarafan, a traditional Russian dress, to accompany mother downtown.

She called to me, speaking in an odd-sounding voice with a bewildered look on her face: "Inna! Look at this cup. Before it looked tall and skinny, but now it looks short and stout."

I laughed. "Mom, don't be silly, how could the cup change shape? It's always looked like that."

"Maybe you're right, but it just seems like it looked different earlier."

"How strange." I thought and couldn't figure out what was going on with her.

Half an hour later, on our way to town, as we were walking quietly side-by-side, Mother came to an abrupt halt, turned towards the sun, looked towards it for a moment, then burst out in alarm: "Inna, go home quickly and take off your sarafan!"

"Why should I do that?"

"The dress is too dark, it's attracting the sun! Look at how crookedly the sun is hanging...what will we do if it falls on our heads?"

I was shocked: "Mother, are you feeling sick? What are you talking about?"

"I feel fine, Inna. Come on, let's keep going."

She accelerated her pace. I followed with a sense of foreboding. What was I supposed to do? If there was only some way for me to contact Father... Mother continued on for a time in relative quiet and did nothing further to alarm me. I began to calm down and tried to put her odd behavior out of my mind.

But then she began again: "The houses are taller and the street narrower today. Do you want to go eat a piece of cake with me, dear?"

Once she mentioned cake, my disquiet evaporated, I hadn't had anything sweet in years: "Cake, of course, are you going to buy some for us?"

"Yes, as much as you want. Let's go to the bakery."

We walked into a large bakery and I ordered a slice of my favorite: Chocolate cake. Mother even allowed me to get a scoop of vanilla ice cream with it. It was like a dream come true as I enjoyed the melting ice cream and warm, moist cake perfectly complementing one another. After I finished, I sat in a pleasant stupor, trying to process what I had tasted, as if I wanted the taste to linger on forever.

A ticking brought me back to my senses. I looked over at a clock hanging on the bakery wall and was reminded of the purpose of our journey: "The police station is only open until noon. We need to hurry, Mother."

"Why then?" She replied. "Our things aren't there anymore. Nyurka paid me a visit last night and told me that she'd gotten away with it all."

"Now you're talking completely crazy again! Are you trying to scare me or make me angry?"

"I don't want to upset anyone. See – Nyurka really did visit me."

Without warning, she stood up and sniffed the air: "What smells so funny in here? I can't breathe." She suddenly grabbed at her chest and ripped her dress, tearing away several small buttons.

She looked around bewildered, and then ran abruptly out onto the street.

"Mommy, Mommy!" I cried, running after her: "Please stop!"

But I couldn't catch up with her as she ran faster and faster towards our home. When I got home, I found her sitting in the middle of the room with a hatchet. My eyes widened:

"What are you going to do?" I screamed in horror.

"Our furniture is growing...Just look at it, the closets are about to reach the ceiling. If they break through the roof, everything will collapse on our heads and kill us." With that she began to swing the hatchet, smashing it into drawers. Wood splintered and flew in every direction.

I ran out to the street and began to scream for help at the top of my voice. Soon, a large group of people stood in front of our house. I followed them to see what they would do with Mother.

"She's gone out of her mind!" I thought, cowering against the wall. In the meantime, she had ripped off her clothes and was dancing wildly in front of the growing crowd of onlookers around the burning kerosene stove. No one dared approach her.

"Make a sacrifice to God - you disgusting pack of atheists – or we're all dead!" She screamed, hurling a burning piece of wood towards the gathered onlookers.

The crowd backed up and someone called for the police.

When mother saw the militia men approaching, she put the "Primus" cooker on the table and said: "Did you bring a black horse for me to ride?" Her eyes were burning coals, and somehow, she'd managed to cut herself and had smeared a streak of dark red blood across her forehead.

I flashed back to mother's nightmare. Tears were streaming down my cheeks as my mother was restrained and led out of the house. Nobody noticed me or cared. The men grabbed her by the arm. She attempted to resist and pull away, but the two men were much stronger and quickly restrained and bound her hands behind her back. One of the militia men swiped up a torn tablecloth, effortlessly ripped a hole in the middle, and gently fit it over her head, and tied a piece of rope around it at her waist so she wouldn't be naked as they led her out to their carriage. I looked around at the surreal, chaotic scene left behind. The small stove stood, still smoking, on the table. The floor wreaked of kerosene and was littered with books, shattered wooden boards, broken dishes, and the odd piece of silverware or broken metal handle from the cabinets and cupboards.

And there, beneath the splinters, to my disbelief and horror, lay the mutilated remains of mother's icons. The hatchet, fresh streaks of blood staining its handle, was wedged crookedly in Mother's favorite, the one she had once prayed to every evening before things had started to change. I drew closer, stood directly over it, and could see that the blade had made a large gash - separating Mother Mary from the Baby Jesus.

Only after the police had left the house did a few of the neighbors turn to me: "Come with us, you poor thing!"

I didn't hear a thing, nothing registered. For a long time, I stood in the doorway and watched as the police carriage disappeared into the distance. That evening my father, who had been told what happened by a caring neighbor, came home.

"We've got to stick together from now on, my daughter."

That evening, the items that had been recovered from Nyurka were returned to us by the police. We unpacked everything and put it all away.

"Mother shouldn't see this all." I pleaded with father.

"Mother will return, my child, and everything will be fine again. I found a better job now and will soon earn twice what I used to earn."

"Oh father..." I sobbed, hugging him around the neck. "Why couldn't you have done that sooner? Maybe things would have been different." After that I told him how Mother had said that she wanted to ask him to return home. With that, I ran to the attic, retrieved the medallion mother had shown me, and handed it to father. He opened it and looked at the photos inside, and I told him how mother had kept it safely hidden-away all these years.

Tears began to well-up in his eyes: "My dear Zina, I knew she had a good heart and that these harsh times had forced her to change into something she had never been before... But it was all too much for her, too much for us..." He said, deep in thought.

"And how will we go forward from here?" He added with questioning concern in his voice. When I looked at him, I understood that this life and been too much for him as well.

Only after a long pause in the conversation, could I bring myself to add: "I don't believe that you love her anymore father."

"I've always loved your mother very much, sweetheart, but I couldn't always show it in these years of misery. It's often the case in life that difficult times drive people who love one another apart."

"You know father – I'm never going to get married! Because if difficult times are enough to break two people apart, then I would rather not marry anyone to begin with."

"You're still too young to decide that. These days there are girls who are already getting engaged at 15, but you should prepare yourself for life, go to school and learn a profession."

"Of course, Father, I've already thought about that all."

“But for now, we’ve got to get this household straightened out before Mother comes home healthy, and you have a lot of work to do Inna.”

“Gladly, Father, but I’m not sure if I can do it all myself.”

Only now did the full gravity of our situation hit us, and for the first time we understood how difficult things would be without her...

Chapter 11 – Departure

"All right then my little housekeeper, keep your head up and don't misbehave." Father said one day and kissed me on the forehead.

"Will you be home soon, Papa?"

"At four o'clock, sweetheart, make sure you cook us something to eat."

"Glady!"

"You've got to hang in there a little while longer, because, for now at least, Mother isn't allowed to visit us without permission from the doctor."

I sighed and accompanied my father to the front door. Then I went back to our room. I hesitantly began to clean up. Today it seemed especially difficult to work. I couldn't stop thinking about Mother and her illness. Even the summer in all its glory, with blossoming flowers and warm sunshine, couldn't lure me outside. Day-for-day I ruminated over what had passed and missed her terribly. Life wasn't the same as before. This day I again sat at the edge of my bed and longed to see her. Memories of my earlier, more carefree childhood ran through my mind. I reminisced about the happy times.

My mother was so young and beautiful back then. She always laughed and found joy in everything, like a small child. In those now distant days, life in Russia was still directed by the policies of Lenin, who allowed for relatively wide economic and spiritual freedom. This relaxed order, known as the "New Economic Policy," was intended to counteract the devastation wrought by the Revolution and civil war. Things had begun to slowly improve for most people with the advent of peace, but Stalin's strict collectivist policies, introduced in 1928, harshly reversed that.

As late as 1926, my father was even able to take a vacation to Berlin under the still relatively open conditions of the time. He brought home many souvenirs for mother, and I still remember how she opened all the presents and the childlike joy with which she embraced father. Finally, she came to a large, boxed present, and I remember how she unpacked it with wonderment and discovered a big, beautiful doll inside.

“That’s for our little Inna!” Father declared. “Oh, how beautiful!” said Mother, taking the doll out and playing with it herself. She loved it so much that she even took the doll with her to bed, and Father, who noticed my protests, took me by the arm and said: “Inna, sweetheart, let your Mom have the doll for today, I’ll give you some other really nice things tomorrow.”

The next day, Mother brought me my “Alice” – and the maid followed with a large box. “Here’s the doll and all her accessories.” She opened the box and showed me all of the clothing father had bought for the doll.

How happy we both were! We dressed her several times. Father laughed when he saw us playing together: “I should have brought back two dolls.” He said and kissed mother, who warmly embraced him. My parents both sat next to me on the carpet and hugged me as well. The door opened and Babushka walked in. Even she laughed at this happy scene but reminded me that my French lesson was about to start and told me I needed to be punctual.

She took me by the hand, and I left the room crestfallen, disappointed that I could no longer play. Nonetheless, having an energetic, intelligent grandmother there to keep order around the house was truly a blessing. I would have been spoiled rotten without her. From the age of four, she saw to it that I learned to read and sew. She kept an eye on me to make sure I behaved myself and minded my manners. She would often say: “There’s nothing like a good upbringing for a child. Times may be peaceful now, but God knows what young people will have to face and overcome in the future." Grandmother was right, and I am grateful for the foundation she provided me. It made me strong, capable and upright in the face of life's many difficult challenges, injustices and temptations.

Mother was only too happy to cede these duties to Babushka. Instead, she kept herself occupied with music, French novels, horseback riding and visits with friends. In a sense, she was a child herself, never taking her duties as a mother and wife all-too-seriously.

Back then, in the "New Economic Policy" era of the mid-1920s, we were still allowed to celebrate Christmas and Easter. Naturally, we had a large, festively decorated Christmas tree each year in our study. But that was all so long ago! Like a beautiful, distant dream, it seemed to float past me. Only a quiet, cherished memory of never-ending happiness remained. How different life had become. All of the contentment and coziness was gone. Now we were happy if we had enough to survive.

I no longer understood why people in times past needed such large houses, or why mother needed to wear jewelry, or why we needed such fancy paintings on the wall or elaborate rugs on the floor. We could, of course, also live without all those adornments.

In my sober, modern assessment of things, I found that one could exist quite adequately in a simple room with minimal furniture and few clothes. As a thirteen-year-old Pioneer, I'd wonder things like:

Why did people put so many dishes on the table when you can eat from one plate? Why did grandmother teach me how to properly hold a knife and fork, when you can eat potatoes with a spoon, and grab meat with your hands and cut it with your teeth?

Why do people need rings, earrings, and jewelry, when you can live without them? Why eat borscht and porridge separately, when it will all end up in the same stomach? Why wash your boots if it's raining outside and they'll just get dirty again?! Why cook lunch if there are canteens! Why think about yourself when you have to live and work for the good of the people? These old things were for the bourgeoisie! Wasn't it all just useless excess, the way we'd lived before?

My thoughts reflected how I had been educated in school.

Now instead of expensive paintings and icons, portraits of Lenin and Stalin hung in the corner, and instead of melodic classical music on the radio, monotone Soviet propaganda blared all around us.

Father supplied me with 3 rubles a day to take care of the household. I had to manage the money properly so that it would provide enough for our meals. But despite my best efforts, even that did not always work out. And because I sometimes failed in my attempts at cooking and other tasks, my desire to keep house gradually diminished, and I began to neglect this or that chore. Soon I began to feel unwell in my own home.

So, one day I went to Father, who was now working at the local comptroller's office, and told him tactfully but firmly that I no longer wanted to care for the home by myself and that I was at the end of my nerves.

"Why at the end of your nerves?" he countered.

"I don't know, I'm just afraid to be alone all the time."

When father, despite my objections, told me to leave his office and go back home, I was suddenly completely overcome by a shaking that seized my entire body. Overwhelmed by what he was seeing, Father took leave from work and took me home. He sat me down and asked me to explain this overwhelming fear. I couldn't explain the feeling, but I told him firmly that I could no longer stand to be home alone. He thought things over carefully, told me to get dressed, and took me to a psychiatrist who examined me closely and shook his head.

"This girl has been through too much for someone her age. She needs to move away – a change of scenery - so she can forget about all that has happened." He said with great empathy.

"Alright – I will write my in-laws!" father replied. "They live down south on the Black Sea. Perhaps they can take her in for a time.

"I would strongly recommend that." the doctor said, nodding his head, and shook our hands.

After that day, I accompanied my father to his office and waited the long hours until he had finished work.

In the meantime, we were now also allowed to visit Mother. The poor thing recognized us, but her speech was slurred, and her mind was still clearly clouded. She thought she was a small child, liked to play in the sand, and told us we should buy her a big ball. After our visit time was over, Mother left us without a word. It was painful to watch as she left, and my heart felt so heavy that it felt difficult to breath, and I felt as if I was choking. I was totally out of it when I got back home and cried the rest of the day.

To my Father's heartfelt relief, my grandparents wrote back and agreed to take me in. I only knew my mother's parents through the rare letters we exchanged and stories my parents told. But the news that I would be going to live with them by the sea made me very happy.

For the first time in my life, I would be able to take long train ride, which seemed particularly adventurous to me. I organized and packed my things quickly and almost forgot my cares in preparing for the journey.

On the day of my trip, my father brought me to the train station with a sense of well-meaning concern. He introduced me to a friend of his, a Comrade Vassiliev, who was traveling the same route and was willing to accompany me.

"This is comrade Vasiliev, he is going to Novorossiysk. He will accompany you to Tonneljnaya..."

"I know," I interrupted, "then my grandparents will meet me at Tonneljnaya, and I'll take a bus through the mountains, through the passes, to Anapa, to the sea! You already told me all that!"

"Well, Olyechka, be a good girl, obey your grandparents, and write often!" he said as he handed me a bundle with my meager belongings.

He gave me a big hug and looked at me as if he knew that this separation would be the last time, we would ever see one another. That thought didn't hit me immediately, as I was too focused on the train and all that awaited me.

Finally, the conductor blew his whistle and raised the green flag. My heart was filled with a strange feeling of joyful anticipation. Only when the train started to move, and I waved to father through the window, did a sudden sense of sadness begin to rise in me. He looked sadly into my eyes, as if wanting to say: "Don't leave me here all alone!" I saw his figure, waving his handkerchief farewell, grow ever-smaller, and finally disappear along with the platform and station behind the tower of the water pumping station.

For the first and last time, I saw my beautiful Poltava from the train window. I had spent my entire life there and had so many wonderful and difficult memories. Its numerous parks and gardens were majestically decorated with luxuriant greenery illuminated by the rays of the August sun. It seemed to me that all the houses were peering back at me sadly with their shining windows. Even the water tower seemed to lean sideways at the top of its old tower in mourning. This town, my home in the world, stood thoughtfully and quietly atop its hillside and bid me its final farewell. I was suddenly overcome by a wave of emotion, and tears ran down my cheeks. I began to loudly sob.

My travel companion Vassiliev, a kind middle-aged man, noticed and took pity on me. He put his hand on my shoulder and said: “Why are you crying little lady? You shouldn’t feel so sad. After all, you’re being allowed to go visit the Black Sea where the summer resort season is in full-swing and the grapes are ripening! Have you ever seen the sea?”

“No.” I replied. I dried my eyes somewhat embarrassed and smiled: “Are you also traveling to the sea?”

“Yes! But unfortunately, I have to come back again soon, my travels are just for business.”

“I’m very curious about the sea. Do you like it there?” I asked.

“Oh yes, definitely. But look out the window...There is another sea out there. Do you like it?”

“A sea?” I said skeptically. I put my face closer to the window and Comrade Vassiliev was indeed correct: Astride our train stretched an endless amber sea of grain, wheat and barley. It extended far and wide to the horizon and glimmered gloriously in the reddening light of the August sunset. When a quiet breeze blew across the fields, the golden stalks would form waves and ripples just like a sea.

“It’s our Ukrainian sea that nourishes so many people.”

“I didn’t know that the fields of our homeland were so endlessly large and wide.” I said, captivated by the scene.

“Earlier it was different. Back then, each farmer had his own small piece of land and worked it himself and the farmland had a totally different appearance. It was broken-up by property lines, paths and villages. Today all the land belongs to the State. The land is all farmed by a collective. And that's why the old farmer's plots of grain have been transformed into an endless sea. It's a peaceful scene today, but not that long ago, many a farmer cried bitter tears when they were forced to surrender their property and join the state collective farm and economic system."

I really didn't completely understand his commentary but looked with an even more keen interest at the site before me.

We stopped at a village station for ten minutes. Outside, along the platform, women and children stood hawking things to eat on small, hastily erected, rickety wooden stands. Comrade Vassiliev told me we should stretch our legs and go have a look, and I was only too happy to tag along, as I was starting to feel intensely hungry from travel. We purchased two apples, a dried red tomato, half a loaf of bread and a few slices of dried sausage. Back on the train, we fixed sandwiches and cut the apples into quarters, which I munched down in just a few bites. I tapped my feet and laughed merrily, and my cares seemed to disappear as I watched the world go by.

The train went faster and faster. The sea of golden grain was occasionally broken up by small green forests and tiny villages. I observed disagreeable scenes of poorly dressed, unkempt village children, who waved kindly up to us. Here and there I also saw Ukrainian women with a wooden yoke across their shoulders with a water bucket hanging from either side. Large herds of cows and sheep passed by. And always the amber sea of grain returned that stretched endlessly into the distance.

I particularly noticed that all of the farmers I saw in the fields and villages went barefoot. Most had old, oftentimes worn-out clothing on. Their hands were black from work. The faces were marked by worries and fatigue. All appeared to be truly poor and unhappy.

This was beautiful Ukraine, my rich, large, fertile and yet, deeply impoverished, homeland. The sun set ever further and soon totally disappeared completely behind the horizon. A gentle, peaceful summer night descended upon the earth. I couldn't leave my window and with rapt curiosity observed the heavenly and solemn beauty of nature and the quiet, small white village houses that shone beneath the moonlight.

In that moment, I had forgotten everything: My parents, my hometown and all the hardships that I had endured.

The train took me ever further from my old life towards a new, unknown future...

Chapter 12 – Anapa

In a peaceful bay, on the upper north-eastern edge of the Black Sea lies the small town of Anapa which, with its long, beautiful, golden beaches, and picturesque seaside cliffs, can be counted among the best-known resorts of the Russian south. The population, in 1935 around five to eight thousand, was comprised mainly of Armenians and Greeks. Some Russians lived there as well. Most had either fled to the Caucuses during the Revolution or had moved there to improve their health on the coast of the Black Sea, known for its many sanatoriums and spas.

The Armenians and Greeks mainly occupied themselves with fishing and vineyard keeping. The Russians, on the other hand, often took jobs as civil servants in town, teachers in local schools, and as employees at the hotels and sanitoriums, or worked in the workshops or wineries. Naturally everything was under State control. No one owned their own villa, and one could only lay claim to a small, single-story clay house as something akin to private property. Even here, as elsewhere, everyone had to earn their daily bread through great toil. And despite every effort and the hard work of the people, poverty was ever-present in Anapa. Life in winter was especially difficult. Most residents had no work in the offseason as the sanatoriums and hotels were all closed. People had to scrape by with what they had earned and squirreled-away over the summer.

And there was little to eat. There was often no sugar at all through the entire winter. To buy bread in this harsh time, you often had to stand in line through the night. Naturally, there was no chocolate, fruit or fresh vegetables, and people were genuinely happy if they just had enough stale bread to survive.

For that reason, everyone waited impatiently for spring to arrive with its golden rays of sun to warm the earth and the sea and bring the little city back to life. The collective mood improved, and people started to prepare for the coming work that accompanied the high season. Then, as soon as the first of thousands of vacationers arrived, the harsh winter was banished like a bad dream. Locals would hastily tidy up their homes and rooms to rent out to visitors. They would live in their kitchens, wooden stalls, or even sleep under the stars to make more space. People had to find ways to make as much money as possible, and tourists typically paid quite well, as one needed money to be able to take a vacation to begin with in the Soviet Union of the 1930s.

It was therefore relatively rare to see a common laborer or farmer among the vacationers. Usually, one would only encounter the wives and children of officials and officers, and other elites including favored artists, scholars and politicians as well as people who, despite the draconian laws forbidding it, knew how to make money trading and speculating on the black market.

The little town itself did not have any particularly imposing or impressive buildings. Only an old Ottoman fortress gate, renamed the "Russian Gate," and the tall lighthouse on the coast, served as landmarks. The streets and paths were paved with smooth, rectangular stones, with the main street named for the famous Russian poet Pushkin. Almost all of the houses were just one story, but always clean and freshly whitewashed. In front of most, stood a large, well-kept garden. There were also alleyways and parks filled with well-cared for flowerbeds.

Best of all was the view of the sea and the fresh sea-breeze. During the sunny summer months, the wide sandy beach, bordered on the south by a rocky series of picturesque embankments and cliffs, drew large crowds of scantily clad bathers. Sprinkled along the sea was a sea of humanity: A panoply of parasols, striped bathing suits, white bathing caps and cotton towels, some propped up on sticks to form make-shift tents, and half-naked bodies of varying hues, ranging from lobster red to hazelnut brown, stretched as far as the eye could see. More than two dozen double-sided-benches - each covered by a shanty roof supported by four wooden beams - formed a uniform row which curved gently along the top of the beach – offering shelter to the sunburned and weary – and perhaps the only sense of uniformity amidst the chaos. A small grassy embankment demarcated the beach from the town, and a path with a sprinkling of kiosks and small tourist stands that sold ice-cream, snacks, grapes and trinkets, ran parallel to it all.

Visitors were also drawn by the fresh fruits available at the marketplace, which was relatively large compared to like-sized towns. Especially great numbers of people jammed its stalls in August and September, when the wine grapes ripened and customers flocked to enjoy the heavenly treat. A newly built four-story hotel on the coast, several villas housing the sanatoriums and guest rooms and numerous restaurants and cafes on the main street rounded out the town. In those months Anapa resembled a giant beehive, and from all sides one could hear the laughter, singing and music that filled the air of this happy place. Even the smallest, most humble rooms had been filled to the brim in high season, which was now in full swing.

I arrived in the midst of this beehive. After a nearly 20-hour train ride that terminated at the Tonneljnaya train station, I had to take an omnibus the final 40 kilometers west through the mountains. In Tonneljnaya my grandparents were already waiting for me. They recognized me immediately as I stepped off the train and called out: "You are the spitting image of your father and don't look at all like your mother!"

I already knew that I didn't much resemble my dark-eyed mother but didn't like to be reminded of it.

"I can't help it!" I said, shrugging my shoulders and stepping out onto the platform.

"That doesn't bother us a bit!" Grandpa laughed. "My father was a hearty young man in his youth, and you also look healthy and vital with your bright eyes and brown hair!" He patted me kindly on the shoulder. Their kind words and welcoming manner immediately made me feel better.

I really liked my grandparents. My petite white-haired grandmother Lydia Pigurenko was still a sprightly lady with dark eyes that looked out at me framed by long black eyelashes and eyebrows. You could see that she had been a very beautiful woman in her youth. By contrast, my grandfather, Joseph Pigurenko, was tall, had broad shoulders and resembled a large bear. He had dark blonde hair that, despite his 70 years, still showed no sign of gray. His eyes were aquamarine, he had a high forehead, and he had a large, fleshy nose. He had a large mustache and laughed mischievously, a true Ukrainian through-and-through.

My grandparents embraced and kissed me, and soon I felt very well and at home with them. We boarded an omnibus crammed with tourists to drive to my new home through the mountains.

Filled with curiosity, I asked Grandpa if we would see the Black Sea soon. "You have to be a little patient there, my dear, until we are out of the mountains." He answered.

After an hour's drive, we had passed through the mountain range with its many curves. I looked out and strained my eyes to catch a first glimpse of the sea but could only make out the vineyards and blue sky.

"Are we still not near the sea?" I asked a few times impatiently. Grandpa just laughed and pointed in the same direction that I had already been looking.

Finally, I was able to distinguish the large, still water from the blue sky. It stretched like an azure strip along the horizon and had nearly the same blue color as the sky itself. Only a tiny dark strip of water, barely visible to the naked eye, divided the sea from the sky.

"I thought the sea would be really dark. It's called the Black Sea after all." I said with a sense of wonderment.

"Just wait until we get closer. It will be much darker up close." Grandmother informed me.

Grandfather added: "It's like a huge mirror when the sea is calm like today. It just takes on the color of the sky. As soon as there is a flood or storm and the waves begin to swell up, the water shows its true color and becomes green or dark green, depending on the size of the waves. In fall and winter, when storms rumble across the lake and the waves look like a big wall and crash into one-another, then the sea does look almost black. It is then so violent and terrible that it resembles a cunning demon. But in whatever state you find it, the sea is wonderfully beautiful." And with that grandfather brought his small lesson to a conclusion.

Soon thereafter, I spotted the first humble houses of Anapa. As we approached the town, it captured my interest so much that I momentarily forgot the sea. Many sunburned people wandered the streets.

"Grandma, do you think that I will also get a nice tan like that here?" I asked, pointing at some people who appeared to have a particularly attractive tan.

"Those are Armenians!" She laughed. "But if you spend a lot of time on the beach lying under the sun, you'll get a nice healthy tan."

With that we arrived at the town marketplace, which strongly attracted my attention. Merchants stood in long rows with large baskets filled with wine grapes, apples, pears, plums, peaches, apricots and other fruit. There was also an abundance of vegetables. Tomatoes and cucumbers could be seen everywhere. Although it was well after noon, new customers kept wandering into the market. Their clothing, bathing suits and parasols presented a colorful scene. Everything resembled a festival. I couldn't contain my enthusiasm and clapped my hands together so loudly that everyone on the bus noticed me, which immediately tempered my enthusiasm.

To my pleasant surprise, the bus came to a halt and the driver called: "Final stop, everyone off!"

We walked 15 minutes through the straight, clean streets and arrived at my grandparents' modest home on the outskirts of town. It consisted of two rooms, which were rented out to guests at the moment, and a kitchen, in which our entire family life would play out for the time-being. The rooms were largely unadorned, but clean with fresh white walls. The unfinished floors were made of simple pine and freshly scrubbed. My grandparents did not have a large mirror or piano like the one we had back in Poltava.

The furniture was all simple and sturdy and the colors and woods used matched tastefully. The tall bed frames were nickel-coated and the beds and pillows had fresh covers. A few family photos decorated the walls. In the kitchen were three collapsible improvised beds, a dining table, a few stools and a large dish cabinet, along with my grandmother's sewing machine.

I wondered at how good this simple abode looked.

"Your grandfather constructed all the furniture himself." Grandmother told me proudly.

"But Grandfather isn't a real carpenter, is he?"

"He's not a carpenter, but there is almost no job he can't do. He is a jack-of-all-trades. Carpenter, painter, gardener, fisherman, vineyard keeper and even a natural scientist. In other words, a man of many talents!"

Unwittingly, I compared my grandfather to my father. How different the two were: Grandfather so rugged and tough, and my father so gentle, soft and sensitive by contrast. I suddenly felt that I had more in common with my grandfather and that I was strongly connected by something to that authentic old Ukrainian. We grew very close, and despite the generational difference, we became something akin to soulmates.

Grandpa worked delivering food to the sanatoriums and hotels. When he wasn't at work, he often snuck away to a makeshift workshop he'd constructed in a nearby barn. Against the back wall stood a work bench with a crate filled with nails and hammer on top of it. On the wall behind it hung all sorts of saws, chisels, planes and other carpentry tools. Rough boards sat in a pile by the front left leg and finished wooden shipping crates sat in a stack to the right of the bench. Grandpa sold these to tourists wanting to mail home bottles of sweet local wine, and with them, happy memories of Anapa.

My Grandmother, despite her efforts as a homemaker, also strove to make extra money by teaching French and German and by tutoring school children in every subject.

"How do you get so much done every day?" I once asked them both. "Wouldn't you rather go to the sea with me?"

"We feel very happy, very happy indeed..." replied Grandma "...when we can have all our children and grandchildren visit us whenever they please, regardless of what time of year. And sometimes all of your aunts and uncles and their kids visit us together, with the exception of your mother. But this family gathering can only take place when we all work together and save as much on the side as we can so that we don't have to worry, even when the whole family is here."

"But why has my mother never come to visit you?" I asked one day, wishing to know more.

Grandma deliberated for a while. Then she said, in a somber and somewhat dejected tone: "There was once a falling out, my dear, between your grandfather and your mother, and afterwards your mother wanted nothing more to do with us. We reached out to her many times since, but with no success."

"What did my mother have against Grandpa?" I asked, taken aback.

Grandma sat down on a bench, pulled me to her side, and began, "Then I do have to tell you the story: When your mother was still young, we all lived together on a large estate near Kharkov. We had our own farm and bred horses. Each of our children received a horse for their 16th birthday. Your mother had a white steed which she could ride masterfully. She was the most beautiful among her sisters and just as proud as her father, your grandfather.

"The owner of the neighboring estate, who was very wealthy but no longer the youngest of men, often saw your mother out riding and fell in love with her. He went to Grandpa to ask his blessing for her hand in marriage, and Grandpa, without so much as asking us, obliged.

"When I heard what had happened, I was very anxious and afraid, because I already knew for some time that your father had already gotten to know your mother, and that they had fallen in love. I also knew that your grandfather would not break his word and would disown your mother if she failed to fulfill his promise.

"So, I went to your grandfather and bid him not to tell your mother about his decision for several days, and used the time to confer my own estate near Poltava with a large piece of land on your mother. With that, I had somewhat secured the future of my favorite child. Then everything that followed happened much as I expected..."

"What happened next?" I asked feverishly, as Grandma paused.

"Then your mother went to Poltava and married your father against Grandpa's wishes without his blessing. Soon the Revolution broke out and your grandfather and I had to flee our estate. Your parents also escaped of course, but our wealthy neighbor, your mother's former admirer, was murdered in an uprising by the rebellious peasants who farmed his land. Of course, when we found out about that, Grandpa was overjoyed that your mother had not ended up marrying him and sharing his fate, and the grudge he had held over her defiance evaporated immediately. Later we invited your parents to Anapa, but they were too proud to accept our invitation."

With that, Grandma concluded the story. I was confused. In my childish naivety, I'd assumed my mother's family was unburdened by the past and had always been living a carefree life by the sea.

"You were wealthy once too, Grandma?" I puzzled, wishing to know more.

"Yes, yes, but that was a long time ago. In the meantime, we've been living here for twenty years like simple workers. Nobody here knows our past."

"I think that Mother is going to want to visit Anapa now." Remembering mother's current condition, I added: "When she is feeling better."

"I hope so sweetheart, at least to visit you if nothing else."

"Not only to visit me. She should visit you again and make amends with you and Grandpa."

"Yes, darling! Then my wish to once again embrace all my children would come true." As she said the word "embrace," I could see Grandmother's eyes slowly begin to well with tears.

Chapter 13 – My Cousins

"Today we're going to visit your Uncle Victor!" Said Grandpa one Sunday morning.

I was happy about this adventure. Mother had often told me of Uncle Victor, my mother's brother, who had also fled to the Caucuses during the Revolution and had two sons: Alexei, who was 15 and Boris, 13. I looked forward to meeting them. Uncle Victor lived in the nearby village of Dzhemete where he and his wife Aunt Sonia where teachers at the local school. Our journey there took us nearly two hours along the coastal beaches on foot. The morning sun was bright and warm, and it was already a habit of mine to go for regular swims.

Victor and Sonia were already waiting when we arrived, but my cousins were nowhere in sight. I impatiently asked where they were. Uncle Victor took me to the sea where they were out for a swim. He called them to come out of the water, introduced me to the two sopping-wet boys, and told them to show me around and look after me. Then he went back home, leaving us to play. We stood a while not knowing what to say. I looked awkwardly at the ground, as I sensed the boys were scanning me with critical, keen eyes from head to foot The younger of the two, Boris, soon broke the ice by asking me if I could swim.

When I nodded yes, both said: "Then come on – let's go swimming!" Upon which I enthusiastically ran after them into the sea. The two were not exactly gentle: They splashed me from all sides and even tried to push me underwater and hold me down for a few seconds. Naturally, I wasn't terribly fond of that. But I showed the boys that I wasn't afraid and knew how to defend myself. Without so much as a word, I grabbed them both by the feet, yanking them beneath the surface, forcing them to take a dive, like it or not.

When the three of us came back to the surface, the two boys laughed and said to each other: "Watch out – she knows how to stick up for herself!"

Then they nodded at each other – as if knowing what the other meant – and disappeared again, I waited anxiously for what might be coming next. Momentarily, both resurfaced close to me, each holding a large sea crab with long pincers. They held them right up to my face in an apparent attempt to frighten me. To their surprise, I grabbed the crabs by their backs and pulled them out of their outstretched hands.

"Ah!" I said, looking the crabs over carefully: "They look quite different from our river crabs! Please fetch a few more! We can dig a pond for them on the beach so it's easier to check them out."

The boys looked astonished: "You are really different from the other girls who come here on vacation!" Said the oldest, Alexei, with admiration. "They are all scared witless and run away screaming when we show them crabs!"

The boys followed me to the beach. We dug a rectangular hole in the sand and filled it with water. Then they retrieved several more crabs of all sizes. I turned over our captives and described the differences between these crabs and the black river crabs of my Ukrainian homeland. The sea crabs were very round and had a sandy-gray color and no tail like our river crabs. Their eyes were propped on two small stands like little sticks and moved around in all directions. They had six skinny feet with which they moved sideways and forwards, which I found comical and different from the river crab, which moved backwards.

And so we played together the rest of the day - and the boys looked for sea mussels and sea spiders and anything they thought might interest me.

Time passed quickly and we were all sad when Grandpa came to take me back home. The boys promised that they would visit me at my grandparents' and kept their word. Not long thereafter, they came to visit us and we immediately went to the sea.

"We want to go out on a boat today!" They shouted.

Grandma gave us a basket to take along filled with the scent of freshly baked bread, cheese and dried grapes. We headed to the beach and hopped in a large rowboat, struggling mightily to pull up the anchor half-burrowed in the sand. The boys, who had grown up on the sea, told me to hold on, and abruptly shoved the boat in the water and rowed us around with ease, with me at the rudder. Soon we were so far out to sea that we could barely make out the shoreline. Alexei unceremoniously threw a lifesaver overboard for me - just in case – and we jumped in the water. At first, I felt extremely unsettled to be swimming so far from shore. The sea was opaque and unfathomably deep, the bottom nowhere in sight. That said, I didn't want to let-on that I was afraid, and managed to keep my composure, trying not to think how far down it was or what strange sea creatures might nip at my heals or even bite me. Soon, we were back in the boat devouring the sandwiches and grapes, having built up a healthy appetite swimming in the cool water. The fresh sea breeze and warm sun gently dried my skin and gave me that refreshed, invigorated feeling like none other.

"Look over there – a ship!" Alexei yelled suddenly and pointed off into the distance. A large freight ship steamed along in the distance. Without a word, the boys sat down at their posts and started to row towards the ship. As we got close, to my terror, we got caught in the ship's powerful wake – and our little boat was tossed around like a bobber. The boys laughed and shouted with excitement. By contrast, I held onto the bench I was sitting on for dear life and could only look on with eyes wide open as this dangerous game played out.

"What if the boat capsizes!" I thought in horror.

Luckily, it didn't come to that. The steamer pulled away and the sea again became calm and quiet. Tired, but exhilarated, I arrived home after this adventure. My cousins promised to visit me as often as possible, to play and go swimming. With that, our friendship was sealed. In the meantime, I had also become familiar with other kids my age around Anapa. But, at first, they were leery and distant, treating me as they might a tourist.

When they first saw me with my two cousins, they joked: "Alexei and Boris must have found a new wife!"

But my cousins wouldn't permit these taunts. The slugged the offenders and told them that we were relatives and that I was no stuck-up city girl, but a "totally cool guy." And with that, no one bothered us, and some of the kids even showed a desire to get to know me better. And so - I spent my entire summer vacation with my new friends, boys and girls, and savored the wide-open, beautiful life of the sunny south. By the time this wonderful summer was over and I went to my new school in Anapa, I had already gotten to know some of my classmates.

The first day of school on September 1 is a day of celebration in Russia. As a student, you would get dressed-up in your best clothing, greet everyone and introduce yourself to anyone you didn't know, and swap stories about your summer vacation. There were no lessons on the first day. All the boys and girls gathered in the courtyard and played, danced and had fun together. There was no separation of boys and girls in schools, all the classes were and are mixed there.

Because I was the "new" kid, my classmates took a particular interest in me. They wanted to know everything: Where I was from, how my grades had been at my old school, my name and where I lived. I had to answer the same questions again-and-again.

In the coming days, as classes got going, everyone was curious to see how I would do. I approached this new school seriously and made every effort to succeed, and soon came to be known as one of the best students, as the demands of the teachers in this small town were significantly lower than in my native city of Poltava. Some of the girls in my class sought to become closer friends with me. But I couldn't form a strong bond. Even though I spent lots of time with the other kids, I was still a loner on the inside.

I always felt very independent and have always been accustomed to directing my own life.

My relationship to my old homeland and parents also began to change for me on the inside. Although I regularly received letters from Poltava, I had a strange feeling when I thought about my old life. I think it must have been a homesickness for my parents. But I never felt like returning to Poltava. I liked my new home, and I began to love the little Black Sea town of Anapa with all my heart. With the start of school, my two cousins could no longer visit so often from their village. And the three of us would wait impatiently for Sundays, when we would often get together. As time passed, their visits became less frequent, as we became ever more occupied with our schoolwork.

I came to feel more and more lonely. A new, and to this point unknown longing began to grow inside of me for someone who would love me. Initially I didn't quite understand this longing and didn't know what was missing. My grandparents spoiled me so much with their love and attention and were always so good to me. But I sought something different and was often melancholy and locked in my own thoughts – which drew the attention of my deeply empathetic grandmother.

"What's wrong dear?" She would increasingly ask. But even that dear old soul had no answer for what plagued me. "Soon your mother will come, and everything will be fine Inna!" She would say, trying to comfort me, when she saw me sobbing.

Father began to report in his letters to us that mother was doing better day-by-day. Her madness had almost totally subsided, and the hope was that she would make a full recovery. My grandparents wrote my father back that he should make every effort to bring my mother to Anapa to recover.

But that letter strangely never received a reply.

At first my grandparents suspected that my mother still held a grudge over the old disagreement with my grandfather – which led me to write a letter to father pleading that it was my greatest wish to see mother healthy again in Anapa. But this letter also received no reply. The suspicion that something had gone afoul in Poltava began to increasingly plague us. Day after day we waited for the mailman to bring a reply, always to be disappointed.

Fear took hold of me as my grandparents began to discuss the possibility that my mother had relapsed and was doing badly. One day when I came home from school, Grandmother handed me a letter from Poltava written in an unfamiliar hand. I opened it, and with tears in my eyes read:

"Dear Inna, Because your father, who has been away now for some time, cannot write you, I wanted to inform you and your grandparents about the condition of your mother: Your mother was issued a full bill of health by us three weeks ago and sent home. In her first days back she felt very well, and when I visited her, she seemed happy and made a very positive impression. She certainly would not have relapsed had your father not suffered his misfortune. They took the poor man away again. After that, your mother had to be readmitted to our institution. I will keep you updated on further developments.

In hopes that your mother will soon make a full recovery, we send our heartfelt greetings,

Sister Lydia"

I looked at grandmother in disgust. "Grandma, why did they take Father away again?! Will life never-ever get better for my parents?!"

"That I can't tell you, Inna. But perhaps they arrested him again because he used to be wealthy."

"Wealthy?! But that was such a long time ago. My father isn't rich anymore, and he was already locked up for 2 years. In school they say that only 'enemies of the people' get arrested. What did my father ever do wrong?"

"No one can prove their innocence in this world we live in today." Grandmother countered.

"And if Father really did something wrong, why did they release him early last time? Did we go to all the effort to nurse him back to health from typhus just so they could arrest him again?" I said angrily.

"My dear child, your father was the son of a noble family." replied the wise old lady.

Now everything came into focus: We had been taught at school that all nobles were the sworn enemies of the people and that they had to be exterminated, otherwise, they would bring back the horrible ways of the past, when children couldn't go to school and slaves had to toil under their oppression. I had imagined as a child that a noble was a fearful thief, a treacherous murderer and a cunning archenemy. My childhood fantasies about these near-mythical villains who tormented the downtrodden proletariat simply did not correspond in the slightest with who I knew my father to be. Nothing made sense any more.

"Grandma, father doesn't look anything like an enemy!" I said with a defiant spirit.

"And he wasn't really an enemy, dear, he was just another unfortunate soul who was unable to bury his past and conceal it from the outside world. And let me give you some important advice: Never say anything to anyone about why your father was arrested. It could come back to haunt you as well. You are the child of a new era in which you have to live and make your way. That's why it would be best if you made your own peace with your father's fate in silence."

And in that moment, as unfair as Father's arrest was, I knew that Grandmother was right, and I had to remain silent. But the unspeakable pain and betrayal tormented me to the depths of my soul, which longed to cry out at the injustice of it all.

Chapter 14 – My First Secret

On a pleasant Saturday afternoon, my two cousins came to take me on an excursion and then to a vineyard festival. The boys worked every year during the grape harvest in their village collective and were allowed to take part in the harvest festival that followed. I gladly accepted their invitation and agreed to go with them the next morning so that we would arrive at the appointed time and location. As we were traveling to the village, we came upon the sea, and Boris suggested we take a boat and row out to meet a passing steamer. Alexei, however, who normally was only too happy to embark on such an adventure, curtly rejected the idea. He told us that he wanted to get home as soon as possible to still be able to go out that evening.

I found this all to be somewhat odd but didn't say anything and followed my cousins. Uncle Victor and Aunt Sonia were already waiting for us with dinner ready. Alexei quickly devoured his food, excused himself, and hurriedly got dressed.

"You don't really want to go out tonight, do you?" Aunt Sonia said, surprised.

"We are taking Inna to the beach to show her the bay in the moonlight. I'm also going to change clothes after dinner." Said Boris, trying to help his brother out.

"Since when did the boys get to be so vain?" Uncle Victor said, scoffing. "On Sundays past, we couldn't get them to put nice clothes on to save your life."

"It's all to impress Inna!" Aunt Sonia laughed.

The three of us finished dinner and quickly left the house. We took a few steps together and then Alexei bid us farewell and took off running towards the park. Boris and I continued on in silence, until I finally decided to ask where Alexei was actually going.

"I can't say! It's a secret!" Boris answered.

"I won't tell, I promise!" I ensured him.

"Girls can't keep their mouths shut. You're all gossips!"

"I can, I can!"

"You swear?"

"I swear!"

"And you promise you won't let Alexei notice that I told you?"

"Yes!"

"Fine, then I'll tell you..." Boris said, his voice growing quieter, nearly a whisper now. "Alexei has, you know, a girlfriend... He wants to meet her in the park."

"A girlfriend? What's the big deal? Why doesn't he bring her along?"

"You don't get it...not a girlfriend...it's not what you think. Alexei loves Nadya. He wants to marry her some day!"

"Aaah! Do you have a girlfriend too Boris?"

"No. You know what, I don't like the other girls, and Nadya is already taken! It's too bad that you are my cousin, otherwise we could be friends like that too."

"And why can't you be friends with a girl cousin, Boris?"

"Because a girl cousin is practically a sister, and have you ever heard of someone marrying their sister?"

"No! Ewwww..."

"Ok then! Now do you understand why that wouldn't work?"

"Yes!" I said, still somewhat confused. We were both silent for a few moments. "So what is Alexei doing with Nadya in the park?" I continued.

"Nothing! He is just going to walk her home."

"Is she pretty?"

"Very pretty! She is the most beautiful girl in the village."

"I'd really like to see her."

"Fine, I'll show her to you tomorrow."

"Is she coming to the vineyard festival?"

"Yes, with all the other girls."

"And Alexei too?"

"Of course! He is coming with the boys, nobody is supposed to know that the two of them are in love."

"How interesting." I was swept away by it all. "Do you think, I could have a boyfriend like that too?"

"Sure! If you love him and he loves you too."

"And then you get married? You know Boris, I didn't know that you had to love the person first."

"Haven't you ever been in love?"

"No, never."

"It will happen one day." Boris said, feeling quite clever and slightly superior: "You just have to wait until you really like someone."

After that we went on without a word, lost in thought, and waited for Alexei, who returned to us after half an hour. My cousins spoke with me as if nothing unusual had happened. They joked and laughed with me, but I wasn't really in a joking mood. When Alexei asked me what was wrong, I pretended to be tired and asked to go home. The next morning, we drove out to the vineyards on a large truck with the rest of the teenagers from the village. On the way, Boris pointed out his brother's girlfriend Nadya.

I didn't find her to be pretty in the least and was irritated that we were missing out on all the fun times we used to have with Alexei because of her. Because after that, Alexei, who had once characterized me as "a totally cool guy," no longer took notice of me. He would endlessly peer over at the girls, where his beloved Nadya cheekily posed and preened. Frankly, I found this girl to be quite ill-mannered. Alexei, however, laughed, when his girl drew everyone's attention with her overt gestures. And Boris stood by and looked at Alexei jealously. My mood was more-or-less ruined during our ride, and the rest of the day felt lonely. Even the beautiful grapevines, from which we were allowed to eat, didn't cheer me up.

That evening, the village boys made a large bonfire. An informal country band consisting of local farmers played the most beautiful Russian folksongs and dances. Everyone danced and sang joyfully around the fire. I was very jealous of Nadya that evening, because she was able to dance the entire time with the tall, slender Alexei. I also tried to dance along to the fast-paced music with Boris, who was short and pudgy, but he couldn't keep up. With a heavy heart, I gave up on dancing. Even though others invited me, I didn't want to dance with strange boys I'd never met. I grew silent and taciturn. As Boris walked home with me that evening, we barely spoke. He soon noticed my disappointment.

"Didn't you like it today?" He finally asked.

"The festival was nice, but Alexei was so rude, he could have at least danced with me one time." I declared.

"Why didn't you dance with the other boys?"

"I don't know – I was scared!"

"Scared? Why?"

I didn't know how to answer Boris. A deep longing was growing inside me. Was it for the lost friendship of my older cousin – or was it perhaps for something else – for someone who I could fall in love with?

After this unusual experience, everything about me seemed to change. Where I was once an open-hearted, happy child, I now became a dreamy, budding young lady. I suddenly began to look at myself in the mirror more often and dress more nicely for school.

My dear grandmother altered my old clothes to fit me and added lace or a collar to some. She had a good sense of style and increasingly praised my newly awakened attention to my appearance. I arranged my once childish pigtails into a traditional Ukrainian-style crown braid. My shoes now never went uncleaned.

I didn't exactly know myself, why I was doing all these things. But soon an explanation for my new habits presented itself. Every day as I approached the school building, I noticed that a tall, blonde boy appeared to be waiting for me. He typically stood by the door and glanced at me full of expectation. As soon as I came close, he seemed to disappear to some unknown destination, and first resurfaced during our midday break, when he would observe me from afar. At first, I didn't like this boy, as I preferred dark hair and dark eyes, and anticipated that any future boyfriend would fit that mold. Still, I observed this blond boy with curiosity and waited quietly for him to finally say something.

But no such luck. He simply went on observing me from afar and occasionally throwing a furtive glance in my direction. Still, his behavior moved me somehow. With each passing day, I thought more and more about this shy admirer. It got to the point where he was all I thought about as I walked staring at the ground on my way to school, only raising my head to scan for him as I approached the building. One day, however, he was not at his usual lookout. This disquieted me to the point that I began to search for him around the entire school.

I went from one classroom to the next, stealthily peeking inside. Only when the first bell rang did I see him through my homeroom window, coming in tardy through the front gate. Today, I had reached his spot before him. During the midday break, he appeared at our classroom door. When he saw me, he smiled tentatively, but his fondness for me was unmistakable. Blood rushed to my head. Embarrassed, I ran back into the classroom and sat down at my desk, hiding my face in my hands.

"He really loves me, he loves me!" My heart was bursting with joy. For the whole next class, I could think of nothing else. Suddenly I heard: "Inna Grinfeldt! Can you prove this theorem?" The geometry teacher called on me.

Startled, I got up and approached the chalkboard in a daze. The problems were new, and the teacher had just explained the theorem. Having been occupied with my thoughts, I had completely missed everything. I was then forced to solve the problem on my own using the geometric figure drawn on the board. I succeeded quite capably but didn't use the same theorem the teacher had just reviewed.

"Your solution is correct." Said the teacher. "I noticed that you hadn't been paying attention the entire hour, and wanted to put you to shame, but I have to at least praise you for your composure and logic in solving the problem."

Relieved, I returned to my seat. "I will never think about that blonde boy during class again!" I silently promised myself.

That evening when I went to bed, I couldn't go to sleep for a long time, and again thought about 'him.' And from the bottom of my heart, I could hear for the first time the soulful ringing of "I love you!"

I didn't want to tell anyone about this first, blissful secret of mine. I had the peculiar fear that someone could take this wonderful feeling away.

One day at school, however, the girl next to me secretively handed me a little note. "A boy from class 8A gave it to me and asked that you answer soon." She whispered.

My heart racing, I took the note to the far corner of the schoolyard and opened it: "Inna, do you want to be my girlfriend?" The note was signed: "Vasya O."

I wondered whether this note could be from my beloved. My heart provided no clear answer. I had long awaited such a sign – but such bad handwriting...! No – it couldn't be. He couldn't possibly write this poorly I thought.

I looked for the girl who passed me the note and asked her to point out Vasya to me. She led me to the second floor of the school, where all 8th grade classes had their homeroom. There in the hallway I discovered my beloved friend, the tall blonde boy, who disappeared behind a classroom door as soon as he spotted me. Excited, I looked at the small sign hanging by the door, which read 8B. A sense of relief washed over me.

I turned to the girl and said: "I want to reply to Vasya from 8A to his face. Please call him over!"

When the boy, who had a crude, displeasing appearance, came over, I said curtly and firmly: "Take back your note and don't ever write me anything else stupid like this again. I come to school to learn!"

The boy's face flushed red in embarrassment and he stutteringly apologized.

"You sure are proud!" said my neighbor. Almost every girl has a boyfriend. You are almost 14 years old. You are allowed to get married at 16!"

"I'm not thinking about getting married that early. From here I'll go to college" I said decidedly. "And anyway, I don't like Vasya one tiny bit."

"Do you like someone else?"

"Someone else? Ah...yes...NO! I don't like anyone at all!"

"Aha! So maybe I can help you. You know, to act as a go-between."

I didn't like that idea at all. "No, just leave it. I already said that I'm at school to learn."

"You're strange!" the girl replied. "Now I know why you don't have any friends." She walked away, leaving me standing there scornfully.

From that day forth I concealed my secret even more deeply in my heart, because for the first time I had come to know the power of falling in love.

Chapter 15 – Renunciation and Indoctrination

"Inna, there are two letters for you!" Grandma called, handing me the mail that had just arrived. This unexpected news interrupted the monotony of the cold winter weather which was stubbornly lingering into late March.

"Two letters at once?" I wondered aloud, examining each carefully to determine the sender. The first was from Mother's hospital in Poltava, where she was still committed. The second was from Uncle Nika, which greatly surprised me, as I hadn't heard anything from him since mother's birthday party over five years ago, my final memory from my old, fairy-tale life.

I opened the letter about my mother first, and it contained some good news. The chief doctor informed us that my mother had made a full recovery and would be allowed to make the journey to us in the Caucuses in the near future. My grandparents studied the letter as well, and as they discussed it, I opened the second letter, which read:

"My Dear Inna! Your father was allowed to write us one last time before his deportation from Poltava to Siberia. He asked us to tell you and your mother that he was sentenced to 10 years forced labor by the secret courts. Up until now, he was denied the right to contact his relatives. Your father, who is concerned with our well-being, requests that you take no steps to assist him, as any connection with him could harm you and your future. He therefore instructs that you should not wait for him and wishes you all the best..."

Although I already knew about my father's arrest, this letter shook me to the core. In that moment, it felt as if my entire past and my homeland had been taken from me forever. Every tie that had once bound me to my earlier childhood had now been permanently severed. I read the letter again and again, but somehow no childish tears came to my eyes. All I could see was a small, first furrow running like a crease across my forehead, no doubt formed from all the worry.

Only a few months ago the news of the trial of the "enemies of the people and spoilers of socialist society", which was taking place in Moscow, thundered through the country. I knew about it from the newspapers. At the trial, the underground anti-Soviet Trotsky-Zinoviev organization, which was allegedly preparing to overthrow the entire Kremlin government, was exposed.

This organization supposedly had its collaborators deep in the Communist Party, the Red Army, and the NKVD. In 1934, the first step of the conspiracy was accomplished when Stalin's closest friend and, apparently, his possible heir, Sergei Kirov, was shot in his Leningrad chancellery. His assassin was a trusted member of the Communist Party, Nikolaev. The Soviet government, which now saw virtually everyone in the world as a potential suspect, began, with the help of the NKVD and detectives, to conduct an investigation that dragged on for three years. Finally, the conspiracy was uncovered, and its perpetrators, after their arrest and trial, were removed from civilian life. Many of them were shot, and the "less guilty" were deported to camps, where they were "re-educated" for productive work and to become "free" Soviet citizens. Among them were many people who had nothing to do with the conspiracy, but who were suspected by the NKVD of having "unstable" political views. They were expelled "just in case" to eliminate the danger that they too might one day become enemies of the people. No one thought about their families, no one felt pity for the lonely wives and mothers who were left behind, or for the children who were losing their fathers.

Trapped in Siberia, in unbearable living conditions, these people had to work as slaves "to build a socialist society". They built new railroads, canals, and cities while living in bestial living conditions and receiving only meager food. And only a few of them, after serving their sentences, returned, exhausted and docile, to their shattered families. Forever unable to resist, they no longer dared to think about living and being happy. Uncle Victor came that evening from his village to discuss picking up my mother from Poltava:

"Such a long journey to a new place will be quite the strain. We will have to see if she's up to it. I don't want to make the long trip for nothing, and money is tight," he said. When he learned about father's prison sentence, he called me over and said: "Sweetheart, your Uncle Nika is right, you've got to separate yourself from the past and make your way in the new realities of the present. It would be a good idea for you to make an effort to join the Komsomol. That could open a lot of doors for you in the future."

To understand why joining the Komsomol was so important, one must understand the central role that education played in the Soviet System: Before the 1917 Russian Revolution, illiteracy was widespread, especially in rural areas. In their effort to consolidate power, the Bolsheviks paid special attention to spreading propaganda, and eliminating competing ideologies. In order to convey the "rightness" of their policies, it was made a priority to stamp out illiteracy to ensure that communist propaganda, in the form of books, newspapers and pamphlets, found a receptive audience and replaced earlier ways of thinking. Efforts to eradicate illiteracy were therefore never motivated by benevolent or humanitarian interests, but by a cold, calculated, systematic effort to establish and maintain the Soviet State's total monopoly over political thought and information.

Along with the organization of collective and state farms, a census of the illiterate began in the country, after which they were required to attend school. Additionally, all Soviet children were first required to attend four, and later seven, years of school. Private schools were abolished, and a uniform, State-controlled education system was developed and installed across the USSR.

Teachers were required to teach only from Soviet textbooks, the contents of which were approved directly by the USSR People's Commissariat or the Politburo. In the corresponding classes of all schools, only one, uniform textbook per subject was allowed.

By indoctrinating pupils in, and censoring facts which ran counter to state ideology, the educational system produced obedient servants to the Soviet system. Naturally, facts about other countries and life abroad were heavily censored and Soviet citizens had little to no idea about life abroad. The Soviet Union did all it could to guard its vast borders and its citizens' exposure to the outside world, with the obvious fear being that they would soon discover that the Soviet "paradise" was anything but relative to other nations. The Komsomol which my uncle now urged me to join was a youth organization that was part of this larger, systematic effort to monopolize political thought. Upon entering school, children were encouraged to join special political organizations which ran through every level of the education system:

From eight to ten years of age, they were Little Octobrists, and their motto was, "Little Octobrist, be ready to fight for the cause of the working class!"

From ten to fifteen years of age, they were enrolled as pioneers, and their motto was, "Pioneer, be ready to fight for the cause of Lenin-Stalin!"

From the age of fifteen, the Pioneers joined the Komsomol, which was their training as members of the Communist Party.

These organizations monitored the ideological direction of each family and, if there was anything "wrong," immediately reported it to the political authorities.

This was a time when the literal poster child for Soviet youth was a thirteen-year-old boy named Pavlik Morozov. The official story was that Pavlik had bravely turned his own father in to the political police for smuggling and forgery in 1932. After his father's arrest and sentencing, family members allegedly retaliated and killed Pavlik, who was then elevated to martyr-like status by the Communist Party – with posters of his likeness plastered everywhere, statues dedicated, and books, songs and plays written about his heroism. A shrine was even placed at the site of his murder. This youth who had betrayed his father – placing loyalty to the State above family – was now held forth as our greatest role model. "That's a person we should look up to," we were told at school: "If a father betrays the people, then the child should betray his father!"

I knew that my uncle was right about joining the Soviet youth or "Komsomol" and took his advice. This was the only way I could distance myself from the checkered past of my family and have a chance to move up in the Soviet system and hope for a better life.

After two weeks, my application for admittance was taken up in an open hearing of the local chapter. First, I was asked to give a truthful and full account of my past. Then I was tested on my knowledge of the history of the Communist party and the teachings and traditions of the Komsomol. After they were satisfied with my initial presentation, individual members were allowed to ask direct questions:

"You said your father was a bureaucrat. What was he before the Revolution?"

"A noble landowner."

"So an aristocrat!?"

"Yes."

Gasps of consternation rippled through the gathering.

"Is your father in Poltava now?"

"No, he was arrested."

"Well then: Do you think it's right that your father was arrested?"

Answering this question was particularly gut-wrenching. After a moment of consideration, I said dejectedly: "If he did something wrong it was."

The gathering became loud, the chairman reached for his bell to call for order amidst the cacophony of excited chatter.

"An innocent person isn't imprisoned in our country!" Shouted the chairman. "We will now put it to a vote. Who is for admitting Comrade Inna Grinfeldt?"

He counted the raised hands out loud: "75 for – 75 against - it is an exact tie! Does anyone want to pose further questions?"

"Yes, Comrade Grinfeldt, do you correspond with your father?" A girl in the group asked.

"No. My mother separated from my father two years ago."

"So, your mother was also against your father? That may change things. Would you be willing to permanently renounce your father...that is for all time?" Came the question, seemingly from multiple people.

"I live with my grandparents in Anapa and will never see my father again."

"That sounds more like it!" said the chairman. "Comrades, there does not appear to be anything preventing us from accepting this applicant into the Komsomol. Let's vote again."

This time I saw a sea of raised hands. "Unanimously approved." Said the chairman. "This meeting is adjourned."

After my initial approval I had to take two additional tests and finally received my Komsomol badge. And with that I had renounced my father and stepped into the new Russian life. For the first time, I felt like a full citizen of the Soviet Union.

The youth organization demanded a great deal of effort and exertion. Because I was a good piano player, I was put in charge of establishing and leading our school choir as a 15-year-old, which I took on with great pleasure. I also put my heart and soul into the theater troupe. Every holiday we would present a play that was typically aimed against the capitalists or religion and always had to further the party's political point of view. The political content of our work was so implicit and all-encompassing that, in a sense, we barely noticed it after a time. It was like our daily life and daily bread – like the air we breathed - ubiquitous. The schools stuffed us full of these ideas starting from very early childhood before we could develop our own thoughts and opinions.

No wonder then, that I too became a true child of Bolshevism. I began to hate the "enemies" of our people with all my heart and genuinely enjoyed theater presentations in which the "capitalist bandits" were taken out and eliminated. The fact that this very system had wrongly imprisoned my father, split apart and taken everything from my family, and driven my mother to the brink of insanity, was wiped from my mind by a combination of the daily brainwashing and wanting to belong so fervently in a society where you had no choice and where the alternative was an abyss of fear and punishment.

I became such a fervent supporter that I even wrote a poem for the school newspaper:

Here and There.
How we love our country,
It's hard to put it into words,

There are no happier children anywhere,
As children here, in the Land of the Soviets!

Here are the next brothers and fathers,
Growing up healthy and flourishing,
Not as they do somewhere abroad,
Life there is very, very different.
In filthy and damp cellars,
Workers' children starve,
And there, in the big factories,
Children are oppressed by the Fascists.
And the children think
That there's another country somewhere
Where life is beautiful for children,
And that's the Land of the Soviets!
How we love our country,
How we love our dear Stalin!
For our lives, we thank
Our dear Leader of the Nations.

Having been inundated with this relentless indoctrination, I waited impatiently for the day of the World Revolution. I couldn't comprehend why we still had to wait for it and wondered how long the workers outside of Russia's borders, particularly in Germany and England, would continue to put up with their abhorrent lives of slavery.

My teachers, along with the plays that we performed, had long-since taught me how things supposedly looked abroad, for example in hostile Germany. In geography, I carefully studied the map of that country and knew of its large industrial cities. But what good was industry when the working people there were treated worse than slaves and dogs?

Daydreaming one evening just after my initiation into the Komsomol, I lay in bed and envisioned the average life of foreign workers: I saw a large city with long, narrow streets, tall buildings and huge factories and workshops. In the large, sumptuous houses lived the capitalists who owned everything. And just one of these exploiters and his family occupied the entire palatial home for themselves. I imaged such a bourgeoise to be a very fat, ugly person with a bald head and angry, sinister face and thick glasses or a monocle.

The workers, on the other hand, lived in the dark, dank basements of the capitalist houses, which were stuffed full of the large families of the impoverished. The poor had been exploited their entire lives and were so poor and miserable that they couldn't even afford furniture or beds. These unfortunate creatures slept on the floor on straw heaped up in piles in the corners of the basements.

Furthermore, all workers were illiterates who were forced to start working in factories when they turned six. They received so little money for their labor that it didn't even suffice to buy stale bread. And in these terrible living conditions, most of these downtrodden people died a premature death of tuberculosis, typhus or starvation.

I shared these stereotypes about capitalist countries with pretty much all of the other young people around me. And that being the case: How could I possibly feel anything other than enormous gratitude for the wonderful homeland and freedom which I enjoyed?! How could I do anything but renounce my father if my homeland had declared him a traitor?

And what more could I possibly want as a hopeful young person than this?

I had nearly dozed off with these thoughts when I was suddenly shaken by a commotion in the house. I heard my grandfather loudly open the front gate, and looking out the window, saw him hurrying to the front door, a telegram in one hand. I heard Grandma opening the front door.

Grandpa stepped in, and in an exuberant, excited voice, exclaimed: "She's finally back..."

Chapter 16 – Spring Returns

I jumped from bed and ran over to my grandparents. "You mean Mama? Mama is back?"

"Yes, Inna, she is coming tomorrow on the train, we will pick her up at the Tonneljnaya station, where we got you." Said Grandpa.

"We will finally see our dear Zina!" Grandma exclaimed, half-shouting and half-sobbing, before breaking down in tears. She embraced Grandfather, who was also overtaken by emotion. I wrapped my arms around them both for joy. The next day I skipped school and accompanied my Grandparents on the bus to the station. Mother was already waiting for us as the bus pulled up, and hastily came over and got on for the return trip. She hugged us all with tears in her eyes.

"My girl, how you've grown up!" She said, looking me over carefully, with her hands on my shoulders.

As if collectively exhausted by the emotion of it all, we sat quietly driving through the mountain passes back to Anapa. When we got home, mother sat down with me:

"Sweetheart, I've recovered." She said, looking me directly in the eyes. Intuitively, I believed her. Her eyes looked more serious and sober, and the childish figure of the past now seemed more grounded.

In the days that followed, I realized that she had, in fact, changed and matured, and we were able to resolve our disagreements now as two adults, rather than as parent and child. She got a job at a local sanatorium, and we approached the coming spring and summer with optimism for a peaceful life.

The end of the school year was approaching, as was one of our greatest Soviet holidays: May Day. By this time in my Russian homeland, we no longer celebrated Easter with its ringing church bells and decorative masses. Instead, we celebrated this great, modern Proletarian holiday.

On May 1, we went to school without our bookbags: The girls all wore white blouses and dark blue skirts, and boys were dressed in matching colors. We lined up in rows of four and marched, singing to music through the city. Scores of red flags and large placards with Communist slogans and images of party leaders accompanied our procession. We came to a halt in the marketplace, where workers, members of the military, and students had all gathered to listen to celebratory speeches, which all contained the same message. It was in this very marketplace that my mother and I had recently waited in long lines nights during the winter hoping to buy bread, sugar or other basic goods, often in vain.

Each speaker emphasized the importance of this special day, on which we showed the proletariat of the entire world our solidarity and how we sought to prove that the day of the World Revolution was growing ever-closer. I was usually relatively bored during these speeches and genuinely happy, in my youthful impatience, when they were finally over, as the remaining holiday activities would be far more enjoyable. In every school, musical offerings were presented by the students after which the older boys and girls were allowed to go out dancing the entire evening.

I had long awaited this evening with great anticipation, because it was my hope that I would finally have an opportunity to get to know my blonde friend more closely. With that in mind, I had put a great deal of preparation into the holiday concert, in which my choir and I would have our first performance. Following that, I was going to sing several Ukrainian songs on my own.

What would he say of it all? Hopefully he would like the performance, I thought with great anticipation.

For my first stage performance, mother had made me a beautiful red dress by hand, and I liked how it looked on me. For that reason, I felt especially confident, and the curious stares of the other students didn't faze me, as all of my thoughts were occupied by him, and him alone. He was sitting directly in front of me in the front row of the theater.

By then I had learned a little about my admirer. I knew his name was Peter Lukov and that he came from a family of respected civil servants, was two years older than me and was a good student. I would repeatedly steal a glance at him from on stage, and to my great satisfaction, saw that he was looking at me, beaming without interruption. The audience liked the choir and the songs I performed. I had to indulge them several encores after repeated rounds of applause. When I finally reached the dance hall, happy and relieved after the concert, several students and teachers came up to me and congratulated me on my success.

Very close to them, waiting modestly off to the side, was my Peter. The band began to play a slow waltz, and in that moment, my deep longing was fulfilled. The young man bowed and requested the first dance.

Without a word, I extended my arms for him to take. He took my hand and put my arm in his and led me onto the dance floor. I could feel my heart pounding as he put his arm around my waist, and we sailed smoothly around the hall to the beat of the music. I looked down at the floor as we danced, but I could feel his eyes fixed intently upon mine. We didn't speak much that evening, but our hearts were overflowing. Dancing together, we forgot the rest of the world and didn't even notice that other students were curiously observing us and then, having understood what was happening, left us to one another. No other boy tried to cut-in and approach me that evening.

After the festivities had ended, Peter accompanied me home. We talked about school and everything else. But neither of us could express our youthful happiness.

"Would you meet me tomorrow for another dance at the resort park?" He asked, before wishing me good night.

"Yes!" I answered, delighted.

After he left, I didn't want to go inside for a long time. Breathing-in the clear air of the spring night, I felt infinitely happy.

The next day we met as arranged at the so-called "little bay." This secluded spot on the coast was formed from the gray cliffs which rose up out of the sea south of Anapa and resembled the gigantic, outstretched wings of a bird.

From the rocky heights, which ran inland all the way to the foothills of the Caucuses, we could look far out over the sea. This evening, the sun dyed the sea a dark green color and the waves swayed gently, weaving together thousands of white foam streaks together along the surface fine embroidered lace.

The setting May sun offered up an enchanting scene. The closer it came to the horizon and the water line, the darker it's golden-red hue became. And when it's round outline finally broached the water, the dark-red fire ball radiated with a powerful, glorious glow which extended across the far reaches of the sea. We watched with quiet delight as the setting star began to flicker and finally disappear. A broad strip of water continued to glow against the horizon for some time.

The most intoxicating May night descended upon the earth. A gentle breeze whispered through the air and carried with it the beautiful scent of the lilac bushes, gillyflowers and early roses growing in the gardens on the city's edge. Numerous dragonflies and ladybugs merrily whirred about us. A bright sheaf of light fell from the lighthouse tower onto the surface of the darkening sea.

As we turned towards the town, we could see the glow of several thousand lights shining forth from the May festival.

We held hands and wandered through the bright streets, which today were filled with happy, singing people, and walked towards the resort park. All of the benches were already occupied. On the square where people were dancing it was so crowded that, as people often say in Russia, you couldn't throw an apple between them. Despite that, we danced nearly the entire night away without getting tired.

During a break, Peter invited me to get ice cream. On the way to the stand, we went through a small, seldom-trafficked side-street. Suddenly, he came to a stop, turned towards me and put both his hands on my shoulders. He looked me in the eyes for several moments. Then he drew me in tightly and kissed me passionately and affectionately.

My face blushed aglow with red heat. I tore myself from his embrace and raced away. He followed me and grabbed me by the hand. "Are you mad at me, my love?"

I didn't answer him, but I could feel the heat of our hands clasped together. He felt it too, lifted my hand to his lips, and looked at me longingly and questioningly. When I smiled back, he pulled me in again and pressed me into his chest tightly. This time I didn't pull away. I closed my eyes and surrendered to the bliss that I long yearned for and dreamt about.

That evening I didn't come home until it was very late. After I bid him goodnight, I went silently into the house. I sneaked over to the window in the room with my bed and looked down towards the front gate, where he was still standing.

"Good night, Peter!" I whispered and stealthily blew him a kiss. Only then did he turn and head home himself, merrily whistling a gypsy tune.

At that moment a light went on in the room. I looked around and only now noticed that my mother was sitting on the edge of her bed fully clothed. Her face was pale and her eyes looked as if she'd been crying.

"What's wrong mother?" I asked quietly. My conscience was not exactly clear at that moment.

"I was worried about you, my child. It got to be so late, and you still hadn't come home. I went out and looked for you in vain – including at the resort park. The dancing had already ended and everyone was going home. And you were nowhere to be seen!"

"I'm sorry mother, I was with Peter in the little bay."

"With Peter? Is that the young man who accompanied you home yesterday and tonight?" Mother asked questioningly.

I couldn't stand her penetrating eyes, which were fixed on me, and had to look in shame at the floor."

"Peter is a good boy, mother, and my dear friend." I answered quietly.

"I don't hold anything against your friend, darling. I just hope that you are sensible enough to know how far a young lady can go and still maintain the respect of her friend." Mother's voice was now gentle and kind.

"You don't have to worry, mama, I'm definitely not doing anything wrong." I answered with conviction.

"I gladly believe you, dear, and I'm ok now. How long have you known Peter?"

Feeling moved by this exchange, I warmly related everything I knew about Peter and his family. The only thing I neglected to tell her about were our first kisses, which still burned hotly on my lips.

"This love of yours is a gift from above, my dear." Mother continued after long consideration: "Be sure to always remain as you are now: Upright, intelligent and pure! When I see you so in love, it reminds me of my own youth. My happiness, however, was very short."

I only knew that all too well, I felt sincerely sorry for mother.

"Can't you try your luck again, Mother? Maybe you will find someone good and get married..." I asked hesitantly.

"I've already thought about that, but I didn't want to risk it because of you." She replied.

"Because of me? Why?"

"I was worried you'd want to leave if I introduced a strange man into your life."

"Oh mother, hadn't you considered that I'll be leaving here in two years? When my schooling is over, I want to go study at a university. Peter is going to Moscow next year to study building and architecture."

"Of course, I knew you'd eventually leave me one day, but I just didn't want to really believe that day would come."

"But that's the way things are, mother, and that's why it would be right for you to think of your own happiness."

"It takes two to marry my dear!"

"You're still beautiful, Mama, you're sure to find someone good."

And it was as if I had known ahead of time: Later that lovely May, Mother got to know a talented musician named Yevgeni who led the orchestra at a large health resort and gave my mother a job as a pianist, and not long thereafter, asked for her hand in marriage.

Chapter 17 – How I Became Independent

It was customary in our small resort town for young people to get a job over summer break. To that end, I attended a two-week evening class on how to take care of children, and soon enough I was in charge of looking after twenty-five kids in a resort day care.

My working day at the resort, where I also lived during the break, began at 7am and ended fifteen hours later at 10pm. Despite the long hours, I enjoyed the work, and I was very happy to receive my monthly salary of 300 rubles. For the first time, I was able to deposit this, for me sizeable sum of money, at the local bank.

Peter did not work this summer. He was preparing for the state exams for the Moscow university of architecture and had to dedicate himself to his books and blueprints hours each day. The long week of hard work and study made the Sunday that followed all the more wonderful. Peter would pick me up early in the morning and we would go for hikes or a swim.

One day he brought a pretty, blonde girl about my age along who looked a lot like him and introduced her as his cousin. Her name was Nastia Golovko, and she and her mother were visiting Peters' family from Krasnodar, the largest city in our region. I liked her from the very beginning, maybe because she was Peter's relative. She would go for walks and swims with us, and soon she got to know a young man visiting for the summer, and we formed a carefree troupe that Nastia's mother, Mrs. Golovko, liked to call "The funny four."

We would alternate our lunches – one day with Peter's parents and one day at my grandparents, where my mother would prepare us all a meal. She was engaged and much happier now. She and Yevgeny already had plans to marry that autumn. The grownups enjoyed seeing us all together in our youthful exuberance.

Nastia also had a beautiful singing voice. We would often perform solos and duets of our favorite Russian songs for family members, who listened with enthusiasm. Evenings we would often go dancing at the resort park, where mother and her fiancé where in the resort band, so we were sure to be on our best behavior. When I looked over to her at the piano, I could see her occasional glances to her fiancé, who was conducting the orchestra. Her eyes sparkled with happiness, and despite the tiny pang at the realization she now loved someone other than my father, I couldn't help but be happy for her after she had endured so many years of misery and struggle.

Other evenings, the four of us would take walks on the beach, sit on a bench and tell stories, jokes and sing our favorite songs.

As is so often the case during the most beautiful moments of our lives, the summer passed all too quickly, and our final day together was soon at hand. To mark this last day, we organized a small celebration and drank a toast with our relatives to our friendship. Nastia, who had to return with her mother to Krasnodar for the start of the school year, promised to write me regularly. Her mother also bid me a heartfelt farewell and invited me to pay them a visit soon. At the time, I didn't realize how meaningful that friendly invitation would be.

The following Sunday, Peter and I were alone again. Things had become much quieter for us, and we were both left deflated by the thought that we would soon be separated by Peter's imminent move to Moscow. Our friendship had grown stronger over the summer. Peter was always so attentive, loving and tactful, and I truly came to treasure him. One occurrence was particularly memorable.

One day we were too tired to go out hiking. We lay down next to each on the beach and silently observed the endless expanse of the mirrorlike sea. Suddenly Peter took my hand, raised it to his lips, and kissed it passionately. Blushing, I turned and threw a glance towards the passing beach goers as if to say: "What will the passers-by think?"

Of course, in that moment, I would have most liked to have grabbed my boyfriend and covered him in kisses. I'd already done it many times in my imagination. But as soon as I was opposite my beloved, I shyly refrained and only responded hesitantly to his caresses.

But this time I came to a firm resolution: That evening I would finally tell him how much I loved him. As the sun sank on the sea horizon, we didn't go dancing as usual. We found a bench in a quiet corner of the park. Peter laid his head across my chest, wrapped his arms around me and simply looked at me in silence. I stroked his wavy blond hair, and consumed with thoughts of his imminent departure, couldn't hold back my tears.

He soon noticed, and we passionately whispered our innermost thoughts about the gloomy future. We swore our unshakeable faithfulness until fate would lead us to be together forever. The next day my beloved departed. He had passed the Moscow University entrance exams successfully and soon began his studies with great enthusiasm.

I also entered my new schoolyear eager to learn.

Not long thereafter, my mother celebrated her wedding. She and my new stepfather rented a home in the center of Anapa with three small rooms, moving me away from my grandparents. I was given one room and the other two went to the newly married couple.

Before that, when they were engaged, I hadn't had much of an opportunity to get to know my new stepfather, who for a time I only knew as Yevgeny. It soon became clear, however, that we did not get along at all.

Yevgeny Petrovitch Serov was a modestly talented, yet overconfident conductor of his choir, and from the very beginning took very strict control of our family life and expected unconditional obedience from me. Having grown used to acting independently from my earliest years, I found this domineering new regime to be unbearable and began to hate my stepfather. Additionally, I refused to call him "father" and instead just used his first name or the formal version of "you" in Russian, which implies distance and unfamiliarity.

I also grew further and further apart from my mother. I increasingly felt out of place and unwell in the new home. My dear mother tried to mediate, but soon had to give up on it. My stepfather and I remained in our stand-off and continued to dislike one another. I wouldn't and couldn't understand what good this man, who was completely foreign to me, was to us.

One day as I was in my room doing my homework, I heard him say:

"Zina, it's really unnecessary for you to hire a cleaning lady. Inna is a big and strong enough to help with the laundry. She doesn't do anything all day other than read her books anyway!"

"Inna has to study a lot, Yevgeni, the school is very demanding, let her read her books." Mother answered quietly.

"What good does it do us?" He replied. "Other girls her age are already at work in factories or offices and earning a salary. How much longer do I have to support your grown-up daughter?"

"It's my duty, Yevgeni, to give my child a good education. In a year she will go to university, please have a little patience until then." Mother responded firmly.

This conversation truly rattled me. It was extremely repugnant to me that this unpleasant man was complaining that he had to "support" me.

I started to think about how I could live on my own and stand on my own two feet. I began to avoid my stepfather even more than before, as the conflicts between us only grew more serious. And it appeared to me as if this hostile man was almost looking for the opportunity to insult and challenge me.

As soon as mother went out and we were alone, he started: "Inna, get out here and wash the floor!" or: "Inna, come clean up the kitchen!"

I replied with: "Mother didn't say anything to me about it." Or: "I still have lots of homework to do."

"Doesn't matter! I'm the head of the house here and you have to listen to me!"

"I live with my mother – not with you, Yevgeni!"

"Your mother is my wife, she doesn't have the say here, I do!"

"But you're not my father and you have no right to force me to do anything!"

"You insolent brat! I won't give your mother another ruble to spend on you. See to it that you get out of here!" He screamed in my face. His eyes were so inflamed with anger that it struck fear into me and I ran off.

Because I didn't want to burden my mother with the chronic arguments of this ever-worsening conflict, I knew that I had to resolve my own problems and take control of my own life. I wrote a letter to my friend Nastia and her mother, Mrs. Golovko in Krasnodar, describing my struggles and requesting that they give me a place to stay until I could find a job there. I was prepared to quit school in Anapa to once again be a free person. I also wrote to Peter in Moscow and asked for his advice and support.

Peter also wrote to his Aunt Golovko and requested she take me in. Shortly thereafter, I received a letter from her and Nastia in which they warmly invited me to come stay with them.

With that, I packed my belongings without so much as a word to my mother, went to school to inform them I was leaving and retrieve copies of my transcripts, withdrew what savings I had from the bank, and made my departure from this inhospitable home. I was now 17 years old, legally an adult by Russian law, and no longer required my mother's permission or signature to do anything.

I got on an almost empty bus and rode to Tonneljnaya. At the train station, I dropped a letter to my mother in the mailbox. I wrote that she should forgive me for undertaking this enterprise on my own initiative and wished her happiness and contentment in her marriage from the bottom of my heart. Then I boarded the train and set out for my new destination: The unknown.

Chapter 18 – My Old-New Home

After a four-hour train ride, I found myself on the unfamiliar platform of the Krasnodar station. Here I was immediately struck by the lively traffic of passengers. Young and old women in headscarves with baskets and bundles, and, in most cases, unshaven men with caps on their heads, were scurrying back and forth, filling all the corners of the station. Many of them sat on the ground outside the station while waiting for their train. There were a lot of cigarette butts, paper, all kinds of cucumber stumps, apples, and eggshells lying around. The waiting room was packed with poorly dressed people. They were sitting and lying on benches and right on the floor. Some of them were smoking cheap cigarettes and tobacco; others were asleep, snoring heavily, with their tired heads lowered down; others were drinking tea and talking and laughing loudly in front of their travel kettles. All this, merging into a muffled hum, was covered with a dense haze of white tobacco smoke.

As I walked out of the station building onto the street, I approached a policeman standing there, asking him how I could find Gogol Street. He explained to me in detail where it was, and which trolley was best to get there. Thanking him, I went in search of the Golovko home. I jumped in one of the trolley street cars, known in Russia as "tram-vai," and rode for what felt like almost two hours through the vast industrial city. Looking out the window, I couldn't help but think of Kharkov in my Ukrainian homeland, where I'd visited Uncle Nika and Aunt Masha. The wide asphalt streets with high-rise buildings and numerous stores and loud, rushing traffic reminded me of my visits there.

Despite that, everything seemed foreign and new, and I couldn't help but feel unsettled. "Would I be able to adjust to life in this big city?" I wondered to myself nervously as I began to feel the first pangs of a guilty conscience over how rashly I'd left my mother's house.

The Golovko's lived at the end of Gogol Street near the banks of the Kuban River in a low, one-story house which resembled a large, well-kept barracks. The owned two long, old-fashioned, yet well-furnished rooms. In one of these, I was given a corner to sleep in next to Nastia. In the second, larger room, which also served as a kitchen and dining room, slept Nadia's parents. I soon felt at home with this lovely family. Nastia's father, a friendly gentleman with graying hair and merry eyes, was an inventor and radio technician. He was very kind to me and also welcomed me whole-heartedly into the family home. After I had had a chance to recover from my journey, we all discussed my future.

"Inna, we are all in agreement that you should continue going to school here," declared Mrs. Golovko.

"Yes." Added Nastia enthusiastically: "With me in the same class."

"But I need to find a way to support myself first." I replied softly. "My savings, about 800 rubles, won't last that long."

"Don't worry about that dear." Replied Mrs. Golovko with a soothing motherly reassurance: "We will support you until you finish school, and you should keep your savings for your trip to Moscow after you graduate here and go on to University to study alongside Peter."

I was eternally grateful to her for these words. I hugged all three. Nastia, who was also the only child of her family, and who had always wanted a sister, was delighted by this decision. So began a harmonious and ordered life, and I began to see a brighter future ahead.

Soon, a letter from my mother in her distinctive, fine penmanship arrived:

My Dearest Inna,

I firmly believe that our journey through life is guided by a higher power and I am therefore not angry with you for your sudden decision to leave. I have two important pieces of information I must share with you: One is tragic, and the other is hopeful. When I returned to Anapa, I couldn't bring myself to tell you, but your Great Uncle Nika is dead. He was arrested last year and charged with counter-revolutionary activities. A month later he was convicted and sentenced to death by firing squad. Great Aunt Masha is devastated with grief and went to live with her children from her first marriage.

My arm fell to my side with the letter still in my hand. I was in total disbelief: Uncle Nika was a 70-year-old man. What "counter-revolutionary" threat could a harmless old man possibly pose? This horrifying news caused me to have one of those disconcerting bouts of doubt that kept recurring when reality contradicted the narrative of the party machinery that we lived in the happiest and most just society on earth.

I read on:

Now the second piece of news: It is a remarkable coincidence that fate should lead you to Krasnodar, of all places. I write that because your father owned a beautiful house on Nikolayevskaya Street for years which he purchased shortly before the Revolution. We planned to move to Krasnodar after our wedding, but we changed our minds after I received my inheritance from my mother, which is the house that you knew in Poltava. After the Revolution, your father thought about going to check on his house, but feared that the neighbors, who knew him well, would turn him in and betray him. I would be very interested to find out what became of that valuable property, so please go have a look my dear, and report back to me what you find out.

At the end of the letter, mother had specified the exact address. Naturally this awakened a tremendous curiosity and I determined to go take a look the next Sunday.

Initially, I hid my undertaking from the Golovko's, as it would have been unpleasant for me to open the can of worms that was my family past before them. After all that had happened, I naturally didn't tell a soul that both my parents were from once prosperous noble lineages. Instead, whenever anyone asked about my family, I typically characterized myself as the daughter of a simple civil servant and housewife.

On a pretty March morning I set out to find the house. I was in an especially good mood, probably because Spring had just arrived, or perhaps because I had an odd inkling that something intriguing lay in store. The snow had only recently melted, and in the countless city plazas and alleyways, the tender green blossoms began to shyly emerge. The flower vendors, who stood with their baskets on the street corners, offered the first, heart-warming bouquets of blue Russian snowdrops. The birds were alive with song and the sun gently caressed the earth's awakening inhabitants.

Nikolayevskaya Street was lined with neatly kept one- and two-story houses with small yards tucked away from the urban bustle. My heart beat rapidly as I approached the garden gate of a two-story house that resembled a small castle. I came to a halt and compared it one more time to the description my mother had provided and confirmed I was at the right location. This had indeed once been my father's property!

A copper placard on the gate read: Dr. B. Heifiz, Director - Krasnodar College of Medicine. I stood stationary in front of the garden entrance and listened to someone playing piano in the house. That reminded me how long it had been since I'd touched piano keys. The thought popped into my mind that I would use this coincidence to ask for permission to play the lovely instrument. Then hopefully I would be able to take a closer look at the house from the inside.

I nervously approached the nicely decorated house door and noticed that a silver-haired, bent over old man was sitting on a bench protected from the wind on the house porch. This scruffy, yet dignified old fellow supported his tired grandfatherly head with his hands, one of which held a cane-like walking stick. His eyes were closed, and it appeared to me that he had dozed off under the warm rays of the March sun. When I walked past him towards the door, he lifted his wrinkled face and looked at me unperturbed with colorless, watery eyes.

I wondered at his large head and long, white beard and thought to myself that he looked like 'Ded Moroz', the Russian fairy tale character who resembles Santa Claus.

As I reached the front entrance and stood a while indecisively looking at the doorbell, the old man got up from the bench and, supporting himself with his walking stick, walked towards me. His eyes grew larger the closer he came. It seemed as if he was opening his mouth to say something, but no sound came out, which somehow gave me the creeps. As this was an old-fashioned doorbell, which actually looked like a bell, I firmly grabbed the small chain attached to bottom of the ball-like clapper and pulled it sharply.

The bell rang out loudly and the piano music in the house came to an abrupt halt. A slender young woman my age approached and opened the door for me.

She thought that I was probably a patient of her father's, and said: "Unfortunately, my father is not here. Would you perhaps like to try back again tomorrow morning?"

I hesitantly replied: “I am not here to see your father. I would really like to ask you something.”

The young lady looked at me somewhat puzzled, then opened the door and bid me to come in.

“My name is Inna Grinfeldt.” I said, introducing myself as I crossed the threshold.

“My God!” came a loud shout from behind me. The young woman looked out startled at the old man, who had just blurted the words out, then closed the front door without another word.

“You’ll have to forgive our old Ivan, Comrade Inna!” She said. “I think he must not be entirely well today. Well, when you consider how old he is, ninety-three, after all...”

As she spoke, the dainty, dark-haired doctor’s daughter, who must have been about eighteen, led me to her father’s waiting room and offered me a seat. She asked me kindly, how she could help me.

Somewhat embarrassed, I asked: “I only wanted to ask if I could play a little on your piano. I’m new to Krasnodar and haven’t had the opportunity to play yet.”

“Gladly! Please come with me.” She replied and opened the door that led to an adjacent room.

I walked into a large, beautiful room decked by a huge Persian rug on the floor and rare paintings on the walls. Heavy old-fashioned furniture, many cushions and ornaments, and plush curtains gave the room the old-fashioned look of pre-revolutionary times. In the center of the room stood a black Bechstein grand piano with a mirror-finish. With shivers running up and down my body, I stepped over to the magnificent piano and gently pressed a few of the keys. A series of warm, somewhat subdued tones flattered my ears. A great longing now suddenly overcame me. I sat down and passionately played the melodious Autumn song by Tchaikovsky in its entirety.

The surroundings reminded me of my long-forgotten childhood in the home of my parents. Memories from those good times came to life again in my soul. In my mind, images of mother's birthday began to play, I saw myself holding the beautiful bouquet of white chrysanthemums in our garden on that beautiful, warm autumn day. Then our many guests and the immense happiness. Mother in her white dress with pearls around her neck. Her beautiful song at the piano and then...

It was as if an icy breath fell upon me as the next thought entered my mind. The memory of that moment – when my life – our lives – changed forever. My hands fell suddenly to my lap, my playing ceased, and hot tears ran down my cheeks. I slowly raised my head and looked around, completely disoriented. Only after a moment did I notice that the doctor's daughter was looking at me in shock.

"Forgive me, I completely forgot myself..." I stuttered: "May...maybe because I've never played such a wonderful instrument..."

"You play so beautifully, Comrade Inna!" She replied encouragingly: "A shame that you stopped, won't you try again?"

Despite her entreaty to continue, I could feel that I wouldn't be possible for me to fulfill her wishes and stood up to leave.

"Then please come again very soon!" She said, inviting me as she led me to the front door.

Only now did I come out with the question: "Does your father own this house?"

"No." She said. "This house is the property of the old man, Ivan Kusmitch, who you saw by the front door. Father often offered to buy the house from him, but the old man wouldn't hear of it. He says he is still waiting for a nephew to whom he wants to leave the property in his will."

"Did he ever tell you how he got the house?" I asked further.

"Never! But the neighbors say that he received the house as a gift from a wealthy man."

"Remarkable!" I said at last.

"Yes! These days it is very rare to own such a house. Had my father not looked after things, Ivan's property would have been seized by the State long ago."

After this, we said our goodbyes and I exited the house.

Ivan Kusmitch was standing by the front gate as I stepped out of the house. When he saw me, he quickly approached and begged: "Please stay a moment, my lady, and listen to old Ivan."

I looked questioningly at this odd old man.

"Please say your name one more time." He continued: "I heard it earlier but can't really believe it."

"Inna Grinfeldt" I answered, feeling puzzled.

"Then I was right! Is your father's name Vladimir...Vladimir Alexandrovich?"

"Yes! How do you know that?"

"How could I not know that? Your beloved father, Vladimir Alexandrovich Grinfeldt, was my master!"

I could feel goosebumps running up and down my body. Initially I thought Ivan wanted to grab me and turn me in to the police. But the exact opposite happened. He started to cry and said, in a muffled voice: "For all these long years I've waited for my master, your father, and took care of this house for him. That's also why I have grown so old, because I couldn't die before I had fulfilled this, my final duty."

With these words, Ivan's kind old face betrayed a great sense of exhaustion and bitterness.

"Come with me inside, Inna Vladimirovna. I want to tell you everything from the beginning."

Deeply moved, I followed him into the house. He slowly ascended the wooden steps and opened a door on the upper floor. He had a small, cozy study with an old, cushioned rocking chair, a sofa, a couple of old portraits and a desk.

Ivan sat in his rocking chair and I sat on the sofa. He began to recall the past, in a calm, subdued voice:

In 1916 your father became engaged to a young lady, Zinaida Yosifovna, the daughter of a fine, wealthy household in Kharkov – and the most beautiful girl in all Ukraine – as he told me.

However, since this young lady had already been promised to another man in marriage, the two lovers determined to run off together. And that is when your father traveled to Krasnodar, accompanied by me, and purchased this beautiful house, so that he could move here with his young wife after the wedding. Your father bid me to manage and look after the new property until his return, and departed with the intention to soon return a married man. In the meantime, however, the Revolution broke out, and my young master has not returned to Krasnodar since, nor did he once look even a single time to see how things were with his property. When the Reds came to Krasnodar, I transferred the house into my name and determined to wait for my master until he remembered his Ivan. But since I could not hold onto the house for myself, I was forced to rent the downstairs to Doctor Heifiz, who has lived with me now for twenty years. During that entire time, I prayed many times to God that he would send me your father or at least a message from him. And finally, in this hour, my prayer has been answered! With unspeakable disbelief, I listened to the story of this faithful servant. And after a lengthy pause, he again continued:

"Tell your dear father, Inna Vladimirovna, that I am waiting here for him to come back. He shouldn't delay much longer – so that I can finally be relieved of my final duty."

Poor Ivan! How terrible it was, that I could not fulfill his final request. As he listened for my answer, I could see the pain in his eyes:

"What are you going to tell me Inna Vladimirovna, that my master has been called to the kingdom of heaven before me?" He asked, his voice trembling.

"My father isn't dead, Ivan Kusmitch." I told him: "He was arrested two years ago."

"Oh, what a misfortune!" He cried out in disgust. "And what is with your mother?"

"She remarried."

"Ah – do you have any siblings? A brother perhaps?"

"No. I am my parent's only child."

"Then I will transfer this property to you Inna Vladimirovna."

Ivan opened a drawer in his stately old desk, took out a piece of paper, scribbled a few lines, and handed me the deed to the house with his name on it.

My house and all the property in it
I bequeath to Inna Vladimirovna Grinfeldt
born in Poltava, 29. 01. 1922
Ivan Kuzmich Dolgovekiy

And so, seemingly out-of-the-blue, I had become the new owner of my father's old house. Was this all a dream? I could hardly believe my luck. I had suddenly been lifted out of poverty.

Slowly emerging from this intense nebula of thought, I could again faintly hear the piano on the first floor. Perhaps inspired by my earlier choice of music, the doctor's daughter was now playing Tchaikovsky's spring. Fate had once again taken an unexpected turn in my life, and a fresh season awaited.

Chapter 19 – The Invisible Bridge

"You're getting your own house? From an old man who you never knew before? Is that even possible?" The Golovko's were stunned. They couldn't believe their ears as I explained, stretching the truth somewhat, how I had met an old relative on a walk through the city, my father's uncle, who needed someone to leave his inheritance to.

"How was he able to recognize you right away?" Nastia asked in disbelief.

"My great-uncle told me I looked so much like his wife, my father's aunt who passed away some years ago, that he had to stop and ask me my name. He recognized our relationship almost immediately." I said, stretching the truth to its breaking point.

Ivan and I had come up with this false explanation to satisfy the curiosity of anyone who might ask, and also to conceal the roots of my inheritance. Besides the two of us, only my mother knew the true story in its entirety. And she was clever enough to keep it to herself, and not even tell her new husband about it. I was therefore able to successfully take ownership of the house without having to reveal my father's past.

When Peter heard about it, I could tell in his next letter that he was concerned that, as a well-off house owner, I might not come to join him in Moscow. I replied that, despite all this, I would keep my promise to fulfill our plans together. But Ivan Kusmitch insisted that I immediately move into my house. He cleaned out two rooms he had occupied containing a small kitchen and glass veranda and moved into a large chamber across from my kitchen.

My new home was not that large. The rooms had vaulted ceilings. That said, everything was so comfortably furnished and cozy, that I soon felt well at home.

Ivan Kusmitch looked after me like a faithful servant and continued to address me as a servant would address his lord in the times of Serfdom. He was so kind and attentive that I soon told him just to call me “Inna” and use the familiar form of “you” in Russian. Old fashioned as he was, he would have none of it, and continued to address me formally with “Madame” and the formal Russian version of the word “you”.

“Madame, you are the daughter of my lord, and therefore also my lord.”

“Ach, lord?!” Such a thing doesn’t exist anymore Ivan.” I countered.

But Ivan had no intention to change and remained resolute in his ways. I continually wondered at the fact that the new way of life in Russia had not influenced the old man in the least. He ignored the new teachings, relations and customs of the time. Ivan was very smart, calculating, and observant. He could pretty much fool everyone. To all people, he was an ordinary man - a plain old commoner - a gardener. His ideal was and remained his master, to whom he would remain faithful to the end, even though no one demanded it of him.

When I was home and had some free time, Ivan would look that no one was listening, lock the doors and windows to ensure no eavesdropping, and tell me of life in the past. He revealed the entire history of my father’s family, which heretofore, had been obscured by fear and whispers, as follows:

Before the Revolution, your father’s parents owned a large, beautiful estate near Odessa. I was sent by my parents to live there as a servant boy when I was just 15 years old. Serfdom had only recently been abolished and had been the way in Russia for many centuries past. Your grandparents, Alexander and Nadieshda, had just married, and I became your Grandfather’s personal servant, and witnessed the birth of your father and his younger siblings, who gradually grew up before my eyes.

Your grandfather was a fearsome Cossack General from a long line of military men. His older brother, Nikolai, was also an officer from the Poltava military academy, and narrowly survived the war, being wounded twice. When the Revolution began, Nikolai and your father joined the White Army Movement as officers in Ukraine and were eventually captured and placed under the watch of the new authorities. After all the fighting ended, everyone scattered...

As Ivan related this last piece of information, my Uncle Nika's peculiar paranoia made more sense, as did my family's stringent disavowal of its own past. Wealthy landowners and tsarist officers were among the most hated and hunted enemies in the new Bolshevik Russia, and I was learning for the first time, to my horror, that my father and Nika had served as officers in the anti-communist White Movement.

Life in old times was quiet and contented for old Ivan, yes indeed. The demonstrations and anarchists in the big cities were of no matter to us in the Ukrainian heartland. Life on the land went on year-for-year as it always had. Then everything changed when the Great War came. Your grandfather enlisted immediately with the Poltava Cavalry, and was appointed commanding officer, and for two years, I only saw him when he was home on leave.

In 1916, came the great tragedy. My master was mortally wounded leading a cavalry charge during General Brusilov's grand offensive: Our Russian army smashed the Austrians and forced the Germans to send in reinforcements and save them. While charging over an open field, a shell exploded near my master, striking him with shrapnel, killing his horse, and sending him careening to the earth. Our last great Russian victory for the Tzar was also the last glorious moment for your illustrious grandfather, who gave his life for victory and Mother Russia.

I remember the last time I saw him... When he died, a part of Russia died, a part of our nation's heart and soul died. It was that day that the world seemed to change forever...for the worse...and we have not seen better days since...

At this, tears welled up in his eyes and he began to wail: "Oh woe our Eternal Russia! How you have lost your way! When will you again find your former glory, dear Motherland?!"

The old man wept. For a moment, he was overcome by emotion, nostalgia and a tarnished but undying patriotism. He pulled a handkerchief from his pants pocket and dried his eyes. After a deep, gasping breath, he gathered himself and continued:

Before he died, your grandfather instructed me to help your father Vladimir manage the estate together with your grandmother Nadieshda. But Nadieshda was strong-willed and would hear none of it. After her husband departed this life, she took firm and complete control of the estate. She also opposed your father's engagement to the beautiful dark-eyed Lida Yosifovna. Hence, the young master felt obliged to move from Poltava to Krasnodar and purchased the house in which we now sit, leaving it in Ivan's care just before the Revolution broke out.

I relayed to Ivan that father's siblings and mother Nadieshda had fled to avoid Communist persecution. I further bid him not to get in touch with them. His duty had been fulfilled with his return of the house to me, the daughter of his master. And through Ivan, I learned about the world of my ancestors for the first time. It was so different than the version of the past taught to us at school. Wealthy people, who I had come to know as the worst thieves, were described by Ivan as humane, kind and generous.

I tried at several points to contradict the well-meaning old man and prove to him that life in the present-day was far better than that in the past. He was never, however, willing to give-in to my views.

"I guess it must have been right for my grandparents to own that entire estate while the workers and farmers received virtually nothing, then?" I asked, spoiling for an argument.

"But of course, it was right Madame. That's why our heavenly father bestowed upon your grandparents the authority to govern the common people. And back then, every honest and hard-working person had more than enough to eat and drink. Nobody wanted to harm the landowners and they looked after the needs of those willing to work. You could buy everything at the market very cheaply. It was a good, easy-going life."

"But today all people are equals!" I attempted to interrupt.

"And what's the point of equality!?" Ivan objected. "A fool will still be a fool, but he'll spend the rest of his life in the rut. A clever man will not sit idly and will strive for a better life, even if they have to send him to Siberia. Equality is invented by people, but from God's perspective, it is nowhere on Earth. Otherwise, God would not give one person beauty and the other ugliness, one intelligence and the other ignorance, one strength and the other weakness! Look at nature: how can you compare a tiger with a cat and a wolf with a dog!"

"I don't know why Ivan, maybe because it's simple, stupid, blind fate." I answered, finding it difficult to formulate a response.

"Because our Lord God, in his wisdom, has willed it to be so Madame." Replied the old man, with a rare certitude: "And this is also why: So that we can all share our passions and talents with one another. Because how could we share, serve, and give anything to anyone else if we all had exactly the same talents, strengths, resources and faculties?"

I didn't like it that Ivan was lecturing me in this manner, and didn't want to accept what he said.

"Peace be with you Madame." He said: "You are still too young to understand old Ivan. Just wait and see what comes of this so-called equality and Godlessness! One war after the other will break out. And like a river, blood will stream across Russian land. I will, thank God, not be alive to see it. But you, Madame, will remember what I have said. The people will bathe in sweat and tears to construct and employ the devil's war machinery. But they won't achieve anything righteous. Our Lord God despises such disobedience, turns his back on the people, and what remains is misery and hellish fear, until they find their own way back to Him."

"I am truly afraid of that – I am afraid there will be war, Ivan." I said with genuine concern.

"That's why you should pray to our Lord, Madame, that he might lead us out of these trials and tribulations."

This well-meaning, heart-felt recommendation still didn't move me: "I can't pray!" I gruffly retorted.

"A terrible mistake Madame!" Ivan said with quiet concern in his eyes.

"But I'll pray for you and ask God our father in heaven to help you find the right path."

He was silent and lowered his gray head into his hands with a sense of resignation.

I had nothing else to say. I could see that the old man was hurt by these conversations, so I stopped talking as well. "He can't be re-educated!" I thought bitterly. "His old soul is forever stuck in the old days and the old ways."

Despite this testy exchange, I held old Ivan very dear. And the thought that I would have to leave him for an extended time pained me. My schoolyear was already coming to an end, and I would soon have to take my final exams. The best students had the right to go to the college or university of their choice without needing to take the entrance exams. For that reason, I took this final schoolyear and my final exams very seriously and often studied through the night, reading my books and writing papers.

Ivan would get up every night around midnight, cook me a strong tea and bring it to me as I studied. He would typically shake his head with its white hair and say: "Haven't you studied enough for today, Madame? Your books won't run away from you and all these long nights of study are leaving you pale. I am worried about you!"

"Just go back to bed, Ivan. I have a few more things to do and I'll be finished soon."

"You are just like your father used to be, Madame. He also never wanted to listen to old Ivan. How will things be in Moscow when you are there all on your own?"

"I'm old enough and I'll make it through, Ivan Kusmitch!" I answered curtly.

"And where are you going to live in Moscow, Madame?" "In a student dormitory." "Oh, Madame, stay here where you are now instead. And wait until you meet the right man."

"I have time before I find a man, Ivan. Marriage won't run away from me either! First, I need to make something of myself."

"A real man doesn't check to see if you've studied ten or twenty years, Madame. Young Doctor Heifiz, who lost his wife some time ago to illness, would marry you immediately and consider himself lucky to have found such a beautiful young wife."

“Young Doctor Heifiz?” I said, wondering if Ivan remembered that his daughter was my age: “Did he say something about me?”

“Yes indeed. He did.”

“Well tell him that he should forget about it and put it out of his mind.” I said, with remarkable calm. “Your young gentleman may simply want to use marriage to get his hands on the house.”

“I don’t believe that, Madame. Doctor Heifiz is an educated man and would certainly not marry out of such calculation. He certainly has enough money, otherwise he wouldn’t be able to pay such a high rent.”

“Oh Ivan...” I laughed: “Just give it up. I respect our dear tenant very much, but I would not marry him for one very simple reason. Namely: I don’t love him!”

“Here you are also very much like your father, Madame! He didn’t want to marry anyone, but the one he loved, his dearest Zinaida Yosifovna. Had he listened to old Ivan, perhaps he wouldn’t be in Siberia today.”

After this exchange, the old man got up. I looked at him as he sadly left the room, and honestly didn’t know what I should do.

In Krasnodar there were several universities that I could attend far more easily than going to study in Moscow. But I truly didn’t want to break my promise to Peter.

There was something else that made me want to leave Krasnodar: That was my secret fear that sooner or later the truth about my past and how I came into possession of the house would come to light. I was often unsettled about the entire matter. Had I acted foolishly? Should I have never accepted the house from Ivan?

I felt out of place. It was as if a mountain of the past had been heaped on my shoulders. I could no longer move easily or freely anywhere, the fear that anyone would find out that I was a "baron's daughter" was keeping me awake at night. "Why is that my fault that my father was a baron? After all, I was born under Soviet regime. I love my motherland with all my heart and am ready to give my life for the building of communism!" I reassured myself. "But what if they won't believe me, what if they'll ask about the house?" Regardless of my agonizing, this is how it had turned out. This is how fate would have it.

And although the conversations with the old man stirred something inside me from earlier times, the Soviet persona inside me was still strong and wide-awake. I wanted to prove that I was a true Komsomol, that my family past wasn't my fault, and to show my readiness "to fight for the good of the people."

With that in mind, I did something extraordinary in this time of intense study: At that time in Krasnodar, there was an Olympiad of children's amateur art activities, where all the talented children showed their ability to play various instruments, sing and recite. I decided to take part and was determined to win in one of the disciplines. But how could I do that? Yes, I could play the piano a little and had a rather pleasant voice, but there were many people like me, and I couldn't count on winning. I had to do something special, and began thinking about it for days.

Finally, a moment of inspiration struck me. I took a piece of paper and wrote a poem in honor of Stalin:

On my native land.
On my native land, the sun shines beautifully,
On my native land, the brook flows bravely,
Under the lucky Kremlin star
We live better and work harder.
We have broken the iron chains
Of oppressive fetters.
We are led by the best in the world,
The wisest of Bolsheviks!

Then, sitting at the piano, I matched my words with a melody and accompaniment and wrote it all down on a sheet of music. I performed this song as a young poet and composer at the Olympics and won first prize for best composition. I also played the song for the leader of my Komsomol organization – who was thrilled - and saw to it that my song and photo were splashed across the pages of all the local newspapers, including the front page of our Komsomol paper. Soon I was something of a local celebrity, and people began to recognize me. I was encouraged to perform my song and to study composition, and people spoke of my great talent and potential. Even Peter got his hands on one of the newspapers and insisted that I attend the Moscow Conservatory instead of going to a technical university as I had originally planned.

And all this because I praised the Soviets and Stalin! If I had written a song about love or nature, nobody would have noticed or cared in the least. And as I had done, many far more talented writers, composers, and artists of the time had turned their talents towards the glorification of Stalin and the Soviet Union just to escape destitution or a checkered past and move up in the system. And the more Soviet propaganda they injected into their art, and the more it penetrated the souls of the desperately needy people, the more Comrade Stalin rewarded them for it!

In this manner, artists who wanted a better life were coerced into actively supporting state policy. And the Soviet intellectual class obediently followed the path laid out for them by the government. The artistic and cultural elite saw and knew full-well that life in the USSR was miserable for the average citizen. But, receiving considerable bribes from Stalin, and living under constant fear of arrest should they step out of line, they reconciled with their fate and took on an active role in in the mass deception of the people.

Now, having played my own distinguished part in this deception, my place in the Soviet world was secure, for the time being. And it seemed that no one had noticed the struggle that had been swirling violently within me between my fearful past and my hopeful future. I felt that I could simply brush the past aside and nobody would ever notice.

But someone did notice.

As the entire world seemed to be standing on its head to align with the brave new world order, Ivan remained fixed like the hand of a compass forever pointing north. Soon after my victory, he came to me and reminded me that no person or government, no matter how powerful or arrogant, could ever erase every pathway to the truth, however terrible it might be: "You see, Madame, the people in power believe that they have completely destroyed the past. But our Lord God created an invisible bridge between the past and present that no person can ever destroy. And you and I are a part of that bridge..."

Chapter 20 – The Prophecy of the White Dove

As time passed, Ivan's health deteriorated. His skin grew yellow and pallid. His face seemed even older and more wrinkled than before. And a stubborn cough plagued him day and night. Despite that, he refused to stay confined to his bed.

When I called upon Dr. Heifiz to examine him, Ivan refused, and would also not take any medicine. All of my pleas and entreaties for him to take care of his health fell on deaf ears. Ivan would stay in bed a while, but as soon as I left the house for school, he got up and did work around the house and yard.

He went to exceptional lengths this year to care for the flowerbeds and to plant beautiful plants around the house. He did all this for me, as he knew how much I loved flowers. Doctor Heifiz and his daughter told me that they had never seen the garden as beautiful before. I was genuinely enchanted by the flowers in all their glory, which were only accentuated by the fragrance of the rosy apple blossoms.

This gardening was such a strain on my Ivan, however, that it became difficult for him to stand up and go up the stairs. He made an effort to hide his poor condition, and forced himself to jokingly chat with me. He was unable to fool me, however, and I helped the weary old man up the stairs to his room. Then I brewed him an herbal tea and saw to it that he drank it. I put his newspaper and a vase with fresh flowers on his table, and bid him not to stand up, but to call me if he needed anything. After caring for Ivan, I went to my room and sat down at my desk to study one last time for my upcoming final exam in Geometry. I was particularly happy that this would be my last test at the Krasnodar High School, because like my father, mathematics had always been my favorite subject.

At eleven o'clock, I finished my studies and, feeling happy, went to wish Ivan a good night. As I quietly opened the door to his chambers, I was very surprised to see a light still on. Ivan was sitting on the edge of his bed and, in that moment, was sealing an envelope with a letter inside.

"What are you doing up so late, Ivan?" I asked in a somewhat accusatory manner as I stepped into the room. He looked up startled, and let the light-blue envelope slip from his hand and slowly drop to the floor like a small sail. I picked it up and, to my great surprise, read my name scribbled on the front.

"Did you write this for me, Ivan?" I asked, already knowing the answer, but needing to hear him confirm it.

"Yes, but you are not allowed to read it yet!"

"Why not?"

"You'll understand later, Madame, when the time is right. Until then, I will keep it." He said, now appearing to be not just elderly, but somehow ancient. With that, he took back the letter and stuffed it under his pillow. A still distant premonition stirred me momentarily, and I looked at him with concern. A serious expression crept across my face.

He was apparently able to read my thoughts: "Don't you worry about me, dear Madame. Your herbal tea did me good. Old Ivan is feeling much better."

I took his hand and felt his pulse. It was regular and calm. Ivan's face now also appeared a bit fresher and more relaxed. I exhaled a little, and the tension in my face slowly subsided. "You see, when you listen to me, Ivan Kusmitch, you start to feel better right away. Promise me now that you'll let Dr. Heifiz examine you tomorrow, won't you?"

Ivan took my hand and pressed it to his lips. "I'll do as you wish, Madame."

His sudden change of heart surprised me, but I was relieved he had finally stopped fighting me on this point. I looked at him with wonder and noticed that his eyes were welling with tears. "You are so good to me!" He said. "And I know, that I have to go on living for you."

I replied with a nod, leaned over and kissed him gently on the forehead. "Good night, dear Ivan Kusmitch, sleep well."

"Good night my dear angel. God bless you." He answered. Then he raised his hand and made a sign of the cross three times across his chest. "God bless you for all times, dear Inna Vladimirovna. Sleep well." With that, he lay back on his pillow.

Deeply moved, I left his chambers. That evening, I couldn't fall asleep for a long time, Ivan constantly returning to my thoughts.

"No." I thought: "I have to stay in Krasnodar and go to college here. I can't just leave Ivan here by himself. If Peter really loves me, he will understand and wait for me until fate opens the way for me to go to Moscow."

I resolved to stay, and only then could I fall asleep.

That night, however, I had an extraordinary dream: On my desk lay Ivan's envelope. Curiously, I opened it, but found no letter inside. Suddenly, as if in a flash, a white dove flew out, circled above me and then came to rest at my feet. I looked down at the bird, not knowing what to think. It opened its beak as if it wanted to say something, but not a single sound emerged from its throat. And now I noticed that the dove was being strangled by a thick, fire-red ribbon around its neck. Suddenly the dove sprung up from the floor and jumped onto my chest, which caused me to rear back and begin to raise my arm as if to fend the bird off. As this occurred, I was aware that the dove was looking at me sadly. As I looked back, to my astonishment, I noticed that the dove's eyes were the light, watery, faithful eyes of Ivan Kusmitch.

"Is that you, Ivan?" I asked, not knowing what to think. "Who turned you into a dove?"

The dove still did not make a sound, but I could see bright tears in its eyes.

"You must certainly want to fly away free." I said. I went to the window, but as I went to open it with one hand, and reached for the dove with my other hand, it suddenly clasped me so tightly that I felt a sharp pain.

"Now blood is flowing out there." Said the dove, in an echoing-voice: "I'm afraid of it. Keep me close to your heart."

I looked out the window and noticed that the entire street in front of the house had turned into a red river. In its violent current it carried many boats and ships filled with soldiers. In one of the boats stood my beloved Peter dressed in a uniform. He waved to me sadly with a handkerchief.

"You'll never see him again once it starts!" Said the dove: "He will be carried off by the river of blood. And you must run away. You should not have a single drop of blood on your conscience. Listen now to what I say, and it will be your salvation!"

With those words, the dove loosened its grip, flew out of the window, and disappeared into the clouds. The red ribbon fell into the river and, as if it had hit a stream of lava, caught fire and vaporized in a thin line of fire.

I suddenly awoke and saw the round sun just piercing the horizon from my window. I looked at the clock and realized my test was just an hour away. Relieved that I had at least not overslept, I hurried to get dressed and go to school. I wanted to tell Ivan about the dream and quickly poked my head quietly into his chambers and whispered "Ivan", but he gave no reply, and seeing he was not awake, hurried out the front door.

On the way to school I met Nastia's mother Mrs. Golovko. "I wanted to come see you my dear!" She said, greeting me kindly. We walked a short way together, and unexpectedly, she said: "Did you already hear that they are calling up all young men in a draft?"

"All young men? But not the university students?"

"University students too."

I proceeded to tell Nastia's mother about my dream and asked: "Can you interpret it? What could it mean?"

"I don't think..." She answered, drawing out her words: "I just hope it doesn't portend war, because Peter has also been called up."

This news shook me to my core. But one small piece of the news put my anguish about leaving to rest: Fate had now decided that I could no longer go to Moscow and had to stay and look after Ivan Kusmitch."

Frau Golovko and I reached the tram station, boarded the street car, and I made it to school with ten minutes to spare.

The geometry exam went well for me, my teacher even had time to grade it, and was very satisfied with my efforts. Happy and relieved that I had cleared the final hurdle of my high school studies, I was able to return home earlier than normal.

When I got to the house just after noon, my first stop was to inquire with Dr. Heifiz. Good day, Sir, would you do me a favor and come upstairs for a brief moment to examine Ivan? He promised me yesterday that he would cooperate. Dr. Heifiz agreed and went with me straight away. We knocked at Ivan's chamber door, but there came no reply. The doctor gave me a look of concern, and when I saw the expression on his face, I quickly opened the door and went inside.

Ivan lay stretched out and motionless in bed. He was holding the letter he had written in his hands folded across his chest. His face was peaceful and hinted of a quiet smile.

“Ivan, why won’t you say anything?” I said, approaching him.

The doctor stepped in and briefly examined him. After just a few moments, he turned to me and said: “Ivan Kusmitch has left us. He’s dead.” I screamed in anguish from the bottom of my heart, fell to my knees and took the cold hand of my faithful old friend and cried bitter tears.

We carried Ivan into the room and laid him on the couch. I washed his face and covered his sad eyes. I put on a clean shirt and crossed his arms over his chest, and with the Doctor and Sara’s help, I began to put the two tables together so that I could cover them with a sheet and lay Ivan on them, according to the Russian custom, with his feet toward the door for his last sleep in the house.

On one of the tables, I found his last letter, written to me.

"Dear Olga Sergeyevna!

May God bless you for many years to come and give you health and happiness. If your father ever returns, bow to him for me.

Your Ivan Dolgovekiy."

The envelope also contained five hundred paper rubles and two gold old coins of five rubles each, which Ivan bequeathed to me. He asked me not to spend a lot of money on him, but to bury him in the simplest coffin.

"No, sweet, faithful Ivan. You deserve an oak lacquered coffin and a small monument over the grave, and many, many flowers!" I said' crying and stroking his frozen face, and it seemed to me that he heard it and smiled slightly in return.

This generous, stalwart old man, faithful to my family and his ideals to the very last, had also foreseen his final day.

Chapter 21 – The Witches' Den

I didn't know what to do. Ivan's passing and Peter's conscription into the military threw me completely off balance. After Ivan's burial, I still couldn't get a grasp of all that had happened, and that I would have to now make my way completely on my own. Good old Ivan had, until the last, taken so many things off of my hands and looked after me.

Even after his death, he proved his loyalty one last time by leaving me his entire savings, 2,000 rubles. In his letter to me, he designated that I spend the money for my journey to Moscow, so that I would have something to see me through my first few months there. He also left me several pieces of advice. He directed me not to sell my house to strangers and told me to continue to rent the downstairs to Doctor Heifiz and his daughter. He further wrote that I should rent the upstairs to someone who would take good care of the house, keep the yard up and clean regularly, in exchange for rent. I could tell that the old man believed that I wouldn't feel better anywhere else but in my own house and hoped that I would return some day.

His letter concluded with the request that I send his greetings to my father should I see him again and ended with many blessings to me for all times. How alone I felt without this loyal, fatherly mentor. Now a painful and piercing question as to what to do next stood before. It was odd that Ivan knew that Peter was no longer in Moscow, yet designated his final savings for my journey there. If I could only ask him why...what had he known?

Feeling isolated, I would often go downstairs to visit Sara, the daughter of Dr. Heifiz, and play the piano, which greatly soothed me and gave me strength. I got to know her better and we became good friends. I could tell that the Doctor, however, still took a fancy to me, as he would look in on us quite often and bring us tea whenever I played. Although he never made any overt gestures, and with Ivan no longer there to watch over me, the Doctor's thinly veiled interest in me was yet another reason for me to leave my house in Krasnodar.

When I suggested to them that I might go to Moscow, Heifiz's interest in owning the house quickly came to the surface, and seemed to trump his interest in me. "Yes, Inna, you should go to Moscow, and experience the city, it's an amazing place! If you sell me the house, you will be able to live quite well there."

I imagined that Ivan would be quite sad to see this come to pass and turned down Heifiz's offer. I'm certainly going to come back to Krasnodar after my studies, I replied.

"As you wish." He said dryly, seemingly repelled by me for once. I could tell that, by rejecting his offer, I had destroyed the doctor's long-held wish to own the house, and from that point on a smoldering resentment reigned between us which made me feel less at home there.

I followed Ivan's advice, and asked Nastia and her family to help me find a renter who could care for the house and take the upstairs. One evening, Nastia's mother introduced me to a very simple, but good-natured woman from the countryside. "This is Tosya Verba, she grew up in the same village as me. Tosya doesn't have much, and has to pay 20 rubles just to rent a corner to sleep in. She would gladly take care of your house if you take her on."

I looked searchingly at this short, chubby middle-aged lady with light blue eyes and long, dark blonde hair arranged in braids around her head in the Ukrainian style. Her face reflected a simple, almost childish desire to please. I honestly liked her.

"What do you live on now?" I asked.

"I work as a cleaning lady in a military school and earn 120 rubles a month."

"Do you have relatives?"

"Just a sister who is married to a farmer and lives and works on a collective farm."

"Can I rely on you to faithfully watch over my house and property when I am away?"

The plump little lady began to blush. "I think you can trust me, I'm not a thief, honest!" She replied, with a plain simplicity. I intuitively knew that she was a good person, and perhaps memories of Nyurka still haunted the peripheries of my subconscious. Mrs. Golovko turned to me, with an expression of mild vexation, and said: "Inna, I can vouch for Tosya, I've known her and her family all my life..." I could tell that Nastia's mother felt that my questioning was slowly devolving into an interrogation of sorts.

"Sorry, I didn't mean to imply that, Tosya. I just don't know you yet and wanted to ask a few questions. Based on everything, I see you are someone I can put my faith in, so let me show you to your quarters."

Tosya and Mrs. Golovko both noticeably relaxed at these words. As I led her to Ivan's former chambers, she could hardly believe her good fortune. To this point she had just had a corner in a dormitory filled with other women to sleep in, and now she would have an entire room to herself and the run of the upstairs after I left.

Soon I realized how good a tenant I had found in her and was glad that I had taken Ivan's advice. Tosya even helped me prepare and pack for my journey to Moscow and accompanied me to the train station on my last day in Krasnodar. I left knowing that my house would be in good hands.

I was surprised when I reached the platform not only to see the Golovko's, but also twenty of my high school classmates who had come to see me off and wish me success in Moscow.

Only now did I realize, how momentous an adventure stood directly before. After all, virtually every young person in the Soviet Union strived to visit and get to know the one great city of Russia, Moscow. And so, with the well-wishes of my friends, I began my journey to the capital on a high note.

For two days and two nights I rode towards the mighty center of the Soviet Union. I looked out the window almost without interruption and wondered at how vast my homeland was. The endless, fertile countryside, giant forests and small, cozy villages of Ukraine floated past and soon the train reached the great central-Russian plain. Here I came to increasingly miss the rich, lush farmland and the deep green Ukrainian prairies and forests. The villages seemed somehow dirtier and more impoverished. A flat land of yellow, dried-out clay stretched for as far as the eye could see.

Shortly before Moscow, grand forests again appeared, which, unlike the varied Ukrainian forest, only seemed to contain needled pine trees and bushes. Instead of the small, humble houses of the many villages we had just passed, Moscow's suburbs were studded with impressive wooden villas and pretty summer houses. Large, newly built factories and workshops greeted me with their howling sirens. For the first time, I saw the large electrified suburban trains with bright, spacious wagons packed with Moscow commuters. The suburban stations were filled with swarms of people, which grew ever-thicker the closer we got to the capital city.

Then my train entered the endless sea of houses and buildings in Moscow itself. We passed many buildings, old and new, of great cultural and historic significance, including dozens of impressive churches built in the Russian Orthodox style with cupolas and domes. Very few, I noticed, were still adorned with crosses as in times past. Instead, a red Soviet flag was typically flying atop the roof.

The train came to its final halt at the Kievsky Station, just west of the city center. I'd never seen so many trains and platforms together in one place. When I stepped out onto the street, I was greeted by the deafening roar of city traffic. A cacophony of cars, buses and trams ran uninterrupted in every direction around me. People hastily walked here and there and spoke in loud voices to and over one another. I was completely disoriented by it all. It seemed as if I had just entered a witches' den. I stood spellbound for a long time in front of the station building, like a new-born trying to make sense of its surroundings for the first time. Somehow, some way, I had to find my way through this boiling cauldron of humanity to my university, and to the future that awaited me there.

Left: Inna Grinfeldt in 1939, at the age of 17.

Chapter 22 – In the Heart of Mother Russia

It was a hot summer day when I arrived in Moscow. The sun still stood above the roofs of the towering sea of buildings and bathed the streets, sidewalks and plazas in its unrelenting rays. The asphalt only reflected and amplifying the heat, giving everything a mirage-like essence, as if it could all melt away at any moment. The cloudless sky was a soft blue. The heavy, dry air was filled with dust and the overpowering smell of leaded gasoline.

Most of the people moving to-and-fro were well-dressed, but seemed to have an unpleasant, anxious, or unfriendly expression of indifference so common in large capital cities. Soon I was able to distinguish the soft, drawn-out Moscow accent of the people from the disjointed concert of noise around me, and determined to ask for directions to my dormitory, which was near a Rizhky Station.

With that in mind, I sought out a handsome looking man in the throng and approached him. This stranger seemed more friendly than most, and as was the custom in Moscow, immediately addressed me with the casual form of "you" in Russian. He told me that I could reach my dormitory one of several ways: Either by taking the tram or the "underground" – in which case I'd have to transfer several times. Or, as he recommended, by taking a taxi, which would bring me directly to my destination.

I followed his advice, got in the long taxi line and rode for nearly a half-hour though the broad avenues of the bustling heart of the Soviet Union. I carefully observed every aspect of the city that came into view, and despite the oppressive heat and street noise, found it to be magnificent beyond imagination. I saw many large, beautiful buildings characterized by their elaborate classical or practical modern architecture. An avenue of large department stores and shops, often housed in multi-story blocks, exhibited bright, large show rooms filled with an endless variety of products and foodstuffs. The many cinemas, theaters and museums that we passed stood out amidst a blinding sea of colorful signs and billboards, many with communist slogans and paintings.

Numerous alleyways, plazas and parks surprised me with the splendor of their greenery, and I noticed several times how flowerbeds had been arranged to look like paintings. These living murals usually grew a political message. Many mimicked portraits of Communist leaders. Seeing Lenin, Marx and Stalin etched into park landscapes with flowers and bushes didn't really perturb or surprise me in the least, nor did it strike me as odd or ridiculous. After all, I had grown up in a society and education system in which the cultish aggrandizement of these men was a ubiquitous fact of life.

On the sidewalks and in the parks, throngs of people moved about briskly as if it were a holiday. The closer we came to the city center, the thicker the crowds of pedestrians grew. We often had to wait at intersections until we could continue because the streets were so packed with cars. I was very glad that I hadn't taken the tram, as I could see that they were so overcrowded that those who liked to live dangerously hung off the side of the cars like bunches of grapes from the footsteps. Unpleasantly moved by this site, I had to admire the boldness of these passengers, who it seemed were risking their lives to arrive at their destination a few minutes earlier.

In the meantime, my taxi driver had advanced into the city center. I had not been in many cars in my life, and this one was how I imagined a battle chariot driven by a fierce warrior might have been. After much jostling, honking, and battling intersection-by-intersection, we had soon advanced to "Red Square," where everything was grand and wide, like a peaceful eye at the center of a violent storm. I excitedly recognized the high castle walls made of ruby colored stone and the star atop the tower of the Kremlin.

Lenin's tomb, of which I had read and heard so much, stood in the middle of the square, and drew my attention. A large, orderly procession of people stood waiting in line before the entrances of this rectangular marble building. I could easily discern that all the people who wanted to view Lenin in his glass sarcophagus were not Muscovites, but outsiders. They wore the varied garbs and traditional clothing of the many peoples of the massive empire and were of every race and countenance. Those who had thronged here where among the few who had the good fortune to see Moscow at least once in their lives. For most citizens of the Union, the richest and most beautiful city in all Russia remained an unreachable fairy tale.

After exiting the square, we turned north, and after another twenty minutes, came to a halt in front of Rizhky Station, near which lay my student home – but where exactly I did not know. For a moment I was seized with panic but remembered almost immediately that I had the exact campus address stuffed in my pocket for just this moment. As the taxi driver looked back at me impatiently, waiting to be paid - I quickly pulled out the scrap of paper with the address, unraveled it, and bid the driver to take me there. At first, he seemed irritated that I was asking to go further, but after considering only a few seconds, nodded and conceded with a grumble that it was less than two blocks away. In seconds we were there: I paid, thanked the driver profusely as he handed me my suitcase, and stepped onto the sidewalk right in front of the main reception building. My journey to the heart of Mother Russia was finally at an end, and now my life as a university student was at hand.

Music students were housed in twelve long, four story dormitory buildings that resembled a military compound. The concrete courtyard contained no flowers or greenery of any kind and seemed uninviting. Around the blocks stood tall wooden plank walls with a heavy wooden door that was always locked. Anyone who wanted to enter this small student settlement had to enter through the security office, where each person's documents were carefully examined. Only permanent students who lived here received an identification document, a sort of passbook, with which they could come and go as they pleased.

I was registered in the so-called "music block" building number 7, girls' room number 12. As I approached the "music block," a musical dystopia assailed my ears: The disjointed clanging, strumming and blaring sounds of students practicing with windows open could be heard from quite some distance. I walked through the wide-open building entranceway, wondering how I would manage to remain sane in this sonic Armageddon, and soon found room 12 on the ground floor. Without so much as a knock, I slowly opened the door and saw a large, bare hall with other girls my age scattered about. Along the walls stood over a dozen steel bedframes. Next to each bed was a small nightstand. I also noticed, with great interest, a large, black-polished grand piano, without which the hall might have easily been mistaken for a women's prison barracks. In the middle of the hall stood a long table with a wooden bench on either side. A spacious common closet shoved up next to the entrance door completed the simple accommodations.

A few of the girls sat on their beds, at the table or piano and were busy reading, writing, or playing music. Without noticing the others, each practiced their instrument, whether it was the violin, flute or piano. I was taken aback by this musical disarray and wondered again how I would adjust to this chaos.

As I shyly approached the table and asked which of the beds was still free, the girls lifted their heads and took notice. One of them clapped her hands together and said: "Comrades look! We have a new classmate!"

As if on cue, the other girls stopped what they were doing and directed their attention towards me. They approached me and kindly greeted me, each shaking my hand and welcoming me. The entire bunch was very curious and, without so much as a moment to unpack and settle-in, I did my best to respond to their questions and best summarize my background and interests. When I told them that I wanted to study composition, they asked if I had composed any works. I mentioned the one song I had written back in Krasnodar which was so well-received and even featured in the local newspaper.

"To the piano – let's hear it! Yes – play it for us!" Without objection, I obliged my new roommates and sat down to play. After I finished playing and singing, the girls gave me a lively round of applause. "A beautiful song!" They shouted: "Did you write the lyrics?" I nodded yes.

"What music school did you attend?"

"None. I prepared myself for the music theory exam."

"Ah! Hopefully you'll make it through." Replied the choir.

To be honest, I was quite afraid of this Moscow exam. If I failed, I would have to go back home. But I had a stroke of luck, because when I performed my song before the stringent commission, they liked it so much that it compensated for my relatively weak theoretical knowledge and they accepted me into the program.

"The young lady will certainly be able to make up what she currently lacks in theoretical knowledge." Said the professor for composition. With that, I knew I would be able to remain and study in Moscow.

For the first two months, things went fabulously in the Russian capital. I went to the opera and concerts several times. Once I even went to the famous Bolshoi Theater. On a particularly nice Sunday, I went to the Central Park of Culture and Recreation – also known as "Gorky Park" - and visited the Tretyakov Art Gallery, where I was able to admire the finest portraits of the modern and classical masters. I also didn't watch my money when it came to food, and soon burned through all I had brought.

It was certainly quite difficult when I had spent my last kopek, and had to switch over to a diet of stale bread and water. I did receive a modest monthly student stipend of 130 rubles, and the Heifiz family transferred their rent from Krasnodar. But life in the capital was so expensive, that these comparatively modest sums barely sufficed for me to make it through the month.

Most of my classmates received supplementary food and money from home. I didn't want to resort to writing my mother, telling her how things were. I certainly knew, after all, that her new husband Yevgeni had no money to spare for me.

I often had to watch hungrily as my roommates devoured sandwiches and vegetables to their hearts' content. My roommate Nina, whose bed was next to mine, soon noticed and often shared her breakfast with me. I knew, however, that this was not sustainable, and increasingly thought about how to earn some money.

One evening, as I sat consumed by these thoughts on the edge of my bed, Nina came over and said that she might be able to help me earn some extra money without too much difficulty.

"You know of a job for me?" I asked happily.

"Job? No. But I want to help you. Listen, why don't you come with me tonight to the grand symphony concert?"

"I don't have any money for it."

"I'll get you a ticket, and we can discuss how you can make some money after the concert." She said thoughtfully and told me to dress up in my nicest dress.

I did as she asked as I was especially thrilled to go to the grand symphony concert, which would be held at the main hall of the Moscow Conservatory downtown. I would be able to hear the most famous soloists in the Moscow Opera. The program contained the Fifth Symphony of my favorite Peter Tchaikovsky as well as Beethoven's Ninth Symphony. The renowned Moscow Philharmonic Orchestra was to perform under the direction of Professor Alexandrov. The soloists included the biggest stars in Russian opera: The soprano Barsovar, the alto Antonova, the tenor Koslovsky and the bass Michailov.

In my excitement and expectation over this once-in-a-lifetime experience, I didn't take any particular note of where the two men Nina introduced to me before the concert had come from. One was named Boris Nikolaiavitch and was, as I later found out, Nina's boyfriend. The other was named Comrade Lushkin. Both were older, and made a rather repellent, burnt-out impression on me.

During the concert, however, I was so immersed in the fabulous music, that I barely noticed the men, one seated to either side of me. As I exited the theater bedazzled by the performance, each of them tried to take me by the arm. I shook myself away and looked upon these intrusive gestures with a questioning look of aggravation. My friend Nina stood next to us, as if cautiously waiting to see what would happen. "Let's all go to a good nightclub I know!" Said Boris Nikolaiavitch: "They have good wine."

"And the best dance music." Added Lushkin and Nina. "We can go have a good time and get to know each other better."

I made no reply for several moments and scanned this odd company with great sobriety. "After that fabulous a concert, I don't need any more entertainment." I said resolutely. "And I am definitely not going to a night club, so I'm sorry, but you'll have to excuse me!"

I saw both men now making long faces. Nina's eyes widened with horror and her shoulders twitched nervously. I was relieved when both men, without a word, reached out and shook my hand, then said goodbye and walked off into the night with Nina.

I stood there surprised for a while and watched the three of them walking away. All the grandeur of the concert and the lofty feeling it had instilled in me had dissipated in the face of this strange scene.

Back in the dormitory hall, I went to bed right away, but couldn't sleep very soundly that night. I repeatedly woke up and looked over at Nina's empty bed. She only came back around five in the morning. She snuck quietly through the room over to my bed and sat fully clothed on its far corner.

"You sleeping, Inna?" She whispered. I reached out for her hand, she leaned over towards me, and I could smell the sweet odor of Schnapps on her breath.

"You're terribly childish." She said with emphasis, scrunching up her face, though I could tell she was not entirely serious.

"Why do you say that?"

"Because Comrade Lushkin paid for your concert ticket and you didn't even go along with us after."

"But where did you expect me to get the money for the ticket?" I replied.

"Boris Nikolaiavitch gives me money every now and then."

"Boris Nikolaiavitch? Are you two engaged?"

"Of course not...He's married!"

"How is it that you can take money from him then?"

"Let's just say he requires a certain degree of obedience from me."

"And you can do that without loving him?"

"I have no choice, otherwise I'd be forced to give up my music studies."

"How awful Nina, I would never be able to do anything like that." I said, deeply shaken.

In that moment I lost my one friend in the heart of Mother Russia – and I realized that this magnificent city was also a cold, harsh place for most of its inhabitants. Never again could I accept anything from Nina. I knew now that she earned her money in a manner that, for me at least, was unbearable and heartless.

Chapter 23 – Released

It was now approaching late fall in the Russian capital. The tired sun now barely made it above the roofs of the houses, steeples of the churches and towers of the Kremlin. The trees in the many parks and avenues began to shed their leaves. The sky was covered by dark, heavy clouds, and a cold wind blew along the streets. The days grew less inviting. My mood seemed to reflect the weather. In my soul, I felt dark and gray. All of my efforts to find a fitting job remained without success. I had to reduce my diet to only the bare essentials, and my empty stomach would often growl in protest.

The constant comings-and-goings of strangers and the constant noise of the city began to exhaust me. I longed to be alone, even if just for a short time, to clear my mind. But it was impossible. The stares of strangers and the noise of the city followed me everywhere. There didn't seem to be any place for peace and reflection.

My fifteen roommates were much less affected by these conditions and dealt with them more easily. They'd all lived much longer in student homes and had grown accustomed to the bustle and racket from their practicing. Most of the girls were able to simply overlook the daily difficulties. And they never missed an opportunity "to live" and take advantage of any possible means to enjoy themselves and blow off steam. Each had a boyfriend or admirer. And they couldn't understand why I didn't want to have anything to do with a man, even though I had plenty of opportunities.

What stood in the way was the promise I had made two years prior to my beloved Peter, and I intended to keep my word. So, I determined to fight the good fight and remain faithful despite all the temptations and difficulties.

Now and then, however, the thought did enter my mind that I couldn't hold out like this forever and that I would have to give-in to life or leave the Conservatory. One evening, the decision was made for me.

My neighbor Nina ran into our hall shouting loudly, holding a newspaper in her hand. "Comrades! Look at this! The new student ordinance just came out. Our scholarships have been withdrawn!"

"How? What? Why?!" All of the girls seemed to say at once, forming a ring around Nina. I also hurried to look and reached my hand out to take the paper. It was the latest edition of the "Moscow Evening Post."

I read the article aloud. Among other things, it stated that, starting November 1, 1940, the payment of scholarships and stipends to university students would be discontinued. From then on, every student would have to pay an annual fee of 500 rubles. Only those who received the highest marks in every subject could still hope to be eligible for financial aid from the state.

Although I genuinely enjoyed my studies and my teachers thought well of me, my knowledge of music theory was still relatively mediocre. It was clear to me that I would have to do without the 130 rubles after November 1. This naturally made me even more unhappy. I let the paper fall to the ground and walked over to my bed. Without saying a word, I sat on the edge and tried to hold back my tears.

Someone gently caressed my hair. I looked up and saw Nina, who looked at me with a concerned, friendly expression, and asked me the burning question: "What will you do now Inna?"

"I think I'll have to give up my studies." I replied sadly.

"If you..." continued Nina: "go with Comrade Lushkin, he will gladly kiss your hand and give you the money for your studies. He loves you!"

"I will never go with that person and sell myself for money!" I said gruffly, waving my hand as if to swat away an annoying fly which I'd already shooed away before.

"Then there is nothing that will help you. But let me advise you one thing: Think about it. Later you may deeply regret squandering your good fortune."

With those words Nina put on her jacket, turned dismissively away, and left the room with a haughty gait.

The other girls left behind said: "She won't have any headaches...her Boris Nikolaiavitch has money and will take care of the new expenses."

I lay down on my bed without a word and took the photo of Peter that I always carried with me out of my purse. I looked at it in deep reflection. A young, fresh face smiled back at me.

"You would have been incredibly disappointed in me, my love, had I gone along with Nina." I said to him in my thoughts. "Have no fear. Your dear Inna will be true to you."

After I had regrouped and taken heart in this manner, I took up pen and paper to write Peter and let him know the news and my decision to give up my studies. I wrote that I planned to return to my father's house in Krasnodar, and that this was the right path for me.

But even before I could send the letter, as if by some wonder, there came a knock at our door. A young man dressed in a neat uniform, accompanied by our campus security officer, stuck his head in: "Telegram for Miss Inna Grinfeldt!"

I got up: "That's me."

"May I see proof of identity?" The messenger said monotonously.

I took my passbook out, opened it, and handed it to him. He looked at it reflexively without so much as reading it, as if he'd done it a thousand times that day. He handed it back, took a folded slip of paper out of his satchel, checked the name, and handed it to me. Both men departed just as quickly as they'd arrived.

I looked at the telegram with intense curiosity. It read: "Coming through Moscow tomorrow 5am. Stopping at Rizhky Station – Peter."

My Peter! I would see my beloved Peter! Suddenly, everything was finally coming together, as if a resolution to these new difficulties had only been waiting, just around the bend.

That night I couldn't get a moment's sleep, my mind swirled with a million thoughts. I tossed and turned restlessly. Hopefully, I thought, the train would be stopped at the station long enough for us to discuss the most important matters. And even if I could only see him a few moments, all of the difficulties that I'd endured studying and living in Moscow would at least not have been entirely in vain. With these thoughts, I reconciled and celebrated the coming meeting in my heart. Soon I could no longer bear to stay in bed: I stood up, got dressed and walked out of my building, across campus, and onto the street. The Rizhky train station was just a few hundred meters to the east, and quickly came into view. The large station clock read three in the morning.

It was still pitch-black outside. A gentle rain fell on the empty streets and transformed the smooth asphalt into an endless blank mirror upon which the sleeping metropolis cast its magical reflection. Under the boundless golden chains of bright street lights, the colorful neon signs of the stores, cinemas and theaters glimmered quietly in the still night like jewels encrusted in Russia's crowning glory, which, by day, was loud, harsh and terrible, yet always majestic.

Only now and then did a random car break the surreal stillness...

I was fascinated by this new manifestation of Moscow - totally asleep. The city was more beautiful than ever. For the first time, I felt completely alone with her, I could feel her spirit, and I wandered around her silent streets for over an hour, inwardly bidding adieu to this part of my life and all of the many impressions it had made upon me. Calm and at peace, I returned to the student home, put on my most beautiful dress and carefully did my hair. I then walked to Rizhky station with a happy heart, spiritually prepared for the meeting.

The platform at which the military transport train was expected was still empty. At exactly five o'clock, a large transport train arrived that included both passenger and freight cars. Tired, half-asleep soldiers looked out from the windows. Before the train had come to a stop, a slender, stately man sprang from one of the cars and ran up to me. I immediately recognized that – despite his changed appearance – this was my Peter. We stood for several moments, looking at one another speechless and bedazzled. Then I threw myself tearfully into his arms and felt his arms firmly embrace me.

"We are only stopped here for five minutes!" He said, beaming with happiness and kissing me passionately.

"I'll ride with you a ways!" Flashed the idea in my mind.

We ran together to his Corporal to gain his permission. At first, he shook his head "no" – but when I began to cry loudly, he quietly said: "OK, you can come along. But only as far as Volokolamsk."

I was delighted, as Volokolamsk lay around four hours train ride from Moscow. And in these four hours I would be able to sit near my beloved and discuss everything. Peter's comrades immediately left the compartment we sat down in and blocked off the entryway from intruders.

We sat across from one another and held hands. I told Peter how things had gone in Moscow and asked him what he thought I should do.

"I know you graduated with honors from high school in Krasnodar, so you could go to a technical college there, and still receive financial aid." Peter recommended.

"Right!" I replied: "I'll go back to Krasnodar and take up my studies there." Then I told him about Nina and her friends Boris and Lushkin.

Peter looked at me seriously and searchingly, and as he took in the end of this sordid tale, he said, quietly and inwardly: "How good you are! And how glad I would be to stay always at your side. But you shouldn't sacrifice the years of your youth for me. Nobody knows what will happen in these uncertain times. And I certainly won't be angry with you, if you find happiness with another man. For that reason, I want to release you. I want to release you from your promise."

"Peter..." I said, upset and appalled: "How on earth could you say such a thing? Don't you love me anymore?" Tears welled up in my eyes.

"I love you more than anything. And that's why I am releasing you from your promise..." He paused. Then, with emphasis: "Because..." he said, nervously prescient: "I have the feeling...that we will never see each other again."

I looked up in dismay and, with strong conviction in my voice, declared: "I will wait for you until your service in that uniform is finished."

"Darling, we're on our way to Poland now." He replied: "to the border with Germany. And I fear things will soon grow hot and bloody."

"A war?? But the Germans are our allies!"

"I don't trust this alliance."

Peter now looked into my eyes and could see the fear in them. He said quietly and kindly: "Maybe I'm mistaken. Then I'll return to Krasnodar in two years. And if you are still available, I will ask for your hand."

"But we promised each other long ago that we would marry some day!"

He quietly smiled and drew me closer. I closed my eyes and forgot the entire world. I no longer noticed how the train rattled and started, no longer noticed that the soft autumn sun had risen and was sparkling through the windows. I also didn't notice when the train stopped and stood still for several minutes.

Suddenly, someone flung open the compartment door, pulled me from Peter's arms and shouted: "Volokolamsk, young lady! The train is departing immediately!" It was the Corporal.

As if awakened from a deep dream, I looked at my Peter. "Thank you for everything. Farewell..." He said quietly.

I managed to utter, "Farewell," half whispering, but could say no more.

The Corporal took me gently by the arm and led me out of the train to the platform. I stood on the station platform and watched as the train rode off and disappeared into the distance. It felt as if my heart had been torn to pieces. The painful realization that we had only met to bid one another farewell and release one another now flooded my soul with grief. And only a tiny flicker of hope helped me, in this dark hour, to withstand the despondency that was taking hold of me.

Chapter 24 – Catherine the Great's Castle

Peter was gone. I was left alone, filled with pain at the Volokolamsk train station, a city completely foreign to me. I could barely comprehend what had just taken place so quickly, as if in a dream. A nagging bitterness remained behind with me. Fate was cruel. Two years I'd waited for my beloved, didn't give any other man the time of day, and was even prepared to wait even longer for him. And all this had produced was one heartrending "farewell."

My dream with the white dove and red river returned to my mind. Peter had indeed become a soldier and been carried off to a possible war. He would and could never be master of his own fate in the Army. And no one considered for a moment that he possessed a youthful heart that longed for love and happiness. And me? What now? I felt like a little boat that was being tossed about by the stormy sea of life - with no land in sight.

I looked around, tired and bewildered, and realized it was ten minutes to noon. A rising feeling of hunger finally brought me back to sober reality, and I determined to find some food. Only now did I notice that I didn't have a single kopek in my purse. When I headed to the station early that morning, it had never occurred to me that I might be leaving Moscow and would need money for the return trip.

"What a stupid mistake!" I thought, angry with myself. "What now?"

After considering my quandary, I determined to go to the local party bureau and request some money for the trip back. But once again, things again played out differently than I'd expected. When I stepped out of the small station building onto the street, a broad-shouldered Russian farmer approached me. He had on a broad fur wool overcoat and traditional Russian felt boots known as "valenki" which rose well above his ankles. Half of his face was obscured by a large black beard.

He came to a halt in front of me, looked at me searchingly: "Are you the young lady from Moscow, the music student?"

I was completely caught off guard: "Why would you think that?"

"I've been waiting here for a few hours already for our new music teacher who I am supposed to take to Yaropolets in this sleigh." He replied.

The village of Yaropolets, as he explained, lay 25 versts from Volokolamsk and was known far and wide for its large and beautiful castle, built by Catherine the Great. The farmer told me that a home of children with tuberculosis was housed there which always lacked personnel, and the student they were waiting for had been assigned there as a music teacher.

"I'm a student and music teacher." I said, unable to believe the coincidence. I've been looking for work for quite some time. Why don't you take me instead?

"Gladly!" The farmer said. "Otherwise our director will chew me out if I come back empty-handed."

I got in the straw-covered country sleigh without further ado, and we drove merrily through forests and fields towards my new destination. We drove past rows of trees, and the merry jingling of the sleigh bells rang out across the snow-covered expanse. The farmer took a big piece of dark bread out of his pocket, broke it into two, and handed me half. Starving, I devoured it and thought that, in this moment, life was very beautiful.

The village of Yaropolets was surrounded by a dense forest and lay astride a small hill. The clay huts appeared somewhat dark and gloomy. As we ascended the hill to the of the upper edge of the sleepy village, a large Orthodox church appeared to my right and then, as if conjured out of a fairy-tale, a majestic, white two-story Baroque manor appeared to our left. The farmer pointed to the manor and nodded – and I understood we had arrived.

Built by a Russian noble to honor Catherine the Great in the late 1700s, the once-sumptuous estate lay in the midst of a giant park bordered by a small lake and river. It's two floors stretched wide from a central hall into two outstretched wings. Along the street stood an elaborate iron gate flanked by what looked like two round, free-standing castle-towers. The gate was open, as if the occupants had been expecting us, and the farmer turned the sled through the wide entrance and we coasted along behind the horses across the sizeable front lawn, now blanketed in snow, atop which sat the bright estate.

As I neared the sprawling steps to the main-hall entrance, I could see its tall, imposing door, with a curved top, flanked by four identically shaped windows on either side. The second floor consisted of rectangular windows, set symmetrically atop the first floor with mathematical precision. Around the windows were ornate architectural flourishes, with a carved lion's head looking down upon me from between two upper-floor windows. Atop the main hall sat a modest, box-shaped belvedere partially obstructed by a wooden sign which leaned slightly in one direction and looked awkward and out-of-place. It read: Pavlik Morozov Sanitorium for Children

I was sincerely happy when the director, a well-liked older woman, kindly received me and said nothing further of the other music teacher who had been offered the position. I was assigned a small living space and allotted a modest salary and daily meals, and had no expenses, which allowed me to save for my eventual return ticket home. I had no intent to stay long, as I wanted to begin the new year at a university in Krasnodar. But this job suited me quite well as a means to bridge the time between now and then.

After I had rested and eaten a good meal, I looked around the castle. Regrettably, the interior of the stately building had been completely rearranged and now resembled a hospital more than the seat of a noble duke or duchess. There were numerous little hospital beds filled with the poor, sick little children. Most of them suffered from bone tuberculosis and had their legs, arms or back in a cast. Only a small number could get up and move around.

My new job consisted of practicing and singing songs to lift their spirits, and an accordion was made available to me for this task. And how happy they were as I would go from room-to-room and sing with them to our hearts' content. Evenings, I again made my rounds and told my little pupils stories and fairy tales. This wasn't part of my duties, but the children loved it and I was well-loved for it in return.

Now and then, there would be ample tears when one of the children recovered and was allowed to return home. In most cases, the children would be picked up by their relatives. In some cases, no family member was able to make the trip to pick up the child, and we had to accompany him or her on the trip home. One day I accompanied a ten-year-old girl named Alla. She lived in a little village about forty versts from Moscow.

We left Yaropolets in the afternoon and only reached our station around midnight due to poor train connections. Despite my urgent telegram, nobody had come to the station to pick up Alla. For better-or-worse, I had to get her home. A solid hours' walk awaited us. Our path took use through a pine forest covered in deep snow. The trees were loaded with ice, and the full moon sent its silver glow to the sleeping earth. I held her hand firmly and walked confidently forward. In the midst of the forest, however, she came to a sudden stop and looked at me with large, sad eyes.

"What's wrong, Allechka?" I asked her.

"I'm so afraid!"

"Of what?"

"Of going home."

"But sweetie, aren't you happy that you'll see your dear mother and siblings again?"

"I am!" She said sadly: "But I'm still afraid. Oh Inna Vladimirovna, if only a magic fairy could come and return us to Yaropolets."

"Did you like it that much in Yaropolets?"

"Yes, it was so pretty. The food tasted so good. And at home I'll get so little to eat."

"What about your father?" I said sympathetically, as we again began to walk.

"He's sick. Mother works alone to support us in the factory. I have three more siblings, and they're all sick."

"How awful. How did you make it to the sanatorium then?"

"We received a single free referral from the health ministry and drew lots at home as to which of us four would be allowed to go." As we were speaking, we emerged from the forest. A small village with a textile factory came into view. We walked a way up the small village street and came to a larger square where several newer wooden barracks stood.

"Do you live there?" I asked her.

"No. We live in an earthen house at the far end of the village." She said quietly.

I couldn't imagine what she meant by an "earthen house" – but I soon found out what she meant.

We came to a large clearing covered by a blanket of snow which sparked beneath the full moon. At the edge of the clearing, I saw a few small white mounds jutting up out of the ground like tiny hills.

"That's our house!" The girl told me, pointing towards one of the mounds.

At first, I couldn't believe that this pile of earth somehow contained a living space. As we came closer, however, I could recognize a low-set wooden door and several tiny round windows which resembled ship portholes.

"Here's where we live." She said, knocking loudly at the door. Soon the door opened. An emaciated, stooped-over middle-aged woman with a small kerosene lamp in her hand stood before us and looked up at us with tired, indifferent eyes.

"Mother!" the girl shouted: "Why didn't you pick me up?"

"For shame! Why have you come home again!" groaned the woman in reply, and turning towards me, sputtered: "Can't you keep her a while longer? What am I supposed to do with all these kids with lung infections?"

As I attempted to explain that I was just a sanatorium employee and had no authority to decide anything, she began to complain and cry more bitterly. "I can't even take them to the orphanage, they only take healthy kids. And my poor little worms are all miserable. It's as if I'm waiting for them to die each day."

"I'll speak with our director." I replied: "Maybe she can help. She is an important party member."

"Yes, please do that, dear comrade! God will bless you for it." She said abruptly, and bid: "Please come in for a moment and look for yourself how we're living."

With these words she took her daughter by the hand and led us through a small entrance into the single living space of the dugout house. The small kerosene lamp provided so little light that it took me a moment for my eyes to adjust. After a while I could recognize a dingy cave.

It was a rectangular room and a large, wooden crate stood against a wall upon which the entire family slept in their clothes without a mattress or pillows. In the corner stood a small, unpainted old table and next to it a three-legged stool. A brick oven rounded out the pitiful little dwelling. I looked around and thought that I had never seen or experienced such wretched poverty.

"How could the children be healthy in this hole in the ground?" I thought to myself. And of the unfortunate mother: "Can't she find a better home?"

The woman looked at me sadly: "My husband used to be a prosperous farmer, a kulak: But we were driven off of our land, and now nobody wants to help us."

This made me feel great sympathy for these banished people.

And when I returned to the sanatorium, I described these terrible conditions to the director. She, however, simply shrugged her shoulders and said: "I can't take every sick person in at my sanatorium. They should be happy, that we at least took one of the children on to recover at no cost to them."

In my inner thoughts, I realized how life could sometimes be so terribly cruel.

Chapter 25 – Quiet Before the Storm

I worked for nearly two months as a music teacher in the village of Yaropolets. I was able to save enough money for the trip home and was genuinely happy that fate had allowed me the means to return to my beautiful home in Krasnodar. On New Year's Eve 1940, I celebrated the coming year along with my farewell to the majestic castle of Catherine the Great and its residents. Because celebrating Christmas was forbidden by this point in Russia, we decorated a white pine tree to celebrate the upcoming New Year and gave the children presents. The adults also received a large, festive dinner and purchased wine and vodka to bolster our holiday spirit. After our little patients had gone to sleep in their beds, the entire staff of the sanitorium gathered close to midnight in what had been Empress Catherine's reception hall to ring in the new year: 1941.

The hall was decorated with colorful paper streamers and fir branches. In the middle of the hall, a pair of colorful electric candles glowed atop a stately pine tree. The hall, which now served as a gym and art room, had very basic furnishings that consisted of several long unfinished wooden benches and a black-polished piano. On the walls hung plain black-and-white prints of the communist party leadership in unadorned, oval frames.

As things looked, one could hardly imagine what a rich and glamorous lifestyle had once prevailed here. Despite that, the high, golden walls, and the uniquely decorated hall ceiling, covered in oil paintings of famous Russian masters, still looked wonderful. The deep window wells and blank parquet floors and crystal chandeliers reminded one of the long-past glory of the czarist empire, and anyone who had a basic understanding of art had to look upon the current kitschy furnishings with at least some disdain. I also looked critically upon the large, brightly lit room and could not feel any enthusiasm for the taste of this new era, although I had grown up in it.

The thought flashed almost automatically through my mind: "What would Empress Catharina say if she saw her castle in this condition?"

The loud chiming of the large wall clock in the next room shook me out of my thoughts back into the present. The new year had arrived. Everyone grew excited and cheered. My colleagues came over and wished me luck in the new year, and I wished them the same. And none of these merry young people had any clue, at this still young hour, how much misfortune and suffering 1941 would bring to the Russian people.

Oblivious to what lay ahead, we drank to our hearts' content, toasted to the future, and danced around the tree. Our director, who had heart problems, soon departed the jovial celebrations and retired to her room. Only now did we feel completely free and at ease, and soon we were all completely drunk.

I began to see the furniture and pictures on the walls take on a life of their own. I looked several times at one of the communist portraits and couldn't comprehend why it seemed to be hanging so crookedly. I went to the picture to straighten it, but the moment I touched the frame, the portrait slid off its nail and crashed to the floor. The other revelers were so drunk that apparently no one took immediate notice.

What I discovered behind the portrait, however, brought me into a great state of confusion. The wall where the portrait had hung had a shallow oval hollow, which was just slightly smaller than the portrait itself. From inside the niche, a wonderful gold relief smiled back at me with a pretty, symmetrical, life-sized face. This face seemed uniquely familiar to me. Around the frame I could make out a golden script: "Her Majesty Empress Catherine II."

I stood, as if spellbound, looking at the relief of the elegant German Princess who transformed into one of Russia's greatest and most powerful rulers. The Empress reminded me of someone I knew. I've seen that face before many times, but where?

The answer hit me suddenly: In the mirror!

When I leaned closer to scrutinize the portrait, the resemblance became uncanny. Did I not look just like the Empress? Only her hairstyle was different due to her powdered wig. I was so absorbed by this observation that I didn't notice that my inebriated colleagues had now gathered around me. I pointed at the portrait lying on the ground and said: "Look at what was behind this portrait."

"Comrades!" I heard from all sides: "Come look at this painting of Empress Catherine. Doesn't she look exactly like our music teacher?"

"Yes – come on – let's look at what's hiding behind the other portraits." Called the others. "Maybe we'll find a duchess or queen who looks like our director!"

In an instant the wild party ran around to all the communist portraits and took them down. Behind each they discovered the same oval niche with a likeness of a member of the royal family. My comrades looked over these paintings from times gone by with amazement. To my regret, I was only able to see some of them, because the director, who had been alarmed by an activist comrade, came stamping back into the hall in a state of aggravation. She gave us a thorough tongue-lashing for indulging in this unsanctioned viewing and ordered us to put the communist portraits back immediately and sent us all to bed. With that, this peculiar New Year's celebration came to an abrupt end.

I deeply regretted that shortly thereafter, the director called workmen into the castle to fill-in these old, apparently dangerous, portholes and the paintings they encapsulated, with plaster. I would have so liked to go back with mirror in hand to compare the facial features of the Empress with my own, because I had my doubts that there could really be a resemblance. After all, I had been in such a fog that evening that perhaps I'd simply imagined the resemblance.

Since it was no longer possible to check, I soon left the beautiful castle with mixed feelings and began my journey home. This first leg took me back through Moscow, where the train would remain at a stop-over for just over an hour at Rizhky station. As my dormitory was less than a ten-minute walk away from the station, I used the opportunity to briefly visit my former roommates and fetch the few belongings I'd left behind. I was interested to see how many girls would still be there after the new law had gone into effect cutting off most financial aid. As I'd anticipated, my dormitory now lay half empty. Most of the students had run out of money and given up.

Nina, I was horrified to learn, had died from blood poisoning only a few days before. She came into difficulties when she realized she was pregnant by her "friend" Boris Nikolaiavitch. She had gone to have an illegal abortion, which was botched by an amateur and ended up costing her her life. Nina's marriage of convenience with a married man she never loved brought her to this premature end.

My sadness over Nina completely erased any petty feelings of annoyance I had once harbored, and all I could feel was sorrow for her and her family. I wondered if there was something I could have said or done differently when we were together that might have changed things, but now it was too late. It was exasperating, and I had to move on. After this depressing news, the departure from Moscow would not be difficult. I gathered my few belongings, went to the front office and declared I was withdrawing, turned in my student passbook, and went back to the station to my waiting train, which would take me out of Moscow for the final time.

When I finally arrived back in Krasnodar, my faithful boarder Tosya picked me up at the station and accompanied me home on the tram. When I arrived and found that my house was in good order, a feeling of warmth and security washed over me. Now I understood why I had to make the arduous and trying journey to Moscow: Never before had I been able to comprehend what a fantastic home I had in Krasnodar in my father's house, and how fortunate I had been that the dutiful Ivan Kusmitch had cared for it for so long and so faithfully and finally bestowed it upon me.

My desire for new experiences and adventures was, for the moment at least, at an end. I now wished for nothing more than to stay in my house and continue my studies. Soon I was accepted to a technical university and even received a stipend for my strong high school transcript and reputation as an outstanding local student. Tosya took care of me and cooked for me. My income from my stipend and the rent from the Heifiz family was enough to live on in Krasnodar, and my life seemed to finally find some stability.

But I wasn't able to enjoy this peaceful life for very long. Fate was about to intervene again, only this time, it would intervene in the life of our entire nation: On June 22, 1941. I woke up at six in the morning as I did every morning, rubbed my eyes and hopped out of bed. I opened the window and turned on the radio, as an exercise program came on that I always followed.

To my great surprise, the Moscow radio broadcast had gone completely silent. I looked at my clock and went to the kitchen. Tosya was also up already and had brewed an aromatic tea for breakfast. I complained to her that my radio didn't seem to be working, not knowing how significant this radio silence actually was.

After breakfast, I went out to the yard, where I was enjoying growing and caring for the flowers. I loved gardening and often thought about Ivan while I was tending the garden, as he once had.

And today, which was a Sunday, a day I didn't have to go to school, I spent the entire morning in the garden and felt close to Ivan's spirit. I could see in my mind's eye how he used to wander between the flower beds and set everything straight. At around ten o'clock, the Heifiz family called me over and asked whether my radio was also broken. They owned a very nice radio and were shocked to find that every channel in the entire Soviet Union had gone silent. From overseas, by contrast, we received music and conversation. "It's nothing wrong with the radio – it's something else!" We concluded.

Suddenly a loud call came from the Moscow broadcaster: "Attention! Attention! Comrades of the Soviet Union! At two in the afternoon the Foreign Minister of the USSR Comrade Molotov will address the people! Everyone is to gather around radios and loud speakers!"

This broadcast was repeated every ten minutes. It was passed by word-of-mouth and spread to the wide reaches of the empire. The people who did not own a radio went to the public parks and plazas, to cinemas and theaters or to their factory, most of which had large loudspeakers set up. The entire Russian nation tensely awaited the appointed hour.

I also walked around my house anxiously and finally I couldn't stand it any longer. I called Tosya and we went together to a neighboring park where many people had gathered during the early afternoon. When we arrived, a boundless crowd of people had gathered around the loud-speakers.

Finally, it was two in the afternoon and a deathly quiet fell over the entire gathering. The voice of Foreign Minister Molotov began to speak in a solemn and determined voice. I remember his words as follows:

Citizens of the Soviet Union! This morning at four o'clock, without warning, German troops attacked our country, violating our entire western border from the White to the Black Sea. A great threat has befallen our land. The enemy is strong, the situation is serious. The stakes are the very existence of our people. I call upon the entire Soviet nation to take up the fight against the invaders! Fight for your freedom as if your life depended on it. Our cause is just! Victory will be ours!

After Molotov finished, a deathly silence fell over the crowd. People finally began to leave with faces downcast, speaking and bemoaning what had just been announced. And as the German people were celebrating the latest conquests of their Fuhrer, the young and elderly in Russia cried in desperation, as they had already been through so much misery and knew that this war would destroy any hopes of a better life for years to come.

I also cried bitterly at the news. I knew that my beloved Peter was stationed on the border with Poland and Germany, and I lost all hope of ever seeing him again. Soon thereafter, I heard the news that Peter had given his young life for Mother Russia on the very first day of the German invasion. I was devastated, but, deep down, the pain was dulled by my premonitions that he would be carried away from me: My dream and then his macabre prediction on the train.

Even with that shattering news, in that hour, I could have no idea how terrible the suffering of the Russian people would be in this war. But soon it came to pass, that I too, would have to shoulder my own full measure of that suffering.

Chapter 26 – In the Line of Fire

Immediately after war broke out with Germany, almost the entire western half of Russia was declared a war zone. Krasnodar stood under immediate threat, especially from air attack. Residents had to cut off their lights in the evening and take other protective measures against bombers. Existing bunkers were inspected, and new bunkers and air raid shelters were built.

The entire city suffered, as almost every family had to send sons, husbands, and fathers off to war. They gathered at the armory, accompanied by wives, mothers and fiancés, old and young draftees. Hundreds-of-thousands of families were torn apart. The women left behind now had to find a way to support their families on their own. They were often forced to take on a tough job in fields which required replacements for the men called off to war. Life became unceasingly difficult for everyone. The Motherland demanded great sacrifices of its people.

Initially, no one in Krasnodar had a clue that the Germans would arrive in a short time, and that the large, beautiful city would become a collection of ruins. But quite quickly, the people noticed that the German enemy was much stronger and more dangerous than the reports from the press and radio broadcasts had indicated.

As the people learned that the Germans were advancing with unimaginable speed deep into Soviet territory, belief in the strength and invincibility of our own armed forces was greatly shaken. And even the propaganda had to concede that the war would indeed be long and difficult and require many sacrifices. The desperate people were reassured that our side had more soldiers than the Germans. It was also hoped that help would soon come from other allied great powers, England, and America. The people, so we were told, simply needed to have patience, as a turning point in the hard fight would soon come and turn victory in our favor.

To ensure that the populace did not fall under any outside influence, it was ordered that everyone voluntarily turn in their radios and receivers. Secretly listening to foreign broadcasts was strictly forbidden and punishable by firing squad. The entire national postal system and all letters were subject to inspection by military censors. Nothing concrete could be gleaned from official broadcasts and newspapers about the fighting. We just heard the names of the largest cities occupied by the Germans and heard of the enemy's heavy losses. There were no reports about our own losses.

And so it came to pass that, as a result of the rapid German advances, the people in the threatened areas could not be evacuated in time. Only the party elites and top political commissars were able to save themselves with their families. Knowing full-well they would be exterminated by the Germans; other party members fled into the forests and hills and formed the partisan bands so feared by the enemy.

I observed the events of the war and, at the time, bitterly despised, with patriotic fervor, the evil enemy to the bottom of my heart. Later, I came to see that everyday German people were not to blame for the war, but that one great, violent, dictatorial power also drove the Germans to occupy Russia and kill our soldiers. I envisioned this power as a giant, evil demon that flew over the warzone like a horrible dark cloud and took delight in sending so many poor and powerless people to their doom. It seemed as if this devil was gladly devouring humanity, spewing flames upon the groaning earth, and rolling his bloody eyes.

At the end of July 1941 all people of German-descent were rounded up and deported to Siberia. It was feared that these people would switch sides and join the German Reich to our detriment. I myself couldn't understand this and asked myself how these poor people could help the fact that they happened to be of German descent. The poorest had to leave their homes and workshops and were only allowed to take very little of their property with them. Nobody knew how they would fare in Siberia.

No one could justify this injustice. And the Russian friends of these people had to look on in silence at this mass incarceration. I often wondered why the people and nations chose to participate in such insanity as this war. If every German and every Russian simply said "no" – then the evil demon of my imagination would be rendered powerless, and peace would rule the world.

Only now did I truly know how wonderful peace is!

Soon, however, Krasnodar stood under the immediate threat of becoming a war zone. German aircraft increasingly flew over the city and dropped the first heavy bombs. As a member of the Komsomol, the communist youth party, I suspected that the Germans would not spare me either should I fall into their hands.

I determined to part with my beautiful house and flee Krasnodar. The only question was: Where to? And the answer: To my mother and grandparents in the small, lovely town of Anapa.

When I turned up without so much as a word at their doorsteps, mother and my grandparents cried tears of joy. Even Yevgeni Petrovich, my stepfather, greeted me kindly and welcomed me back into his house. I now found out that my mother was expecting her second child soon and was happy that I had come at this particular moment of greatest need. I took on the most difficult household chores for her and was able to care for her as her pregnancy neared its end.

At the end of October 1941, my half-brother was born and named Vladimir, in honor of my father. And while we celebrated the birth of a new citizen of the world, the Germans occupied Krasnodar, where my father's property was left alone without a caretaker. I worried about what had become of my faithful tenant and caretaker Tosya, who I had left behind, and the Jewish family Heifiz. I asked myself what would become of these people who were near and dear to me. I didn't even know if my house was still standing or if it had been damaged or destroyed in the fighting.

With that, I would have to stay with my mother for the foreseeable future. As I didn't want to become a burden on her and her husband, I immediately sought employment. It wasn't easy in Anapa as there was no more tourism and all of the sanatoriums and hotels were occupied by the military. As the front drew closer, the wives and children of the officers were evacuated and so I didn't even have the option to work as a music teacher as before. But soon I came upon a very nice job completely out of the blue.

At that time a military doctor, Comrade Dr. Timko, was quartered in my mother's house. He could play the piano very well and would often join my mother and her husband in an impromptu music session. Doctor Timko asked my mother if it would be alright for me to accompany him to a club of straw-widowers. These were officers and party officials who had been separated from their families by the evacuations, and who were now quite bored in their social club. Dr. Timko suggested I go with him and take some music along to sing and perform.

My mother was understandably strongly opposed initially. Dr. Timko assured her that she could trust him with her daughter, and that he would watch over her like a father. So mother gave up her objections, as I also wanted to go. Dr. Timko took me to the club at a hotel on the coast where the officers lived. We walked into the bright dinner hall where several high-ranking officers and commissars, as well as the city commandant had gathered at a table.

Dr. Timko introduced me, and the gentlemen invited me to have a seat with them. I sat down with them at the table. I didn't find it difficult at all to entertain this illustrious group, and spontaneously began to tell amusing stories, and soon a good vibe filled the room. These old lions looked very tame to me and gladly listened to me. Later, I was invited to play the piano, and played to my heart's content to repeated applause and requests for more songs. I performed pieces from the latest movies and operettas with gusto and also threw in some good folk songs, which only increased the enthusiasm of the thankful audience.

The wide-shouldered city commandant praised me loudly, and the stylish commissar asked: "What are you doing at the moment Comrade Inna? Do you have a job?"

"Nothing at the moment, unfortunately. I had to give up my university studies because of the war for the time-being." I replied with regret.

"Wouldn't you like to direct a military choir in the town?" asked both men simultaneously, as if speaking with one voice. "and prepare it for the New Year's celebration?"

It was only three weeks before new years by this time. Still, I was overjoyed at the offer, gladly accepted and promised to do my best. Everyone in the room was excited at this good news, and the next day I began my work with the Black Sea Marine Division choir.

Almost two-hundred young marines had signed up for the new choir. I tested how well each could sing and selected the seventy-five best voices. Then I stood facing this large choir of men as the only woman and sang and practiced the best folk and Soviet songs for the new year with this enthusiastic group. My singers were highly motivated and made my job easy and pleasant. I was also glad at their discipline and respectful and decent behavior. Because of this, I was able to lead the choir with great success at the New Year's party. I also sang several songs in the program.

In this manner I became well-known with my choir in all of Anapa, and it was a small sensation that a 20-year-old lass was directing such a large male choir. Many of the soldiers and officers admired me and even offered me their heart and hand in marriage. I did not accept, however, as inside I was already forming a vision of my still distant, unknown love. I suspected I already knew how he would look. I also knew that he lived somewhere and, just like me, longed for a grand, pure love.

And that is why I did not respond to any advances, I wanted to wait for that special person. I would never have imagined then, however, that my great love would be one of them...

Chapter 27 – Return to Krasnodar

Although the population of Anapa had still been spared from the thick of the fighting during 1941, the mood of the people was still very downcast. With secret fear we noted from the radio broadcasts that the Germans had already occupied all of Ukraine and central Russia and were closing in on the heart of the Soviet Union, Moscow. Soon enemy troops were within striking distance of the capital, bringing it into grave danger. The city of Volokolamsk and the village of Yaropolets with Catherine's castle, where I had lived less than a year ago, as well as my hometown Poltava, had all been seized by the enemy.

When I looked at a map of the Soviet Union and realized what large swaths of territory had already been occupied by the German armies, I felt heartache and anxiety. Compared to the great expanses already taken over, the distance to the little town of Anapa was just a small hop. Subconsciously, I began to doubt that we would win the war. And many other Soviet citizens began to have the same doubts. But no one dared to say it out loud, because it would be condemned as a betrayal of the homeland. Indeed, the Russian people now stood before a truly massive crisis, and nobody really knew, how this terrible war would find its end.

I often tried to learn something more concrete about the state of affairs from the officers and commissars, with whom I was in good standing. The comrades and functionaries held with visible confidence that we would still prove victorious, although the sacrifice would be great. We just had to avoid losing our courage.

That's why it was important for me to lead the choir and lift the spirits of the young marines with new Soviet songs and to get them in a better frame of mind. They saw in me a person who understood them and in whom they could trust. Often, one of the choir members would come to me after practice and sadly tell me: "My fiancé or my family was left behind in the occupied territories. What will become of my loved ones?"

There was no easy answer to these questions. It was therefore incredibly rewarding for me to see these men forget their worries and feel joy again during our choir practices. My mother and step-father also asked me often whether I believed the Germans would occupy Anapa. Since I had no answer, they began to think about what they would do should it come to pass.

"If we lose the war and the Germans occupy all Russia, it's pointless to run from here," thought my stepfather.

"It's best that we remain here where we are and leave our fate in the hand of our heavenly father," determined mother.

"But without me!" I replied: "Because if the Germans find out that I'm a Komsomol and worked for the Russian military, they will certainly have me shot."

With that I walked over to the radio in the corner and turned it on. The Voice of Moscow broadcast was on. I listened a few moments, and said with relief: "Moscow still speaks, not all is lost! Now that it's winter, maybe the Germans won't be able to advance any further."

When one day the report came over the airwaves that an entire German army had been destroyed before Moscow and that the enemy had been thrown back several hundred kilometers, hope rose that we would be spared by the dark fortunes of war. Because even nature, it seemed, seemed to be aiding the Russian side: A cold winter like that of 1941-42 had been seldom experienced by the Russian people. Even where we were on the mild Black Sea coast, temperatures dropped under 20 degrees below zero Celsius. We also read in numerous reports that German soldiers had frozen to death in Russia's ice and snow.

When I imagined these German soldiers frozen to death, I couldn't bring myself to feel happy like the other people. I painfully sensed that even the Germans were still human beings, who suffered and felt as we did, and that the dead also had mothers, wives and children left behind waiting for them in vain and mourning them in their homeland.

It became less and less clear to me why people and nations prosecuted such evil wars and why they couldn't live in peace. After all, wasn't all this human life worth more than the conquest of a piece of foreign land? The death and destruction were so horrific and foreign, that no further wish occurred to me than that humanity would somehow be helped out of this giant calamity.

For that reason, I couldn't condemn or hate anyone. I would have most liked to place myself between the warring camps and tried to get them to reconcile their differences. But what could a single woman do in the face of the dark power of a world war? My aspirations for peace had about as much a chance of success as a tiny drop of rain falling into the endless Black Sea had of transforming the salt water into fresh water. I certainly could never express my feelings or say that I felt sympathy for human beings on the other side. The others would have never understood and would have thought that I had turned against the Motherland.

After the first German defeat before Moscow, things improved on our southern front as well, and the city of Krasnodar was also liberated from the Germans. Finally, the harsh winter neared its end and the rays of the spring sun slowly warmed the sleeping earth. In April 1942, I received my first letter from the recaptured city from Tosya, who had survived all the dangers during the enemy attacks, occupation and Russian counterattacks and reconquest. She advised me to return to Krasnodar to care for my house, which despite all the heavy fighting was still in good condition.

The Heifiz family no longer lived there she further wrote. What happened to my Jewish tenants, however, was indiscernible, as many lines of the letter had been redacted by the military censors with heavy black streaks.

Soon after, upon the advice of Tosya, I arrived in Krasnodar. The city was in a sad state, the streets were empty and covered in ash and ruble. The many bombed out and burned out ruins stared back at me from their empty window frames like skeletons and conjured an eerie feeling inside me. Torn cables and wire hung everywhere. Trees and telegraph poles were knocked over and splintered. The stores were empty and closed and the street cars nowhere in sight. That evening after I arrived in my house, Tosya and I sat by the light of the kerosene lamp and drank tea together.

"I'm so happy that you are here again, dear Inna Vladimirovna. What was I to do all alone in this house ever since the Heifiz family left me?" Said my faithful helper.

"Why did the Heifiz's move out Tosya?" I asked, surprised by the news. I had noticed when I arrived that the downstairs apartment was empty, and furnishings gone.

"The family didn't leave voluntarily,Inna Vladimirovna," said Tosya somberly. "They are no longer among the living..."

"How? Were they killed in the bombing?"

"No! Killed by the German Gestapo and SS!"

"Gestapo and SS? What's that?"

"A German unit that is their version of the Soviet NKVD – the feared political police – except they hunt down Jews and Bolsheviks instead of capitalists and Kulaks."

"But why did this unit have to kill the Heifiz family, Tosya?"

"All of the Jews in the city shared the same fate at the hands of the SS men. I not sure, however, that the other Germans would have agreed to all the killing..."

"How would you know that?" I asked in disbelief.

"The daughter Sarah Heifiz could speak German. Soon after the Germans marched in, she befriended a German soldier named Rudi, who fell in love with Sarah and one day asked if she was of German descent. She admitted to him that she was a Jew. The young man cried like a child and when Sarah asked him why, he only answered that German soldiers were strictly forbidden to fraternize with Jews. But he wanted to put in a good word for her with his superior officer. After that day, Sarah waited for him in vain. We never saw his face again."

"And what happened to Sarah and her father?"

"Ach, it's a terrible thing. Soon after the Germans arrived, all of the Jews had to register with the German military authority. They were told that nothing bad would happen to them, and that the Jewish population was simply being conscripted to carry out work.

A Jewish spokesman was even appointed, and he advised his people to show the German authorities that they were friendly and obedient. He wanted them to give a good account of themselves.

This spokesman collected signatures and handed a petition to the Germans requesting that the Jewish population not be deported from Krasnodar. This feel upon deaf ears, however, and the Jews were ordered to pack their things within 24 hours and prepare themselves for an eight-day journey.

"Miss Heifiz..." said Tosya after a small pause: "asked me to help her pack: Valuables, clothing, jewelry, and plenty to eat. When she and her father left the house, I accompanied them to the German headquarters.

The street that led to the building was lined with SS troops. All of the Jews had to cross through a sealed checkpoint. Russians were turned away. Even Russian men and women there with their Jewish husbands and wives were separated from their spouses and left with their half-Jewish children.

"I certainly believe..." sobbed Tosya: "That had the poor Jews known what lay in store for them, that they would have tried to make a run for the Russian lines with their wives and children, even under German fire. When the Jews had all gathered at the headquarters, the SS separated the children ten and under from their parents. These little ones were led directly to the basement and given a poison that quickly took their lives.

The older children and adults were driven out of Krasnodar in trucks. They were lined up along the deep anti-tank ditches the Russians had dug earlier and mowed down with machine guns. After the victims had fallen into the ditches, no one bothered to check whether they were all dead or whether there was any movement or not. They simply buried the mass of humanity in the heavy black earth. There too, the Heifiz's found their end."

After Tosya finished her account, I sat a long time in silence, unable to find the words.

I finally asked: "How can a person help it if they are born into this world as a Jew?!" The Heifiz's were good people and didn't deserve a fate like that!"

Tosya didn't know how to respond. We both fell silent and what I had learned filled my heart with loathing for the Germans. Didn't these savages, these murderers, have any humanity at all?

Only later would I gain more perspective and realize that not all Germans supported the Nazi regime, and not all Germans knew of or would have approved of the horrors being committed in their names...

Chapter 28 – First Contact

Tosya supported me with a great deal of love and attention in this bitter time. She did everything possible to make me feel at home, and often begged me not to leave her again. But it simply wasn't possible for me to fulfill her wishes, as I was soon compelled to flee again. The Germans had begun their 1942 summer offensive which was aimed at the southern front: Ukraine, Crimea and the Caucuses, of which Krasnodar was a part. Yet again, the city found itself in immediate danger of attack and re-occupation by the Germans.

The violent thunder of the artillery guns drew ever closer. Enemy planes bombed the city continuously and the howling air raid sirens filled our hearts with deathly fear. The civilian population as well as the party organization and the various military units of the Red Army fled the threatened city in great disorder by the most direct paths.

I also packed my suitcases and bid Tosya farewell, who again had determined to stay put. She tried with all her might to convince me to stay, and was very sad when she realized that everything she said was falling on deaf ears. She continually repeated that I had nothing to fear from the Germans, and that they would certainly have no reason to do anything bad to a decent young lady. She also claimed to have already seen the Germans and how strong their army was. She had become convinced that this powerful armed force was unstoppable, and that fleeing was pointless.

Her last statement to me made me very angry, and I impolitely replied: "It isn't fitting for a real Russian to wait around for the enemy and believe in his victory!" With those words I left the house and went to the main road to try to hitch a ride out of town with a passing car, as trains no longer ran from Krasnodar. Most of the bridges and tracks had been damaged during the fighting.

I soon noticed, however, that it wasn't so easy to get a passing car to stop. They were so packed full with people that you couldn't throw an apple between them, not to mention a grown person with two suitcases. I stood there several hours without success and my mood grew worse and worse. I was truly envious of the people sitting in the cars who were able to flee and was angry with myself that I had come back to Krasnodar at all.

"This is all because of my father's house!" I thought. "If only I'd never seen it!" Finally, I could no longer stand by the side of the road. Disappointed, I took my suitcases and went home.

When Tosya saw me, she was overcome with joy. She went right back to work on me: "Please do stay here, Inna Vladimirovna! I heard from the retreating Red Army soldiers that the Germans are no longer far from Krasnodar. Who knows if you will even make it through, even if you find a car that will take you. It's so dangerous riding out in the open, you'd be in constant danger of being shot at or bombed from above."

"But Tosya, what about the fighting that will take place here in Krasnodar? Where and how will we save ourselves then?" I replied, defending my plans.

"Our basement is deep and sturdy." She countered. "We will be well-protected there."

"And what are we supposed to live on Tosya? The stores are all closed."

"I've stashed many things down there that will keep us above-water for the time-being." She admitted to me secretively. "And after that, we will see. God, our Lord won't abandon us!" With that, Tosya retrieved a candle and the basement key and led me down to her hidden treasures. In the farthest corner, I saw sacks of flour and corn skillfully concealed behind old crates.

"Where did you get this all?" I asked in amazement. Tosya told me how, during the first Russian withdrawal, she had taken it all out of a state mill and dragged it home. She promised to always take care of me if I stayed.

Despite everything, I couldn't immediately conclude that the best course of action was to intentionally stay and allow myself to fall into German hands. So, I said: "I'm going to try my luck again one more time tomorrow, Tosya. Maybe I'll be able to find a way out. If not, then I'll stay here. I don't want anyone accusing me later of voluntarily allowing myself to fall under German occupation."

Fate would have it otherwise. That very night, heavy fighting began in the city itself. There was shooting from all sides, and the shells and mortars flew over and past our house without interruption as we fearfully listened to the impacts all around us. Even in the basement, where we sat quietly close together, we could smell the burning ash.

Early in the morning, women and children from neighboring houses who had remained in their homes begged us to allow them to take shelter in out basement, which we gladly did. The fighting for the city lasted several days, and some neighboring houses fell victim to the fighting, collapsing into dust and rubble. My sturdy basement became filled with more and more people looking for safety. Soon we counted twenty-five in the narrow room. Hunger and thirst began to plague the tightly packed group, but no one dared to go to the well for water. When we could no longer bear the thirst, however, we drew lots to decide who amongst the adults would fetch the water.

A woman drew the lot who was the mother of four small children. She anxiously took the two pails Tosya had made ready and, crying, said goodbye to her little ones. "My poor children!" she wailed: "if I don't come back, they won't have anyone left!"

This scene broke my heart. "Give me the pails." I said: "I'll get the water." Tosya stood up and added: "I won't let you go alone, Inna Vladimirovna, I'm coming too."

She grabbed two more pails and joined me. As we opened the basement door, a large shell struck our yard and exploded with such force that every window in the house shattered and flew from its frame. Tosya dropped her pails and pulled me by my dress back into the basement. I could feel myself trembling uncontrollably.

We regrouped and made ready to run to the well. Before we opened the door, Tosya put down her pails, fell to her knees, and began to pray: "Oh lord God, have mercy on us! Dear heavenly father, protect us and help us in our time of fear and need!"

All of the women in the basement followed Tosya's example, and soon I heard them all fervently reciting "The Lord's Prayer" in unison: "Our father in heaven, hallowed be thy name, thy kingdom come ..."

Had I witnessed such a scene earlier, with the atheist views that had been instilled in me, I would have certainly lost my mind. But today I felt quite differently. I suddenly felt a deep longing to pray from the bottom of my heart in fellowship with these women. I turned with my face to the wall so that no one would see, and following along, reciting "The Lord's Prayer" for the first time in my life. I felt goosebumps wash across my body, and a wave of peace came over me: For the first time in my life, I could feel God's presence.

During our prayer, the terrible din of battle suddenly ceased. There were no more explosions, and in that moment, I felt that God, our lord and father, was there with us in this hour of greatest danger to help us out of our terrible distress. Emboldened, I went with Tosya up to the street and fetched the badly needed water. Calm and unshaken, we returned to the basement. Not a single shell had fallen. Our prayer had been answered. In that hour, it became eerily still around us. We no longer heard shooting in the distance.

Finally, a few of the women determined to go out and check on their houses and belongings. They soon returned and announced: "The Germans have occupied Krasnodar! They are very close and searching every house and basement."

In short order, our basement door was torn open. Two German soldiers and a junior officer with pistols in their hands looked down the stairs. When they saw our fear-filled faces, they laughed. One of them who could speak some Russian said: "Have no fear good people. We mean you no harm. We're just looking for Russian soldiers."

We assured them that no soldiers were with us. The Germans seemed satisfied, closed the door and left just as abruptly as they'd appeared.

I was very surprised: I thought for certain that these men would assault and shoot us. Could it be that they didn't want anything?

After the women and children had left and disappeared to their houses and apartments, I wonderingly asked Tosya: "Are all Germans like that?"

"It was sometimes the case, Inna Vladimirovna, that the SS and Gestapo troops set upon young girls and attractive women." She replied: "You'd better stay down here until things in the city quiet down."

Then she went up to our living quarters to bring the house in order and prepare a warm meal. I remained in the basement and nibbled hungrily on Tosya's roasted corn kernels, which had served as our main source of sustenance over the past few days. Then the basement door opened again, and a young, skinny German soldier descended the stairs and approached me.

I fearfully crept over to the furthest corner of the basement, where I hoped that he wouldn't discover me. He held his flashlight aloft and looked the entire basement over thoroughly. Then suddenly, he stood before me, shining the light in my face. I was petrified, but instead of the snarling monster I anticipated, a youthful, handsome face peered back at me.

When he saw the plate of roasted corn near me, he shook his head and said in a broken mix or German and Russian: "You eat maiz? Maiz no good. I get you brot."

With that he left. As I barely understood a word of German, I didn't really know what he meant by "maiz" and "brot" and was shocked to see him return in short order with a loaf of bread and a few slices of sausage. I was so confused by his actions that I forgot to say thank you, or anything for that matter. I looked at him questioningly with wide eyes. He smiled and said: "Lasse es Dir gut schmecken!" – which I later found out meant "Bon appetite" in German. Then he left again.

Frozen, I watched as he departed, unable to move for quite some time. If only all Germans and Russians were like that – there would never have been a war to begin with...

Chapter 29 - Occupation

I was very lucky in the first few days of the German occupation. Both my house and I were spared visits by the infamous Gestapo and SS. And other than the first three men looking for Russian troops and the friendly soldier who had brought me food, I did not receive any further visits to my basement hideout by the Germans. Soon a city government was formed consisting of the German military command and a Russian mayor. Things stabilized and I was able to emerge from my subterranean hideout.

The first time I hazarded out for a walk through the streets, I encountered a lively chaos. Gray green uniforms swarmed around us. Thousands of military vehicles and tanks raced uninterrupted through the city and headed south. The German airplanes continued to drone through the air, but no longer troubled us, and now no longer instilled fear in the locals.

The new authorities issued an order that the entire population of Krasnodar was to immediately register with the military command. The occupation force was determined to arrest any communists and Komsomol who had stayed behind. But who was going to voluntarily turn themselves in? All party members naturally concealed their past. I also didn't volunteer that I had been a Komsomol but lived in constant fear that someone would betray me.

Truth be told - the Russians stuck firmly together, and it was very rare that anyone would rat out a fellow Russian. After all, we were together in the same boat, and nobody wanted it on their conscience that they'd brought someone else to harm. Russian people are, in this respect, very true of heart, and the humblest people had a saying that reflects one of life's great truths: "Whoever digs a grave for others will fall in themselves!"

Things being as they were, I stayed away from the Germans as long as possible. I didn't even understand their language. Soon, for better-or-worse, I had to get my hands on a German-Russian dictionary: The downstairs apartment vacated after the murder of the Heifiz's was seized and billeted with two German officers. Tosya was employed cleaning their rooms, doing their laundry and repairing their clothing. The Germans paid well and also gave us enough bread and food to eat. Tosya was very happy to have this work, as almost all the Russians left behind were put to work for the Germans, most assigned to clearing rubble, which was strenuous and poorly paid. The Russian ruble also depreciated more and more and had only a 10 to 1 exchange value with the newly introduced occupation mark.

Any Russian with any talent for trade now had a golden opportunity to make money trading and selling things. The price of food became nearly unaffordable. For example, a plate of white flour cost 15 to 20 rubles. The Russian people came anew to a time where they had to endure hunger. The bread, which was now baked from corn flour, was rationed at 200 grams per person a day.

The citizenry of the city of Krasnodar was very disappointed with these developments. Some believed that the Germans would bring freedom and bread after the harsh communist rule. Things didn't turn out that way. The Germans handled the Russians like second-class citizens. For that reason, many went over to the partisans. And as the Germans pushed ever deeper into the North Caucuses and towards Stalingrad, the partisans fought behind their lines to liberate Soviet land. At the end of August, Axis forces captured Anapa where my family remained, and I was unable to write them as no postal service existed in the occupied territories at that time.

Soon that all changed one cool September morning. Tosya had gone to her home village to visit family. Both German officers who lived with us had also left for duty. I was alone at home cooking borscht, a sort of unofficial national soup consisting of red beets, cabbage, carrots, potatoes, and tomatoes. As I was mincing the beets, I was filled with sadness over a newly issued directive to all able-bodied girls and women, forcing them to register for forced labor in Germany. I had often thought of fleeing Krasnodar to avoid it but had not found an opportunity to leave.

The decision was made for me. I had heard several airplanes circling overhead that day, but assumed they were German and thought nothing of it. Suddenly, through the open window, I saw an aircraft diving directly towards me. To my horror, I saw two red stars on the wings: "A Soviet plane!" raced through my mind – which meant it was attacking. As if moved by an unseen force, I ran down the stairs, swiping my purse along the way, and dashed out of the house as if carried by wings of my own towards the air raid bunker in a neighboring yard.

Sirens began to howl from all sides, and bombs fell right behind my house. Before I could reach the bunker, a bomb with a sharp whistle flew very close to me. Everything seemed to slow down to a crawl. Seconds seemed like minutes. I dove for cover, and pressed my face into the earth as I hit the ground. The ground trembled and a violent concussion swept over me, sucking the air out of everything. Dust and gravel rained down for what seemed like an eternity, caking me in dirt and debris, making it impossible to breath. The world disappeared in a cloud of ash. I stayed down until I no longer heard any sign of the plane and the dust had dissipated. Before I even stood up, I somehow knew: My house had been hit. Luckily, other than a few scrapes, I had survived unharmed, but I was covered in dust and ash which made me cough uncontrollably.

I finally stood up and dusted myself off as best I could. When I turned around hoping to see my house, a pile of rubble was all that was left. Exhausted, I sat in the yard listlessly next to what remained of my father's only legacy. I finally went over to a large stone near where the entrance had been, took out a piece of chalk that I carried in my purse, and wrote: "Tosya – I'm alive. Leaving Krasnodar for good. Farewell."

Then I said goodbye in my heart to my old family home one more time, and said, looking up to the firmament above: "If there is really a God who rescued me from this grave danger, then please guide me further!"

Without looking back, I went to the main street and began to walk the long distance from Krasnodar to Anapa. I was then still twenty-years-old when this fateful turning point in my life arrived which would lead me to my distant destination.

For ten days I walked along the endless country highway, from village to village, and met almost no one along the way. It was as if I had embarked on a surreal hike through an abandoned, haunted country, and the only sign that something was amiss was the occasional burned-out wreck of a car, truck or tank, and craters and pockmarks left behind in some of the buildings from previous fighting. Only rarely did a German military vehicle pass, as this territory was already taken. If one did appear, it was usually hurriedly racing towards the front, and I didn't dare to try to flag one down.

In the villages, few people were outdoors wandering the street. A farmer or shepherd could occasionally be seen tending his field or livestock. Towards evening, I would often approach one of these country-folk, and they would often kindly offer me something to eat of the little they had, and offer me a place to spend the night in a barn or shed. As soon as the sun rose, however, I doggedly continued my pilgrimage. I soon realized that my shoes were not designed for such a long hike, and my feet increasingly hurt and burned with blisters. It got so bad that I could only limp along the final two days.

When I finally caught sight of the Black Sea on the tenth day, I gathered my last strength and pushed on towards my beloved Anapa. "It's not much farther" I told myself: "In a few hours you will see your mother."

I hoped that I would find my mother and other relatives as I had left them a few months before. But to my indescribable horror, all I found of the quaint little town was a field of ruins. Not only my mother's house, but everything around it had been destroyed, burned and smashed, and not a single living thing was to be seen. At this sight I was so overtaken by despair, that I would have liked to have died in that moment. Hopeless and dead tired, I looked at my blistered, swollen feet, my filthy clothes, and I knew that I couldn't go one step further. In that moment, I regretted that I had not simply been buried in a pile of rubble with my house.

The world seemed to be coming to an end and I saw no way out...

Chapter 30 - Rescued

"Hello young lady! What's wrong with you? Wake up...Wake up!" Someone shook me by the shoulders, lifted me, and tried to help me stand up. "My God!" I heard, as if listening to a voice in a dream: "It's Inna Grinfeldt!"

When I heard my name, I tried with all my strength to open my eyes. A middle-aged woman with a kind face was bending over me and sobbing: "Finally! I thought for sure you were dead!"

I looked around dazed. The broken buildings and stones littered all about brought me back to this sad reality. Immediately I thought of my painful journey over the past days. I looked at the women's face fearfully and asked: "My mother...is she still alive...?" I closed my eyes again, because the thought that I would never see my mother again was unbearable.

This woman, who was a former neighbor of my mother's named Marina, reassured me: My mother and husband were living with my Uncle Victor in his village. They had both managed to safely flee the air and ground fighting. This news gave me renewed hope and I felt my strength starting to return. The lady saw my swollen, bleeding feet, and when I told her how I had walked from Krasnodar for the past week and a half, she was amazed at my courage.

"For heaven's sake!" She shouted: "And you weren't ambushed by the Germans or partisans along the way?"

"I didn't see a single partisan." I replied: "And the Germans I saw were all in a hurry to get somewhere, and simply drove past without paying me any attention."

"You were incredibly lucky."

When she said that, I realized what an enormous risk I had just taken and felt there must be some otherworldly force protecting me. Emboldened by that thought, I got to my feet with her help, and said: "I want to go to my mother's!"

Marina offered me her arm, but even with her assistance, I was only able to hobble slowly along. It took us over three hours to walk the seven kilometers to my Uncle Victor's house.

On the way, she told me that my Uncle's village had been spared from the fighting and that everything was intact there. Anapa, by contrast, had been subject to heavy fighting, and that the destruction from the attacking German and Romanian air and ground forces had been so great, that much of the population had fled to neighboring villages, and many civilians had been killed. My family also suffered a grave loss: I learned that my grandfather Joseph had died under the ruins of his house. My grandmother Lydia was pulled from the rubble in one piece but had received such a shock that she was unable to hear or speak for several days. She had since recovered somewhat, but was still in deep mourning, and also living with Uncle Victor. I took in this news as if in a waking nightmare, and when I heard about the death of my dear grandfather, and had no feeling left to even cry with.

Marina pointed out that it was exceptionally lucky that she found me in abandoned Anapa. She would go most days to the still intact houses to work for the Germans and lived in constant fear of being ambushed along the way by Russian partisans and taken and executed as a collaborator, when she was just trying to earn enough to avoid starvation. She saw me lying motionless near what had been my grandparents' house and at first assumed such a fate had befallen me, and her first instinct was to run away. But then she looked and could see I was probably still alive and needed her help. She came closer to get a better look and was now happy she had, otherwise she would have not been able to sleep in peace with me on her mind.

By that time, we had reached my Uncle Victor's house. The neighbor knocked at the door and called in to my mother: "Zina Yosifovna, your daughter Inna is home!"

A parade of footsteps ran to the door: My Uncle Victor, Aunt Sonia, Grandma Lydia holding my little half-brother Vladimir and my stepfather all came.

When they saw me in my miserable condition, they began to sob and moan to one another. My mother ran to me and called out: "My child! My poor child! I could sense that you were doing poorly, and my senses didn't deceive me. But you are alive, thank God, and have made it back to us. Heaven has answered my prayers for you! Come and lay down and we will all nurse you back to health."

Marina was also ushered in by my family, and as she recounted how she had found me laying in the ruins, my mother led me into her room, helped me to take off my shoes and the rags I had left for clothes, and gently bathed me from head to toe as if I was a small toddler in a tub. My mother's gentle touch and care did me a world of good, and how fortunate I felt after all the danger and distress to be in the company of my family. Thanks to her care I quickly recovered and soon stood healthily back on my own two feet.

My relatives shared their meager food and humble clothing with me. Autumn was already at hand, and I had to find a way to contribute and earn something so that I would have something to get through the winter. I didn't want to be a burden to my family in the long term. I looked around and soon found work.

At that time, the Germans were building a theater near the village to hold performances for the German and Romanian occupation troops, and they were looking for young women to sing and dance. I introduced myself to the director and sang a few songs I knew and was immediately offered a spot as a singer. I learned my first two German hit songs: "Komm zurück" and "Peterle" and could soon perform them with a small band consisting of German soldiers. I began to learn German with the help of my dictionary, which I always had with me.

In this time, I had the first opportunity to get to know average German and Romanian enlisted soldiers, and not all of them were the blood-thirsty monsters depicted by our Russian propaganda. It was remarkable how ordinary they were, just as human as anyone else. I found many to be decent people caught up in events beyond their control. Not hatred for Russians, but homesickness for their own distant countries and loved ones colored most of their sentiments. Many of them told me that they hated the war and would be happy to see this inhumane suffering end soon. Naturally, all of them wanted their country to emerge victorious in this fight. They had also believed very faithfully and patiently that the sacrifices they were making were not in vain.

I received a modest, but decent pay and, as luck would have it, had much success with my two little songs, which I sang in a very broken German. Many in the audience admired my voice and perhaps some even admired me as well. Despite that, I was not looking for any romantic relationships, and the enlisted men did not push things with me.

As someone who found myself in the midst of the fighting, first on the Russian, then on the German side of the lines, I was later very surprised to hear accusations from around the world that the German people carried a massive collective guilt for what happened. After all, what could a common German soldier who was 20 years old have done to avoid getting pulled into this fight?

Soon, however, I would encounter the darkest side of this force up close and personal. I would come face-to-face with the force most dreaded by Russians: The SS.

It came to pass on a frosty December day. The director came unexpectedly to where I was living and said that he had just received an order to drive to Anapa and put on a performance there for a “special” unit. As I packed my dress a dark premonition washed over me. We got in a truck and began the drive. I couldn’t shake a foreboding sixth sense the entire way. And my sixth sense didn’t deceive me. A dark gray cloud with two streaks of lightning was fast approaching that would forever cast a shadow across my life...

Chapter 31 – Into the Storm

Our theater troupe rode in a tightly sealed truck with no windows towards the commandery. When the truck halted after a short ride and we were allowed to get out, we were standing in front of a partially collapsed former sanatorium building. To my great surprise, I recognized this place. Just over a year ago, I'd directed my Russian marine choir in the same building.

And today? Today a German SS company was here – men who were our greatest enemies – and we were obliged to perform for them. Truly strange, I thought, life is full of bizarre twists and turns.

I anxiously followed the other performers, men and women, as we were received by an SS officer and a translator. I could barely recognize the rooms in this building that I had known so well. The Germans had rearranged everything to meet their tastes and needs. In the large, well-lit main hall, the windows had been carefully blacked out to protect the building from air attack, and numerous rectangular tables had been set up. Every seat at these tables was occupied by young and old SS men, who drank wine, smoked, joked and loudly and haughtily conversed with one another. Our theater troupe was received with such a storm of enthusiasm, that I began to feel unwell. I could hear them shouting rude and inappropriate comments directed at me and the ballet girls. A strong desire arose in me to escape this place as soon as possible.

But it wasn't that simple. There was a strictly enforced curfew for civilians in the town, and so I had no choice but to patiently wait until I was permitted to leave with the entire theater troupe and ride home. The Germans had no intention of letting us go soon. And after the final performance on our program, the company chief invited us to dinner and dancing. As a consequence, I had no choice but to accept the invitation. I was also obliged to accept that the company chief, an Obersturmführer named Max Strang, took a particularly keen interest in me, and selected me as his dance partner, and no other soldier dared to cut in and pull me away.

I didn't like Max. Despite his stately and well-groomed appearance, there was something repulsive about him. But what was it that kept me silent and unable to interact with him warmly the entire evening? He did look very handsome and made an effort to treat me very politely and kindly. Perhaps it was because I simply detested the SS to begin with. Max Strang was tall and blonde, with very light, cool gray-blue eyes, a slender, somewhat long nose, and fresh, narrow lips. His face was clean-shaven and full of energy. He also wore a much better uniform than the others, and his well-polished boots shone like a mirror. And on his collar were the unmistakable SS runes and the deaths-head, or skull and crossbones on his hat.

"You sing very nicely!" He began politely and, after clearing his throat, continued: "Are you nice in other ways?" I made no reply, and he became even more direct: "Could you be nice to me tonight, young lady?" He whispered suddenly to me in my ear as we danced a tango.

This question made me shudder: "I don't understand you!" I said curtly. "I want to go home on time."

He just laughed at this reply and led me firmly by the hand to a neighboring room. There he ordered a bottle of sparkling wine and I had to drink with him.

"Let's drink to you...with a kiss!" He said.

"Please no!" I implored.

Amazed, Max put his glass down on the table and tried to forcefully kiss me. I jumped out of my chair and ran away into the dance hall. He angrily pursued me.

"What? You can't behave yourself?" He said, confronting me with a bitter, angry glare.

"Please let me go home." I said firmly.

He seemed to direct his stare even more firmly into my eyes as he heard my plea. Then, after a moment's reflection, he growled: "Fine – you'll have your way today. But we will see each other soon, and I hope that you will be more sensible then!"

With that, he led me out of the building and ordered his driver to take me home. In this manner I returned home at three in the morning unharmed. I learned the next day that the other young female performers had all been set upon and molested by the SS men. This news was deeply disturbing, and reminded me of Max's parting words to me, that we would meet again soon. A bitter anger and silent fear arose in me.

Of course, Max Strang kept his word and sent a car with the translator and two military police to pick me up. "Take all of your documents with you," said the translator: "The boss wants to thoroughly check you out."

"Check me? Why?" I said terrified, thinking silently: *"I hope no one has betrayed me and told them that I am a Komsomol."*

Max received me in his office. He carefully examined my documents and asked: "Miss Grinfeldt, where is your true father, your current father is just your stepfather, isn't he?"

"My father was deported to Siberia in 1937."

"For what?"

"He was a noble by birth and served the Russian Czar before the Revolution."

"And you? What is your standing with the Communists? Were you a Komsomol?"

"Me? No!" My face froze as if petrified as I spoke. I looked him boldly and firmly in the eye and thought he certainly didn't notice that I was totally agitated on the inside.

"That's good!" He said after this brief examination. "I can certainly imagine that you wouldn't have been allowed into the Komsomol because of your father. But how did you come to us? Do you want to work for us?"

"How do you mean?"

Max looked at me with penetrating eyes: "Do you know the residents of this town? There are a bunch of partisans and it's our mission to catch and neutralize them. You could help us with that. So - tell me – what are the names of these men?"

With that, the chief set several photos on his desk in front of me. I looked at the photos coolly and indifferently.

"And...do you know any of these people?"

"I've never seen any of them."

"Really? Do you want to reconsider that?"

I very firmly answered: "Chief, I have not lived here for more than three years, I've been in Krasnodar during that time. How could I know who these men are?"

My answer seemed to convince him.

"Ok then. That's enough for today. But you'll leave your pass with us."

Shocked by the second part of this statement, I looked questioningly back. "How am I supposed to carry on without my pass? As you know, the German troops stop civilians all the time and ask for documents.."

"I'll make sure nothing happens to you." Came the answer. Strang looked me sharply in the eyes as he spoke. Momentarily, however, his face became more relaxed, he stood up from behind his desk, locked my pass in a drawer, and said, turning towards me in a calm, almost friendly tone: "You'll stay with us here for the time-being. You'll be well taken care of. Now follow me!"

With that he led me to his private quarters, where a table for two covered with food was waiting.

Strang closed the door behind me and explained with a polite manner and hand gesture: "This is my apartment and here the two of us will discuss private matters."

He requested that I join him for lunch, and as I had no other option under the circumstances, I complied and sat down at the table. To my great surprise, he now began to speak Russian to me. He clearly had a very good mastery of the language and asked about all different aspects of my life. I couldn't help but ask why he needed a translator to speak with the people when his own language skills were so good.

"You!" He replied strictly: "No one is to know that I understand Russian – otherwise you are finished!"

With a fearsome expression he pointed to his pistol. I sat the entire time in this violent SS man's room as if I was walking on coals. But now I was shaken by a horrible fear of this sinister man.

"When can I go home?" I asked quietly after we had finished eating.

Then Strang got out of his chair and stepped to me. I also got up from my seat and looked at him with hostility. Suddenly, the thug grabbed me, wild and without restraint, locking me in his iron grip. For several moments, I could feel his hot, rapid breathing on my face. He awkwardly tried to press his lips against mine. A great tussle broke out between us. Like a bird caught in a net, I swung my arms wildly. Finally, after a brief, intense struggle, I was able to free myself from his violent embrace.

I then stood tall and hot with anger and adrenaline and shouted: "Leave me alone! I despise you!"

The domineering chief looked me from head to toe: "I'll make you obey me! Do you hear? I must and will have you!"

"Never!" I shouted back defiantly.

Then Strang stepped towards me with a dark look in his eyes and wagged his finger in my face: "Your stepfather is a Jew. I've got you all in my hands."

"You're lying!" I shouted back. "My stepfather was never a Jew, he's Russian!"

"But I'm telling you that he's a Jew. And I'll shoot him if you don't...! The choice is yours. Him or you!"

I now understood that he would stop at nothing to reach his object. And I did not doubt for a moment, that he could certainly carry out what he was threatening.

"So, what will it be?" He said coldly after a short silence as we stood glaring at one another: "You or your stepfather?"

Weary and unable to fight any further, I collapsed into my seat. My tormenter approached me again and held his hands out.

"Please not today!" I finally whispered. "Give me time!"

"Fine!" Strang said, relenting. "You can go home now. I'll give you three days to come to your senses. But don't try to flee. You won't get far without your passbook and will be quickly arrested as a partisan." Then he added ominously: "Don't tell anyone anything about our conversation. Otherwise know that your days will be numbered." With these words he led me to the door, returned me to the reception area and turned me over to the translator.

"All right then, until we meet again in three days!" With that I was released, but still imprisoned.

Chapter 32 – In the Clutches of the Demon

My mother was waiting for me to return from the commandery in Anapa with great concern. It was already pitch black out when I reached our home. When I walked into the room dejected and absorbed in thought, my mother looked at me searchingly. She asked nervously with a shaky voice.

"Did something happen to you dear? You look so tired and pale. I wasn't able to relax the entire time you were away."

"It's nothing mother, I just have a terrible headache and want to go to bed." I hoped to simply avoid any further questioning. I couldn't tell her about what had happened, and she couldn't help me either, especially considering how hard her life was already.

Mother still followed me and, after I had laid down, stroked my forehead with her warm hand: "You don't have a fever Inna, but I noticed that something isn't right. Don't you want to tell me what's tormenting you?"

I tried with all my might to make a pleasing expression and replied: "It's really nothing mother! I was just thoroughly questioned at the commandery whether I am a Komsomol and where my father is. I told them father is in Siberia and I denied being in the Komsomol. The chief believed me and even invited me to dinner and wine."

"You drank wine with him? My God!" wondered Mother.

"Yes, I couldn't say no."

Mother shook her head, and sobbed: "But you won't go back again my child, will you?"

"Yes – I must – the chief wishes to see me again soon."

"What does that man want from you?"

"He...He loves me!" I said quickly. My face turning bright red.

"I think you must have gone insane!" Mother said outraged: "You're not going to start any affairs with that man, are you?"

"Affairs? What kind of affairs? Aren't I allowed to have an admirer at twenty-years-old?" I asked, batting my eyes.

"I thought you were much more sensible!" She said sternly, got up, and abruptly left the room.

I hid my face in the pillow and cried long and bitterly, as I saw no way out of my predicament. It was unthinkable for me that my stepfather would lose his life because of me. How awful it would be for my mother to lose her second husband and father of her small son Sergei. And I would have to carry that guilt around in my heart for the rest of my life. How awful, how unbearable it all was. That night I decided that I had no choice but to go along with what Max wanted, there was nothing I could do, I was trapped.

The three days of waiting were dark and difficult and mother didn't say a word to me. I paced restlessly back and forth around the room and grimly looked at the clock. The horrible moment of reckoning drew closer and closer.

When the third day arrived, mother came to me. "I see that you are suffering, my dear! And I don't think you can do anything but go to the chief. I have thought it over through sleepless nights and can no longer bear to see your suffering. I won't be angry with you. I just want to tell you one thing: I warned you and you have to live with your own fate. I just ask that you think everything through one more time."

"I've already thought it through mother, and I'll go the way that I've chosen this evening."

Sad and yet lovingly, mother looked at me and said: "I understand, my poor thing – you love him!"

"Yes!" I answered, like a cry from deep inside: "Yes! I love him, that man!"

And then I just had to cry again, cry...And mother cried too from the bottom of her heart in the belief that my first great love was for such a person. If only she had known, what was really going on inside me! But she could never, never know the truth.

That evening, a large car pulled up in front of our house. I could see through the window how Max Strang and two heavily armed military police and the translator got out. Strang knocked loudly at our door. Mother opened and welcomed them inside. He greeted her politely and then stepped in towards me.

"So Inna: Have you decided to go with me?" He asked confidently. He knew full-well that I would never refuse.

I offered him my hand with quiet calm and said, glancing over to mother, who I didn't want to give any suspicions: "Yes, let's go."

My new master smiled happily and led me to the front door and out of the house. We got in the car, and on the drive to Anapa, this loathsome man kissed me and said triumphantly: "I knew you would come to your senses, my little Russian darling!"

I gave no reply. My body was lifeless. My thoughts numbed. When we entered his room, wine and a meal complete with sweets had been prepared. That evening I intentionally drank very quickly and was soon completely drunk. In that state, I could barely understand what was going on around me.

My head grew ever heavier and a heavy fog obscured my vision. I soon completely stopped thinking and feeling. I only remember an almost unbearable heat and a short, sharp burning pain, that abruptly passed through my body and caused me to scream out. Then everything went dark and silent.

The next morning, I awoke at a late hour.

I saw myself half-dressed lying on a couch. Max Strang sat dressed near me and bent forward towards me with a bizarrely altered expression.

"I understand now Inna." He began slowly, as if choosing his words carefully: "why you defended yourself so vigorously. I couldn't have imagined that you would still be pure and untouched as a twenty-year-old."

Horrified, I looked at him and then closed my eyes, deeply injured. I hated this person to the core of my being. And it seemed as if my assailant understood my numbed-out thoughts. He took my hand, caressed it and said with a soft, muffled voice: "I love you very much Inna. Do you really hate me?"

Without a word, I turned my back to him.

"I'm sorry, that I tormented you so. You truly didn't deserve it." He continued and covered my hand in kisses.

I tore my hand away: "Leave me alone!" I shouted disdainfully.

Max was quiet for what seemed like an eternity. Then, he suddenly spoke in Russian: "Inna, listen...please...just listen..." He started to stammer, a sort of frail hollowness replaced his usual cocky tone: "This life and this war have made me into the animal that I am now. I haven't felt anything for anyone for a long time. But when I saw you lying there... When I saw you lying there, I felt something again through the numbness...I felt...I felt guilty."

Again, I wondered, was this man German or Russian, or even human? Could it be he was a demon sent to torment me?

Max continued in Russian: "Inna – I know you hate me. But truth be told...we aren't so different, you and I...

He cocked his head and looked me in the eyes. Then he revealed the past that he had been concealing for so long: "You see, I grew up speaking Russian just like you. My parents are also descended from a noble family of Cossacks. When the Revolution broke out, my father joined the Don Republic when they declared independence from the Bolsheviks. He fought in the Cossack cavalry alongside the White Army. One day, the Reds came to our home village, not far from where you were born in Poltava, looking for him, but we were already gone. Instead, they killed his brother, my Uncle. They strung him from a tree in front of his wife and children and riddled his corpse with bullets. When the White Army was at its end, my father took us into exile in 1920. We didn't wait around like your family to be deported, displaced, starved and killed by the Bolsheviks like obedient sheep.

My family moved to a village near Konigsberg in East Prussia, and we changed our Slavic last name to 'Strang' to fit in with the Germans. Nonetheless, my mother always spoke Russian with me and my siblings at home, so that we wouldn't forget our past. My father made me promise that, if the chance ever arose, I would one day avenge his brother and restore our family's honor and land.

That's why, when Hitler came to power, I joined the party and the SS – that's why every time I shoot a communist pig in the face – it's an act of vengeance, an act of justice – for my family - and for yours too Inna. I've known all along you are Komsomol – but I also knew that you had no other way to move up in the communist prison they've constructed. I don't judge you Inna, so please don't judge me too harshly.

Now you know who I really am...I thought I owed you that much after what I took from you...but this has to stay between us...or you know what's going to happen..."

I was stupefied and it took me what felt like minutes to absorb it all. Thoughts that I'd had for years, suppressed thoughts, repressed thoughts, rushed into my mind. I had nothing more to lose, and like a bursting dam, they came rushing out:

"I don't judge you. I can't judge you...only God can do that....

But how is this horrific war with all its innocent victims...a just revenge? What have the Jews and the innocent civilians got to do with it? And how does violating me and others who've done you no harm bring justice and honor to your family? You're just replacing one evil, Godless killing machine with another Max. And you're just another cog in that machine. Communism and Fascism are two sides of the same coin: Each marching in uniform columns of uniform people shouting uniform slogans – mercilessly stamping out freedom and humanity under their boots wherever they tread. They both have the same goals: Fear and conquest.

Nothing will change in this world until people remember that truth, honor and respect still mean something. Nothing will change until we return to the eternal from which we came. A wise old man once taught me that."

I suddenly remembered my guardian angel Ivan Kusmitch as I spoke these words, and a total sense of security enveloped me. Whether I now lived or died, I was at peace with the outcome.

Max listened, completely disarmed and now seemingly at my mercy, with his eyes to the ground. It was as if what I had said had struck a deep chord in him, but he was too entrenched in his way of life and thinking to change, and I could see that he was hardening his heart again. He had gone too far down the path of darkness to turn back.

He slowly looked up, and quietly said: "This isn't some Hollywood drama, Inna, where there are good guys and bad guys and a simple, happy ending: There are no good guys here – there is no freedom – and there is no God."

Immediately, those words took me back somewhere familiar and primal: In my mind's eye - I could again hear the voice of my first school teacher...

Chapter 33 – My Only Love Sprung from My Only Hate

After this descent into hell, my only thought was leaving Anapa and the local theater for good. Since everyone knew I was working for the Germans and had seen me being driven about in Max's car, I'd be branded a traitor and shot by the NKVD if the Soviets ever came back. It didn't take me long to ask Max if he could send me somewhere farther from the front, so that I'd at least have a better chance to escape arrest or death should the battle lines shift again. He told me he'd handle it, and after leaving for nearly an hour, came back with my passbook and a signed letter. "With this you'll be able to go to Germany as an "Ostarbeiter" or laborer from the east. You'll be a refugee there, but there's nothing left for you here, and chances are you may drag your whole family down if you stay and the Bolsheviks return."

I opened my pass and saw a stamp inside designating me Ostarbeiter – essentially a work permit and a way to get out of the Soviet Union. I opened the envelope and found a letter of passage to Simferopol, the capital of the Crimea, where there was a hub for eastern laborers to be sent to Germany. Max called the translator and ordered him to take me home and collect my things and return immediately. He did so and I packed my few belongings together and hurriedly said farewell to my mother and family.

As I was stuffing my small suitcase, Mother hurried over and held out her hand. "Take this my child..."

I looked over, and immediately recognized the golden medallion she had promised me years ago. She opened it, revealing the two smiling photos of her and father from so many years past.

"Mother, it's better if you keep it, they are sending me to Germany to work and I promise to write you when I can. You can give it to me when this war is over, and we see each other again. I love you!" We embraced, kissed, and said our farewells. Heartfelt tears were shed, as we knew we might never see one another again.

As much as I wanted to stay, I couldn't loiter around town after all that had just happened. The head of the SS was not someone you wanted to trifle with or be associated with, as local partisans would be looking to take your head.

Upon my return, Max drove me to the harbor to board a German transport ship that would take me across the Black Sea to the Crimea. He bid a young corporal who was also heading to Simferopol, the capital of Crimea, to accompany me and ensure that I was given documents to continue onto Germany and assigned "volunteer" status so that I would not be treated as forced labor. Then he bid me farewell with words that echoed with an undertone of shame for what had passed between us. As the ship set sail, I could see him watching us a long time as we grew ever more distant. I sighed a huge sigh of relief that this dark chapter of my life was behind me.

The young corporal charged with escorting me enthusiastically gave me his full attention and saw to it that I wanted for nothing on the journey. I soon learned that his name was Wolfram and that he was also a singer by profession. He began the war in the Luftwaffe *(or German Air Force)*, but his plane was damaged in a bombing run over Stalingrad and crashed attempting to land, breaking several of his ribs and damaging his liver, rendering him unfit for combat. He was subsequently transferred to work as a singer and entertainer at the military radio station in Simferopol. He was slender and of medium build. He had dark black hair, and thick, distinctive eyebrows crowned his sparkling dark eyes. Dimples adorned his happy, mischievous smile.

When I heard this, I told him: "I've also performed songs for soldiers and even directed a choir."

"Really!" he said with a lively interest: "You'll have to sing something for me."

I didn't want to immediately indulge the request of this still unknown young man. I remained silent as we approached the bow of the ship, which looked out onto the open sea. Then he said, freshly and with a playful confidence: "All right, then I'll sing something for you!" He sang a beautiful German song with a deep, inwardly warm voice. The broad sea rushed and whirred along, and gave his song a special, festive accent.

Wulfram Zimmermann in German Luftwaffe uniform

I stopped in my tracks, my breath taken away by the depth and soul of his voice, which was among the best I'd ever heard, even at the Moscow Theater. I could feel the salty spray of the sea breeze coursing along my skin, which tingled with goosebumps.

When he had finished, my reservations had been melted by the warmth of his performance. I replied with a beautiful, nostalgic Russian song. As I sang, I felt keenly the seemingly endless well of emotion inside me. My Slavic spirit was a wild force of nature, like an unstoppable, fearsome Russian blizzard. Its force had helped me withstand great trials and sorrow, but now I felt it raging with fire and passion.

A powerful, indescribably blissful feeling arose inside me. What was this? As we stood exchanging songs at the bow of the German ship, alone and unseen, I was, without a doubt, falling in love with this young, dark-eyed, hot-blooded, German soldier.

He must have felt something similar, because he suddenly said: “It would be a terrible shame if you went to Germany as a common laborer. I want to see to it that you can continue your career as a singer in Simferopol at the theater there.”

Those words rang in my heart like a deliverance. I thankfully looked up at my rescuer, and it was like I was in a beautiful dream. His large, dark eyes sparkled like two stars. I knew that my destiny was looking back at me and that it would finally be good.

When we arrived in Simferopol, I was employed by the “Propagandastaffel Krim” or “Propaganda Division Crimea” with Wolfram – assigned to music and theater – and received a position with the Ukrainian theater, which was performing around the peninsula at that time. Strange, that as people who performed music which diverted people’s attention from war with ballads about love and home – that we were still just another division in a vast war machine.

I was assigned a quaint little apartment and provided enough food to live on. Wolfram visited me almost every day. We sang together, discussed our concerts and performances and talked about how our days had gone. I still didn’t speak very good German, but we still understood each other quite well. He was a soldier in a war – but with his voice and charisma - he had that special something that few people have – he had star power – and it turned me on to no end.

As time passed, I increasingly realized that I didn’t want to live without this man and that my love for him knew no bounds. I could tell that he felt the same, but intentionally tried to remain cool and reserved. Nonetheless, he was drawn ever-closer to me with each passing day, and I knew full well that he loved me.

The sense of it all seemed to elude me, because nothing in life seemed to make sense: First my family's travails, my father's arrest, the war and my torment at the hands of Max. And now, in the midst of a world gone insane, what could this indescribable romance mean? After all, what could it mean when the whole world wanted us to hate one another – and we just wanted to make love?

Sooner or later, we had to come to an understanding. It happened on a normal day in early 1943. That evening he came to see me, and we ate dinner by candlelight, as Russians were not allowed electricity. Wolfram sat next to me on the couch, and looked at me repeatedly, longingly. I looked down at my plate, as a burning desire to throw myself into his arms was overwhelming me.

As if aware of my own guilty feelings, I finally looked over and my eyes met his and I felt myself melting inside. He smiled, as if he knew what I was thinking, and opened his arms to embrace me. Now there was no holding back. We drank in the sweet intoxication of the moment and swore our love to one another forever.

We woke up the next morning in one another's arms. It was the first time I'd felt this way or experienced anything like this, and it was like I was on a different planet. I sat up and could see myself in a mirror near the bed. It was me, but somehow, I looked different, somehow, I'd transformed into a different version of myself. It felt good, disconcerting and permanent at the same time, and I intuitively knew I had crossed an inexorable boundary in my life. More than anything, I felt as if I'd been with this man forever, like being with him was as natural as breathing and eating.

Wolfram sat up and stroked the side of my chin and cheek sensuously with his fingertips. "Inna, we were meant to be together.

You have to go to Germany to my parents and wait for me there until this war is over."

He seemed to believe that his parents, who viewed him as a well-behaved, upright son, would give us their blessing to marry, and wrote them a detailed letter that evening and included a small photo of me. How great was our disappointment, then, when the reply came that he should get the idea that he would marry a Russian woman out of his mind, and that they would never tolerate it, and if they were forced to, they would notify his company commander of his folly if he didn't come to his senses.

We read the letter in agony. Wolfram said: "We've forgotten that people have built-up a wall between nations."

Dejected, he remained silent a while. Then he got up, looked at me, and said determinedly: "I'll never, ever leave you Inna!"

I couldn't share his confidence, and felt it was painfully clear that this wonderful dream could not continue and decided to let both of us out of this hopeless situation.

I went secretly the next day to the work authority and renewed my application to be sent to Germany as a voluntary Ostarbeiter. The head of the authority, who knew me from my work at the theater, wondered at my intentions and my request to leave as soon as possible. He assumed I had good reason, and without further questioning, gave me a personal attestation to take with me to Germany to give to the work administrator.

After that had all been taken care of, I went home and packed my things. I told Wolfram I was going away on a concert trip and promised to be back in a few days. I didn't want to tell him the truth and ask for forgiveness until after I had left. We said our heartfelt goodbyes, and deeply moved, I left my cozy little apartment in Simferopol, where fate had bestowed upon me so many happy memories.

Chapter 34 – Stopover in Vienna

I boarded a transport train with three-thousand other Russians, most of them forced laborers bound for Germany. It consisted of freight cars without windows or seats. During the trip, we sat or lay on the floor of the cars. There was little to eat or drink. We often went without warm meals, as we never seemed to reach our designated stations stops on time. We had to yield to other, more important trains. Our train often had to wait hours each day until the rails were open and we were allowed to continue. This endlessly long journey became a torturous imprisonment for us. Many of my countrymen and women were near the end of their nerves. Some attempted to flee but were swiftly captured by the train guards and locked in the "sabotage car."

"If they're handling us like cattle now, what was going to happen when we got to Germany?" asked the other passengers.

I had little time to think about that, however. The tragedy of my destiny and the fact that I had voluntarily plunged myself into this situation overwhelmed me to such a degree that I barely noticed the present state of my surroundings. All of my thoughts swirled around Simferopol and Wolfram. An enormous, burning longing plagued me. And day and night, just one question accompanied me: What would he do? Would he understand and forgive me that I'd taken this course without telling him?

The occasional quiet hope that perhaps he would look into what had become of me and try to find me led me to think that perhaps everything could still turn out well. At times I would daydream about my memories of recent days gone by, and it became more and more evident, that I would never be able to forget this great love. And even if we never met again, I still wanted to remain faithful to this man.

But the longer the train trip stretched out, the more I lost hope. We had been underway for over three weeks and were still in Soviet territory. Often there were air raid alarms, and our large train would be the target of attacks by Russian fighter-bombers. There was also the talk of air attacks growing ever worse in Germany and that we could be heading to our deaths. On the twenty-fifth day, we finally reached the German-Polish border. We were put in a temporary holding area in a compound where we were examined by a doctor and thoroughly disinfected. Then we were informed of our final destinations.

When I gave the compound director my documents from the authority head in Simferopol, he told me that my marching orders had already been there for several days, and that I had been assigned to head to Vienna: "Since you are a volunteer, you don't need to wait for a transport. We will put you on the next train transporting troops home on holiday."

I was separated from the large group of Ostarbeiter and handed my documents along with a train ticket to Vienna. The director even gave me a car ride to the train station after he had finished processing all the laborers. When I arrived in Vienna, I was to proceed to the work authority for my assignment. I was surprised at how much trust was given to me and wondered what the fates now had in store. When I arrived in Vienna, someone was already waiting for me when I stepped off the train.

The employment office official received me immediately and said: "Miss Grinfeldt, you have been assigned a household here. Your lady is already waiting for you. Follow me to my office."

We went to his office near the station, and he immediately rang her: "Lady Maybach, the Russian from Simferopol is here, please come right away." I waited with curiosity for my new overseer. After a short wait, the friendly official introduced me to a petite, still quite young and elegant young lady who looked me carefully up and down.

I seemed to pass her inspection. She gave me her hand and said: “I’m happy that you made it safely to Vienna, Miss Grinfeldt. Now please follow me.”

I gladly wondered at this pleasant treatment. I immediately came to love this small, elegant lady who was now my mistress, and the thought that I had to serve as a housekeeper and Ostarbeiter no longer seemed so repugnant.

We soon reached her apartment, which was in a nice, modern house. When I saw the large rooms and the refined furniture, I was impressed but skeptical. This lady, I thought, must certainly be a wealthy capitalist. I could hardly believe it when she told me that she had been doing all of the housework alone as her husband was an officer currently stationed in France, and they didn’t have a large income.

“I thought” I said shyly: “...looking at this house, that you were a very wealthy lady with a large staff of servants.”

She laughed. “It’s not such great wealth, but if you save your money, you can still live quite well here in Vienna.”

“Do workers live here in the house?” I now inquired, with a little more confidence: “maybe in the basement?”

“In the basement? Why would you think that?” she asked, amused. “Nobody lives with us in the basement, and every worker has his own proper place to live.”

I replied: “I thought that in Germany and Austria that the workers didn’t have their own homes or furniture. We learned at school that they live in basements and sleep on straw.”

Lady Maybach replied kindly and firmly: “We are much more technically advanced than the Russians, my dear, every part of life is more advanced.”

Soon, however, it would be her turn to be amazed. We walked into a music room and encountered a large, glistening grand piano. Spellbound, I stood before the magnificent, well-loved instrument and carefully raised the lid.

Lady Maybach observed me with curiosity: "do you know, what that is?" She asked.

"Of course! May I play?"

"Gladly!" She said, surprised: "You can play the piano? Please go ahead." She looked at me amused again, which I took to mean that she didn't believe me. I sat down and began to play the *Pathetique* by Beethoven.

"Beethoven?" She said, greatly surprised. "But you're from Russia."

"Yes, of course."

"And you play Beethoven? How is that?"

"I learned it."

"I believe you, but to be honest, I didn't think that there were pianos in Russia, at least not outside Moscow."

My bright young lady soon sat at her telephone and called all her acquaintances. She invited them to come have a look at her new weird and wonderful creature. Most of the Viennese who came to see me were of the mind that, if all Russians were like me, that they didn't need to have any fears of their coming. I gradually came to understand how the lie-filled propaganda from both sides had deceived and blinded the two peoples now locked in a merciless world war. Wolfram was right - walls were being erected between peoples and nations - built brick-by-brick with false narratives and caricatures. I soon noticed that the Viennese had a strong aversion to Adolf Hitler, and only a few still believed firmly in a German victory.

Lady Maybach always treated me especially well, and never made me feel that I was her servant. My German had become fluent enough by then, that I was able to converse without difficulty. I often told her and her guests stories about life in Russia. I tried to give them an accurate picture of life there.

During such conversations, it was often very painful for me when I noticed that the Viennese viewed my homeland as a fully uncultivated nation and land. I tried to correct this perception and tell them that the Germans had made a big mistake in that they, with their ever-advancing technology, had underestimated the values and strength of the new Russia. They would have done better, as I saw it, to seek a true understanding and honest peace with the Russian people.

In Lady Maybach's house and the houses of her friends, I did see many useful gadgets and furnishings that I'd never seen in Russia. I also noticed the fashionable clothes and shoes. This led me to the conclusion that, although the average Russian person was less wealthy, that the cultural and educational development of the Russians was not far behind. I found the Soviet regime with its Marxist materialist worldview to be quite similar to the Hitler regime.

Lady Maybach and her guests allowed me to discuss all these things with them with great interest. Afterwards, they often asked me to play the piano and sing them Russian songs, which I always enjoyed. One evening, when I was feeling especially homesick and longing for my beloved Wolfram, and could no longer hold back my tears at the piano, Lady Maybach called me into the living room and asked compassionately what was causing me so much anguish.

I told her all about my heartbreak and my great love.

"Where is the man you love now?" She asked when I'd finished.

"He's with the military broadcaster in Simferopol."

"Can't we write to him and request that he take leave and come visit us?"

I looked at her imploringly: "You can't write to him dear Lady Maybach. Perhaps he has already forgotten about me, and I don't want to trouble his heart again."

I briefly explained what had happened with Wolfram and how I had felt compelled to secretly leave him. When she understood that I had become an Ostarbeiter for Wolfram's sake, she took my hand and looked deep into my eyes: "You poor dear, I see you need my assistance. I am going to write your Wolfram right away. Such a great love can't be allowed to simply die!"

She immediately retrieved a pen and paper and sat down at her desk to write. I sat across from her, suddenly immersed in new dreams of bliss.

Wulfram Zimmerman – a picture from early during the war, location unknown

Chapter 35 - I Become a German

Several weeks went by. Lady Maybach and I waited impatiently for Wolfram's reply. Going back and forth between joyful hope and anxious worry, I made an effort to use this time to learn about every aspect of German life. Lady Maybach helped me as much as she could. And when I told her, I wanted to learn German more thoroughly, she bought the few German-Russian books she could find and studied with me most evenings.

We were overjoyed, when we received a telegram from Wolfram: "Coming in a few days on my leave to Vienna."

I was beside myself with happiness and hugged my lady again and again. She beckoned me into her room and gave me some of her own elegant clothes to try on.

"I want you to look beautiful." she said in a chatty voice.

She even took me to the hair stylist, and I emerged looking like a fashion model. When I looked at myself in the mirror, I could barely recognize myself. The braided Russian girl had transformed into an elegant Viennese lady. I laughed at how unlikely it all was. How lovely she had unexpectedly made my life in such a short time.

And soon the hour was at hand that I would stand face-to-face with my beloved. I couldn't find the words. The reunion was so overwhelming that we forgot the entire world in a long embrace.

Lady Maybach was genuinely happy for us both. That evening, we discussed our future. Wolfram wondered if it would be possible for me to remain with Lady Maybach and attend the Vienna Musical College part-time to continue the studies I'd begun in Moscow, at least until he returned from the war.

"Will Inna be allowed to study here as a Russian?" Lady Maybach inquired with concern.

"We'll go first thing tomorrow morning to the director of the college and discuss it with him." Wolfram declared. "But let me suggest that this evening, that we make music together and select what Inna should perform tomorrow."

We happily went to the music room and sang and played to our heart's content deep into the night. It was a wonderfully harmonious house concert. Wolfram's sang several grand Schubert songs with such an enchanting voice, that both Lady Maybach and I were moved to tears.

The next morning, full of apprehension, I had to demonstrate my ability to the director and other musicians: This included playing the piano, singing, and also performing my own compositions.

The audition went very well. Afterwards, the director requested Wolfram and I join him on his walk home for a special conversation. As we made our way through the streets of Vienna, the director took on a look of concern, and he informed us that, despite my abilities, he could not accept a foreigner into the program. I had to get German citizenship. Austria had been annexed by Germany in 1938 and remained a part of greater Germany, so only German citizenship would remove any barriers to my acceptance.

"A German?" cried Lady Maybach, at a loss.

"Yes, that would set things straight." Wolfram said: "If we got married now, then she would legally become a German citizen."

"But dear Wolfram..." she objected: "You must know that no German is allowed to marry a Russian."

I listened to this painful conversation and said with resignation: "I don't need to study here, anyway..."

"You will!" decided Wolfram: "Your talent won't go to waste." And then something occurred to him: "Wait a minute... I've got it!"

He said it so loudly that both Lady Maybach and I paused, waiting to hear what surprise solution he had in store for us.

He turned searchingly to me and asked: "You were, I remember, born in Ukraine in Poltava, were you not? So that means you are a Ukrainian and not a Russian!"

"Indeed." I confirmed.

"I've heard," He continued triumphantly, "that marriages between Ukrainians and Germans are permitted. I will look into the exact details immediately."

Both Lady Maybach and I praised Wolfram for this insight. But I still wondered: "What about your parents? What will they say about our plans? Did you forget the letter they wrote?"

"We won't say anything to them for now, as they have no ability to judge from such a distance. After we are husband and wife, things will resolve themselves with time."

Lady Maybach heartily approved. And then I knew how much my chosen one loved me and I firmly believed that we would find a way.

The marriage preparations, however, demanded great effort and many nerves. Day after day, Wolfram and I had to go from one bureau to the next and take care of all the forms and formalities. His remaining vacation days were filled with struggling through this red tape, and the days flew by. Our impending separation drew closer, and we began to despair as we still did not have all the necessary papers. Finally, on the next-to-last day, we received the most important document in our lives, the permission to marry.

With Anne-Marie, as we now called Lady Maybach, we celebrated our humble wartime wedding, and, glowing on the inside, were unspeakably happy.

This small celebration was also a farewell party. The next morning, I brought my young groom to the train station. He was pale and sad as he embraced me for the last time before boarding the train back to the front. "When the war is over, we will be the happiest two people on the earth." He whispered in my ear.

Then he left me alone and rode away eastwards towards my former homeland. I remained in Vienna, now a German lady.

Inna Grinfeldt Zimmerman, c. 1945, possibly taken at the time of her wedding to Wulfram.

Chapter 36 – Sent Away

"So, you're saying that your husband is a Stuttgarter by birth?" Asked the small, hunchbacked bureaucrat with a small, shrunken face, looking at me with fatigue in two eyes enlarged by his thick glasses. Then he paged through several thick regulation books and finally told me, in his unpleasant, chirpy voice: "I'm sorry, we cannot issue you a residency permit for Vienna, you have to go to your husband's hometown."

I'd heard this line at least a dozen times already since Wolfram's departure. "But I can't go to Stuttgart, sir! My in-laws still don't know a thing about our marriage!" I replied in exasperation.

The jaded bureaucrat looked back at me amused. "It's not our responsibility to settle your family matters." He replied, twitching his shoulders. And pointing to the door, he added morosely: "Other people are waiting out there, young lady. Your time is up."

Having lost all hope, I left this unwelcoming place. As I was no longer an Ostarbeiter and had become a German through marriage, I was no longer allowed to remain in Vienna due to the extremely rigid Viennese residency laws. Without a residency permit, I was also unable to obtain ration cards which allowed a person to purchase basic necessities. Like it or not, it seemed I had no choice but to go live in Stuttgart. Even before this problem with my residency, I was already extremely anxious about meeting Wolfram's parents and explaining to them that I, a totally alien Russian woman, was their new daughter-in-law. After the letter they had written, my apprehension was certainly not unfounded.

I therefore determined to do all I could to stay in Vienna and went from one authority to the next. But the local bureaucrats were all implacable and had no sympathy for my pleas and tears. I thought to myself that these people had no hearts at all.

Anne Marie, my beloved, indispensable friend, followed these developments with concern and tried to support me as she could. But even she was unable to achieve anything. I didn't want to weigh down Wolfram with these problems, as he couldn't help from so far away. So I decided that I had no choice but to take these difficulties upon myself and travel to Stuttgart to meet with Wolfram's parents and try to talk to them.

I told Anne Marie: "I will ask his parents to forgive us both and tell them how deeply and truly I love their son."

With a heavy heart, I bid farewell this wonderful dainty lady, who could have been my unfeeling master, but had grown into my greatest friend and confidant. As for Vienna, this supposed world city had closed its gates to me – so I bitterly departed and caught a night train to Stuttgart. The journey would take me across most of Austria and southern Germany.

I was so nervous that I didn't sleep a wink that night until I had imagined everything that I would say down to the word to explain the situation to my new in-laws. I also knew that Wolfram had a younger sister, Ilse, who I hoped would relate to me and maybe even become a close friend. I wanted to present myself to them as a good daughter and sincerely request that they forgive us our trespasses. If they would only treat me well, I would love them as much as my husband. My heart was truly filled with love for these still unknown parents.

Around noon the next day, I arrived in Stuttgart, a city nestled in gentle, rolling hills, with quaint houses and vineyards, and immediately set out to find Wolfram's family home. I was soon able to find it in a quiet residential area, at the end of a long street lined by a ridge of houses. Wolfram's family lived at the end of the street, which curved not far past the house in the face of a sunken railroad track. I stood a long time staring at the front door and listened as several trains clattered past. I could see "Richard Zimmermann – Instructor for Music" engraved on a small metal placard next to the doorbell, and it seemed completely familiar and foreign at the same time. The longer I stood thinking, the more nervous I grew, my eyes fixed on the doorbell button, which seemed to be growing in size the longer I stared at it, and I felt like running away.

Feeling that it was now-or-never, I pulled myself together, took a deep breath, and shyly pressed the button. I waited for the door to open. My heart was pounding so quickly and terribly that I could hardly breathe.

Several moments passed. It felt like an eternity. I finally heard steps approaching and a dog's shrill barking. A faint male voice called: "Bonzo, back! Sit!" A hand grasped the door handle, I saw it turning, as if in slow motion, and the door opened...

Before me stood an older, gray-haired, yet well-groomed and stately looking gentleman, who looked at me questioningly. I knew without a word, that this was my husband's father Richard.

"What can I do for you, young lady?" He asked, in a friendly voice.

"I'd like to speak to Mrs. Zimmermann."

"Mrs. Zimmermann?" My wife is unfortunately not available at the moment. Could you perhaps come another time?"

"I've come from Vienna and I'd like to report something about your son Wolfram." I replied quietly.

"You know our Wolfram?" He shouted, pleasantly surprised. "Then please come in!" he said, opening the door widely and motioning with his hand.

As I stepped inside, a small black-and-white spotted little dog sprang towards me. He sniffed my clothes with his broad nose and stood up on his hind-paws and hopped happily about in a sort of dance in a circle around me, barking loudly and trying to lick me.

My father-in-law was astonished by this outburst of happiness from his little "Bonzo." Then he commanded him to sit.

"That's remarkable." He said, turning to me: "Bonzo normally can't stand strangers. He only behaves like that when Wolfram comes home to visit."

With those words, he led me into the large, bright and cozily furnished living room and invited me to have a seat. He sat down across from me, waiting patiently for me to say something. Despite my endless reflection on the train the night before, I didn't know where to start or what to say.

He made things easier by breaking the silence: "So you are from Vienna? May I ask your name?"

My face flushed a deep red. I looked down at the ground and answered shyly: "My name is Inna Zimmermann."

"Come again?" I heard his voice ringing in my ear.

"Inna Zimmermann." I said more firmly. "I'm Wolfram's wife."

With that the ice was broken – smashed to pieces in fact. I slowly raised my head and looked at my father-in-law. He sat with a pale, downcast face across from me.

"Are you the Russian from Simferopol who Wolfram wrote us about?"

"Yes!"

"I couldn't imagine a Russian very well, but now I can see why my son liked you." He said with reservation.

I was relieved by this remark, and with a warm voice, I recounted all of the trials we had experienced and admitted that I deeply loved his son. Then I asked him to forgive me for our headstrong actions and for this manner of relationship, so rushed by circumstances, and to bless our marriage.

My story visibly moved the old gentleman. He gently put his hand to my face, looked in my eyes, and said: "Mother Klara is taking a nap, but I will go to her and let her know you are here."

I remained in the living room feeling both encouraged and anxious, waiting for Wolfram's mother. My mother-in-law was, as I later learned, extremely upset by her husband's news. She could barely contain herself when, at her husband's request, she stepped into the living room and extended her hand to me.

Klara had intense dark eyes and curly dark hair with wisps of gray, and I could immediately see that Wolfram took his appearances from her. She scanned me with a curious, unwelcoming look, and I knew right away that something was wrong. I looked over to my father-in-law pleadingly.

"You'll stay with us today." He said in a friendly voice. "We will discuss together, what we should do going forward."

After those words, however, Klara tilted her head and motioned for him to speak privately in another room.

When the two returned, the well-meaning Richard was completely unsettled. "Mother says..." he said hesitantly... "that we don't have room in the house for you. I want to ask a neighbor if they have a place you can stay."

I silently wondered how there was no room for me in such a large house, and soon understood that the husband didn't have much to say in the matter. I soon came to clearly understand that my mother-in-law would have most liked to see Wolfram and me separated immediately. But there was another thing that bound us firmly together in addition to our great love: I was carrying our first child.

When I told the parents about this, it still didn't change things. And although I soon found a place to stay with friendly neighbors, my mother-in-law was determined to see me leave the city as soon as possible to a location in the greater countryside. The parents wrote Wolfram a bitter letter castigating him for marrying a completely foreign woman, (yes, an enemy!) so young without a solid means of supporting himself and without their permission.

I cried a great deal in this bitter time, particularly when I noticed that Wolfram wrote me less often and enthusiastically, and accused me of going to his parents without first informing him. I finally felt forced to compose a long and detailed letter and Wolfram's reply gave me renewed hope and strength. He promised to visit me when our child was born and to reconcile his parents with me.

I waited impatiently for this long-hoped for day. As my child began to show more and more, my mother-in-law registered me at a home for soldier's wives who were pregnant or had children in Calw, a small town about 40 kilometers west of Stuttgart in the Black Forest. As my due date drew close, I was temporarily transferred to a large hospital in Tübingen, about an hour southeast of Calw in late July 1944, as it was the nearest facility with a maternity wing.

When I arrived in the hospital it was towards evening and, as if by clockwork, my water broke and I went into labor. I hadn't even been assigned a room and was sent directly to the delivery ward. There was still blood on the floor from a woman who had just given birth before me which was being hastily mopped up by a young girl orderly.

The nurse assigned to me was a young woman who took my hand and looked at me sympathetically. She looked exhausted but still managed to mumble a few reassuring words to me. As the contractions grew closer and the pain greater, she asked me if I wanted any morphine, but I refused.

Finally, a doctor came in to assist. I could hear the nurse starting to prompt me to push. This went on for about 45 minutes when I heard a loudspeaker announcement and then the distant blaring of sirens. It all seemed like a surreal dream. The eyes of the doctor widened and the nurse turned pale. She began: "It's an air raid...we've got to get to the shelter...!"

The doctor and nurse rolled me to the hospital exit and then had two young male patients assist me. Each put one of my arms over his shoulder and half-dragged, half-carried me along the cobble-stoned courtyard to two storm-doors protruding like open arms from the ground about a half block from the hospital. Despite the intense pain of my contractions, I could hear the distinct sound of heavy guns firing in the distance. The men dragged me down the steps as best they could, and I was laid down on a hastily thrown-together pile of blankets and jackets. Minutes later I could hear loud concussive thuds. Luckily, the doctor and nurse had remained dutifully near me the entire time and, as my contractions continued, tended to me in the dank cellar full of frightened people, with the two men who had carried me keeping curious, frightened children at a distance.

The pain became so intense that all I could focus on now was the face of the nurse and the feeling of her hand squeezing mine. The only other thing that registered was a final, thunderous concussion from above, which violently shook dust over us all like some gray, suffocating confetti. And in that moment, as death rained from the sky, the cries of my first child became audible. Then all went dark...

Chapter 37 – Minamama and the Visitor

I awoke again back in the hospital. The sun was streaming in through an open window. Outside it was a beautiful summer day, and green leaves rustled gently in the breeze. Luckily, the hospital had been left unscathed by the previous night's bombing raid. I was assigned a bare room with three other women. We each had a bed with a table next to it. As soon as I was fully awake, the nurse brought my healthy young baby boy to me, and as I had already promised Wolfram, I named him Alexander.

That day I sent three letters announcing the happy news: The first to Wolfram, whose unit had been redeployed from Crimea to Romania. The second to Lady Maybach in Vienna. And the third to Wolfram's parents. Wolfram and Anne Marie answered immediately with letters wishing me and our new little world citizen all the best. My husband again promised to come for a visit on his next leave. My in-laws, however, made no reply.

For the time being I was alone, had no visitors and was confronted with a chaotic and completely uncertain future...

As my discharge date neared, I received a letter from the women's home: Good news! You have been placed with a local family. The letter gave me a date and time. I had one week to have my room cleaned out and things packed for my departure. I really didn't know where we would be going or with whom we would be living. I was both relieved and anxious.

Baby Alexander and I were adopted by a farmer's wife named Wilhelmine Schönhardt living in a small village near the women's home named Sommenhardt with her invalid husband and five children ranging in age from 7 to 16. The house was a simple, wooden, two-story farmhouse on the main road through the village. It had no running water, just a well and an outhouse. Wilhelmina, or Minamama, as we always called her, was a quiet, humble, no-

nonsense peasant woman. Like so many people in southwestern Germany, she was thrifty, hard-working and tidy. There wasn't much adorning the house except a simple cross hanging from the wall in the living room. The cross, despite its lack of adornment, reminded me of my mother's icons.

Life was simple and revolved around subsisting from day-to-day. I would help Minamama collect vegetables from the family garden, prepare food and do the laundry. She was stern and didn't allow me to speak a word of Russian. Despite the war, I didn't feel that she hated Russians, she just wanted me to adjust to my surroundings for my own good. As I learned more German, I could ask local farmers for a little extra milk for Alexander, and some would even oblige. In this ideal, rural setting, few signs of the war were to be seen, with the notable exception of bombers loudly flying past towards nearby cities. Now, despite the uncertainty of the war, I had a relatively safe place to stay, and reason to hope the future could be better.

But things did not go as planned: In late August 1944, when Alexander was just weeks old, days after moving in with Minamama, the Romanian King Michael, who had largely been on the sidelines in his country, re-asserted himself, led a coup against his country's Fascist leaders, and sued for peace with the Soviet Union. All German soldiers stationed in Romania were interned and the country soon fell into Russian hands. All I received in the midst of this political turmoil was a disheartening message: "Missing." What a terrible word! Only the heart of a woman in love can understand the depth of its horror.

It was as if a part of me was torn out. I broke down in unspeakable agony at the sight of this one short line. My life now became empty and pitch black.

Tortured by uncertainty, I dragged myself through each day and only my little Alexander, my blonde, healthy little baby, brought me happiness in these lonely hours. He developed splendidly day-by-day and I thought how impressed his father would be with him. I was often so distraught that I could barely eat.

Whenever I prepared something for myself, I could only think of Wolfram missing, and was tormented by the thought that at this moment he might be starving. Like a hunted pigeon under fire, I flapped my way through the thorn bushes of these days and weeks and could barely stand to wait until the father of my son finally came home to set things right. I often knelt at the foot of my child's bed and prayed to God in my intense desperation to protect my husband and son's father.

Although Wolfram's fate was unknown to me, I did finally receive a piece of good news. His younger sister, Ilse, responded to my message of Alexander's birth, and promised to come visit me. Apparently, after hearing Wolfram had gone missing, his parents' conscience had tormented then after their callous treatment of me, and they bid Ilse to check up on me. This also allowed Ilse to get away from Stuttgart, now a regular target of Allied aerial bombardments.

I wrote back to Ilse about how we had been taken in by Minamama and now lived in the heart of little Sommenhardt. A week later, she arrived. She was five years younger than Wolfram, but at 19, already stood over six feet tall and had blonde hair and blue eyes, quite in contrast to Wolfram, who looked more like his mother. By this time, Alexander was two months old and a cute baby with blonde hair and blue eyes. Ilse was proud of her little nephew, which made me very happy.

I thought, "Maybe this grief will bring me closer to Wolfram's family, and if God lets him come home, all will be well!"

But these hopes were soon dashed: Wolfram's parents, having sent Ilse to visit, considered their familial duties satisfied. They remained cold and alien toward me. They could not empathize or understand how hard it was for me to be alone with a small child in my arms in a foreign land, far from my homeland and family.

I had no one from whom I could get moral support other than Minamama, who had her hands full with her own children, home, and husband. Only a little Alexander, and the hope that Wolfram would return after the war ended, kept me going.

From time to time, Ilse would visit my rustic country home and its relative safety away from the now daily bombing runs on Germany's urban centers, which were subjected to increasing destruction. On one visit to my rustic little country home, she arrived shaken by the horrors she had endured. The Zimmermann family house at which I had had my encounter with Wolfram's parents had been damaged by a bomb. Ilse was noticeably upset and anxious, and I tried my best to make her feel at ease. Even so, I was never able to truly connect with her.

I concluded that Wolfram's parents and sister could not forgive me for not being German. I thought bitterly, "Will they never change their attitude toward me?" I was struck by their political conviction: Even though Hitler had subjected the German people to tremendous hardship during the war, and many German cities had been reduced to rubble thanks to his lust for conquest, many Germans believed until the final day that they could win. The thought that they might lose seemed impossible to them.

I often argued with Ilse on this point. I asked her, "Can't you see that the German army is defeated? Isn't it constantly retreating?"

She replied, "That's nothing. The Fuhrer said that new secret wonder weapons will soon be used and we will win!"

I assured her, "I don't believe it. No weapon can destroy the entire world! Germany is too small and now that her allies have abandoned her, Germans are fighting alone. Victory is impossible!"

"Only a non-German could think that. It cannot be that our Führer would subject us to such sacrifices in vain. We will win!"

"Just wait. You will see for yourself who is right! The Germans are bleeding. If they were smart they would stop the war and save what is still intact for their own people!"

"You say strange things! To sacrifice so many young lives in this war for nothing? To lose our homes and fortunes aimlessly in this war, and not win? Impossible! The Germans cannot give up their fight!"

I said confidently, "Then they will be forced to do so! It is clear to me. The only concern that occupies me now is Wolfram! I know that only after this war is over will he be able to return to me, which is why I wish for it to end as soon as possible."

But it was impossible to change Ilse's mind, even as the combined forces of Germany's enemies began to penetrate deep into the country, she was still waiting for some miracle to save Germany.

As the war neared its conclusion, Ilse visited less frequently. As the fall turned to winter, I became so physically and spiritually weakened, that I could barely stand up at times.

Then something happened on a bright, sunny, early spring day that was both wonderful and incomprehensible. I was particularly downcast that day, cried for a long time over my husband, and felt so despondent that I thought I wanted to die. Without having eaten anything, I lay down in bed around noon. My thoughts were consumed by my distant, lost love. In that moment, I was also tormented by thoughts that I would never see my homeland or mother again:

“What would happen next? Where would I find a way out of this situation, who would protect me? Oh mother, my dear, sweetheart, why are you not with me in such a difficult moment? I am suffering so much; if only I could press myself against your chest and cry, and you would put your hand in my hair and comfort me!”

At times I was ready to drop everything and run day and night, to run east to my mother, looking to her for salvation from this heartache.

"God, why do I have to suffer so much?" I asked. And I thought I could hear his answer:

"Wait, you sinful servant of God, you have much more to see in life! You are still a very young woman, and there are many, many torments and trials to be endured. Every person must bear his or her cross and suffer many sorrows! Only then can a person pass the way of perfection of the soul. Submit to your destiny and wait for what comes next"

And I waited...

Suddenly, I heard a quiet knocking at the door. I wanted to stand up to open it, but my body felt as heavy as lead, and I couldn’t move. At the same time, I felt as if I rose up out of my own body, and I could see myself dressed and lying on the bed right in front of me. I seemingly floated to the door and opened it.

In walked, in full uniform, with a fully packed rucksack on his back, my beloved Wolfram. Completely taken aback, I looked at this and couldn’t believe my eyes. Crying, I whispered: “Is it really you?”

“Of course it’s me!” He replied brightly, stepping into the room. “If you don’t believe me, just touch the rucksack here on my back.” I touched the rough, rugged pack and felt it between my fingers. In my heart, I felt and knew that the wearer of this pack was truly my husband.

"Why?" I passionately asked: "haven't you written me in such a long time?"

"My love…" he replied: "That's why I've come to visit you now, to tell you that you should no longer mourn. I am alive and well and I will come home!"

With those words, the spirit wanted to take me in his arms and embrace me. But before my beloved could touch me, my spirit turned towards my resting body and the two reunited.

With that, this odd occurrence came to an end. Was it a dream? A delusion? Had I seen a ghost? Spellbound, I lay with my eyes wide-open, looking up at the ceiling, and I firmly believed from that moment on that my husband was alive and would come home.

This encounter brought me back to life and to the world of the living and gave me the strength to carry on a new, ordered existence filled with hope.

Chapter 38 – The War Ends and a New Struggle Begins

The war had by this time began to wind towards its bitter end. Where once German forces had advanced on every front, they now stood in retreat, and the opposing armies advanced irresistibly from all sides into the heart of Germany. Large swarms of heavy bombers passed overhead in such numbers that they seemed to block out the sun, making a tremendous amount of noise. People's belief in their leaders was completely shattered. Time and again the starving, impoverished and homeless asked one another why they had made all these sacrifices of countless human lives and property and why their faithful, brave sons had to fight for a lost cause to the bitter end. I shared this feeling and was only happy that I did not have a drop of human blood on my conscience.

In the second half of April 1945, the American and French troops approached my quiet, peaceful Black Forest hideaway and soon occupied all of the surrounding towns and cities. Only the little village in which I had been living for 9 months with Alexander was remarkably untouched by the war. Not a single bomb or mortar disturbed the quiet rural serenity in Sommenhardt, and not a single foreign soldier found his way there.

When the complete surrender of Germany was finally announced in early May 1945, most Germans were stunned to the core. But the fact remained: Germany had lost the war and was now under the occupation of four great powers – America, Britain, France, and the Soviet Union. The end and loss of the war brought much moral depravity to the German population, and many women became involved in prostitution. Others, having lost hope of the return of their missing husbands, found new lovers, and when husbands unexpectedly returned home, divorces followed, which skyrocketed after the end of the war.

Germany had sunk to its lowest point since its foundation.

Despite this, I believe that Germany will rise from the ashes. The Germans are amazingly clean, talented, and hardworking people. They are one of the most civilized peoples of Europe. Although they are suffering after having fallen to the bottom of the world order, they are trying to recover with all their strength. With the help of the Western powers, they will certainly succeed, if they do not go the way of Bolshevism. If, however, communism wins and Germany becomes a Soviet republic, it will not escape its poverty and misery, because the people of the Soviet Union know only the backbreaking and miserable labor of "national defense."

Hitler's gravest mistake was choosing war and aggression against other peoples and nations instead of peace and trade. That is why he failed. The Soviet rulers make the same mistake by starving their own people, forcing them into an endless cycle of privation to pursue the task of defending communism and destroying all other rival systems in the world. For that reason, peaceful cooperation with the Soviet Union will never be possible. It is increasingly clear to people all over the world that war with the USSR is inevitable. The Russians are pursuing a policy of both foreign and domestic violence, and violence breeds resistance. And if the peoples of the USSR, clutched in the grip of Bolshevism, have no opportunity to resist, there are enough strong fighters for freedom and democracy on the remaining 5/6 of the globe!

Tragically, freedom has never been experienced by the Russian people and they will have to suffer a great deal more before they get a chance to taste its sweetness. But the Russian people aspire to freedom and happiness. Who has the right to subject them to further deprivation and torture?!

After Germany surrendered, I decided to visit Stuttgart. As I walked through the broken streets after months of living in the countryside, an incredible longing came over me. I thought of Wolfram, of how it would hurt him to see his homeland in such a miserable state. The usually well-cleaned and groomed streets were littered with piles of rubble from shattered buildings, and the windows of the streetcars that had been damaged in the bombing were boarded up. But this did not stop traffic in the city. It somehow lived on. It seemed that this huge giant, whose body was covered with blood and wounds, was beginning to recover again from the battles it had suffered.

I visited Wolfram's family, who now lived in a private apartment in one of the surviving villas on the outskirts of the city. My mother-in-law Klara, upon seeing me, waved her hands at me as if to shew me away:

"You're crazy, coming to Stuttgart at a time like this! We have nothing to eat ourselves, we can't feed you too!"

I calmed her by telling her that I had only come for a day and had brought food to share with them. When I pulled a jar of butter out of my knapsack and set it on the table, she immediately calmed down, and we managed to share a fairly tolerable day together.

We talked a lot about Wolfram. We speculated that he had been taken prisoner by the Russians, which I dreaded even considering. He, the spoiled son of his parents, who had never experienced need and lack, would not bear the trials of imprisonment well. Wolfram had given me his hand in the worst of times, and now that bad times had come to Germany, I felt it was my duty to help his parents any way I could, even though they did not like or accept me. I again proposed to Ilse that she come with me to the countryside for a few weeks and added that she didn't have to take any food with her as we had enough in Sommenhardt.

Although I was much poorer than the Zimmermanns, I made sure that Ilse had a good time, and I saved the food I had previously received and fed her well. Ilse reminded me of Wolfram, and I forgave her for her youthful ignorance, remembering his wild love and affection. “Maybe they will appreciate me as a human being someday, if only for doing well by them!”, I thought and tried to be conciliatory toward them.

Ilse had also learned to sing from her father. Her voice, though small, was pleasant enough. But Papa Zimmermann considered her an extraordinary talent. He was infinitely proud of his musical children. Despite that, my compositions and singing found no appreciation with him.

“You are a wife now and must keep house, you have no time to think about singing!”, he said when I asked him to give me a few lessons. I noticed that they harbored some jealousy towards me as a musician, so I never brought up the topic with them again.

“When Wolfram comes back, it will be different!”, I thought and looked forward to hearing from my beloved. I couldn’t tolerate the thought that Wolfram might be dead. "I consoled myself, “Fate is never so impenetrably cruel! Wolfram certainly thought of me and tried to save himself for his family and little son, whom he had never had the chance to see!”

Alexander had already begun to walk and babble in German. He was a chubby, blond baby with big blue eyes and rosy cheeks and was admired by everyone who saw him. I was proud of my little son and could not wait to see him with his father. I was unceasingly following the news of the prisoners and stopping every soldier I met on my way back. But most of them were returning from America, England, and France. I could not find out anything about prisoners from Romania.

From time to time I met prisoners who had come to Germany from Russia. All of them were sick and exhausted by their impossible ordeal. Their faces, hands, and feet were swollen, and many of them were dying by the time they arrived back in their homeland.

Ilse told me, "You see! You see how your Russians treat people!"

I answered, "I know it's harsh, but it's not their fault. Russian people are kind and willing to share their last piece of bread with the hungry. But they are doomed to starve by their own government!"

Inna's in-laws: Richard Zimmermann, who was first violinist with the Stuttgart orchestra, and Clara Grieshaber Zimmermann, with Inna's daughter. Picture dated from after the war

I did not think about the possibility of returning home, even if Wolfram was not destined to return. I knew life in the Soviet Union all too well, and I knew that now, after the war, which had brought great destruction to Russia, life behind the iron curtain could not be better than it had been before the war. I saw pictures of destroyed Russian towns and cities, with poorly dressed Russian people in need, drowning in dirt and poverty even more than before the war.

I often thought of my mother and brother, of all my relatives and acquaintances, and my soul ached with longing and concern for them. I wish they didn't have to go on starving as they did in 1933!

At present, I did not feel any foundation under my feet. I had not yet settled in Germany and had not found a home here but had been uprooted from my native environment and thrown outward. Will I ever adapt to life in a foreign land? Maybe when Wolfram comes home! But weeks and months passed, and still no news of him arrived. I waited patiently, longing for him and picturing the possibility of our meeting as my greatest happiness on earth.

I was also very interested in what was going on in the Soviet Union after the war ended. So I sat by the radio every spare minute, listening with curiosity to Moscow's latest news.

As before, Moscow talked about the heroes of the Soviet Union who had now defeated fascism, about the fulfillment of plans for agriculture and industry, about the further development of the socialist economy, but not a word about what life looked like for the population now, after the war. This remained, as before, unclear to anyone.

I knew that in 1946 a new Supreme Soviet of the USSR was elected and that at its session a law on the "Five-year plan for the restoration and development of the national economy of the USSR for the years 1946-50" was passed. And I knew very well that this plan would bring only oppressive labor to the exhausted people of Russia but would not give them a better life.

Here is what the Russian-language newspaper “Posev” abroad said about the Fourth Five-Year Plan, with which I agreed: "The Soviet newspapers print the text of the law on the five-year plan, the speeches of the deputies who spoke in the debates on the law and devote several articles to this question. Thus, "Pravda" of 21.04.1946 contains the full text of the law and printed an editorial entitled "The New Stalin Five Year Plan". This article proves, in stereotyped phrases so familiar to a person who systematically reads the Soviet press, that the plan for the development of the national economy "is the great program of socialist construction, developed on the instructions of Comrade Stalin, the inspirer, and organizer of the world-historic victories of the Soviet Union", that the five-year plan is a historical document which defines both the main political tasks of the new plan and specific tasks in the growth of production and capital construction. “Pravda” writes that "the country already knows the majestic scope and high tempo of the past five-year plan, but the tasks of the new five-year plan surpass everything that was in the past... It must be concluded that from the population of the USSR the state will require an enormous exertion of effort, and probably also many hardships..."

Thus, the Russian people, who have not yet had time to recover from the hardships of war, are again exposed to many hardships! When will there be a rest from deprivation? Or will the Soviet people, after this new deprivation, be threatened with war again? So, from war to construction, from construction to war, will they spend their lives in deprivation?

Stalin's May Day order does not give hope for the possibility of permanent peace between the USSR and the capitalist countries. In it, Stalin stresses "that in the past war the whole world could be convinced of the power of the Soviet Union and the decency of its policy. However, in the interests of a peaceful socialist government, the USSR will not lose sight for a single moment of "the intrigues of international reaction and, full of hatred, its plans for a new war." The order speaks of the necessity of intensified development of military affairs and of the study of the military experience of the war which has ended, and of the further development of military science and technology. It speaks of the leading role played by the

USSR in the struggle against fascism for peace and security." (Neiss Zeitung)

I was particularly struck by the news from the Soviet Union that churches were being reopened there. But this, too, soon became clear to me. Having been in trouble during the war, people had turned back to God on their own, seeking His protection and help. The people began to grumble against the godless, who were responsible for the Lord God's anger at them and for sending such woe upon the Soviet country. And the government had to make concessions! But even here the government proved its "genius" mind and took the church under its control.

Here is what the Moscow newspaper *Izvestia* wrote in August 1946: "Stalin is one of the greatest defenders of the church," said Orthodox Archbishop Alexei during a visit to Vienna. Everyone who wishes to become a priest has the opportunity to do so. The position of the Communist Party toward the church is loyal." While in Vienna, the Archbishop visited Catholic Cardinal Innitzer and informed him of the actual situation of the Church in the USSR."

After the end of the war, Russian officers arrived in Germany and organized the return of the “Ost Arbeiter” workers taken by the Germans from their homeland to work in the Reich. I expected Radio Moscow to speak enthusiastically about the return of those who had fallen under the violence of fascism to the Soviet Union. But I was wrong. Moscow was silent on the matter.

These people had seen life abroad. They had seen things that didn’t correspond to the Soviet propaganda narrative about capitalist countries. Therefore, it is unlikely that they would simply be reintegrated easily back into Soviet society. They would certainly be put into "re-education" camps first. And when their heads were finally filled with communist ideology again to the point where they forget everything they had seen abroad, maybe they would be released. But would their loved ones and relatives still be there by then?!

When I thought of being extradited to the Russians and having to return, I could only shudder! I never wanted to go back to that horrible situation, to again experience the constant fear of being arrested "just in case." I never again wanted to experience the horrible Soviet poverty and political oppression. The worst thing about the USSR is that the people have no actual freedoms. The freedom of speech, freedom of the press, and freedom of the individual that the Soviet constitution speaks of are completely unenforceable in practice in the face of the all-powerful state.

I know that after seeing life abroad and having developed my worldview, I would be the unhappiest person if I ever returned, even if I were not condemned to a life in the gulag. And whether they placed me in a "re-education" camp or not, I could never forget what I had seen abroad and could never again believe that the Soviet Union was the happiest and most beautiful country on earth.

I had given up hope of returning home or becoming a famous actress forever and accepted my fate. The only thing I hoped for now was to finally escape this constant waiting and uncertainty.

Chapter 39 – Over the Final Mountain

After this momentous shift in the course of history, I felt as if my life also stood before a major shift. Since my waking dream, I had come to believe more firmly that fate would finally smile upon me after all my suffering and lead me to a newfound happiness. I still couldn't contact my family in Russia, as there was no postal service, and even if I could send a letter, my family probably wouldn't want to receive mail from someone likely branded a traitor. After the end of the war, I decided to settle in Stuttgart. The state had stopped paying me my allowance as a soldier's wife, and I had to look for a job. I rented a small room with a piano in a working-class neighborhood and began giving music lessons to beginners.

Alexander grew up and delighted me immensely with his amazing musicality for his age. One day I took him for a walk, and when we came home, Ilse was waiting for me in my room with a smiling face: "Inna, I have good news for you!" she said.

"Wolfram is alive!" I exclaimed, guessing the reason for her joy. She nodded her head and handed me a letter written in his hand. Tears of joy filled my eyes as I took it out of the envelope with a trembling hand.

"Dear Parents! I am alive and well in Salzburg, Austria..." I was overcome with gratitude as I read further about how he had made a dangerous and adventure-filled escape from imprisonment in Romania, pretended to be an Austrian and changing his last name to "Mildenburg," and made his way to Salzburg, an Austrian city on the border with Germany in the midst of the Alps.

To be able to return to Germany, he still needed his true German identification documents, as he had destroyed his old documents in Romania to disguise his identity.

Now I stood facing a seemingly impossible task: I had to get my husband his papers without compromising him, as Austria was still occupied by Soviet authorities. Should they intercept his papers and arrest him, he stood a good chance of being deported to Siberia.

What was I to do? It wasn't possible to send a registered letter, and a normal letter would take weeks to arrive and ran the risk of being opened and read by Soviet censors. As the border itself was closed and heavily guarded, only very few travelers and known border-crossers who lived in one country and worked in the other were allowed across. I didn't want to trust this letter to a stranger, either. How easily Wolfram's papers could be lost or confiscated.

I paced the room as if in a dream, listening to every knock and rustle. It seemed to me that he was close to me and that he was about to knock on my door.

After much serious consideration, I decided to take the documents to Wolfram myself. I was out of patience, and I began to pack for the border and Salzburg. Somehow, I had to get to Wolfram and get him back into Germany. I didn't quite know exactly how I would do it, but I knew there had to be a way, and I was going to do everything to reunite what family I had left or die trying. "If the mountain does not go to Mohammed, Mohammed goes to the mountain!" an Armenian proverb says – and I was determined to go to the mountain.

I placed Alexander back in the care of Minamama and returned to Stuttgart to retrieve Wolfram's documents from his parents and also to request a visa to travel abroad from the American authorities. The Americans were unable to issue me a travel permit, as they had no jurisdiction over Austria. Wolfram's parents, on the other hand, were unexpectedly helpful, and retrieved his civilian identification card and handed it to me along with a local residency document. With that I went to the Stuttgart station and got on a train that would take me clear across southern Germany to the border town of Freilassing, which lies directly across from Salzburg, Austria in the Alps.

On the way, I met some Russian immigrants from Munich, who offered to let me stay with them for the night. I had to change trains in Munich anyway and would have had to wait all night at the train station, so I willingly accepted their offer. I told them of my intention to find my husband in Austria.

"How long has it been since you last saw your husband?" One asked me.

"Two years."

"I wish you luck, but your husband may have changed a great deal in that time. Does he even know that you are coming to see him?"

"No. I want to surprise him. That's the only way I'll know if he is still serious about us, about our marriage."

"You shouldn't. If I were you, I would at least get a hold of him first and allow him time to prepare for this reunion."

"But why? If he loves me, he will be delighted to see me. Besides, there was no way to reliably contact him."

"And what if he doesn't love you anymore, what then?"

"Then...? It can't be! That would be terrible!"

"Well, may God bless you, but let me say that in life things usually turn out differently than one expects!"

That night I could not sleep, the thought of "what if?" kept me awake. At seven o'clock in the morning, I boarded the train. It was about one o'clock in the afternoon when I arrived at Freilassing, on the German-Austrian border. I went straight to the border crossing and begged an American soldier to let me through into Salzburg, if only for a few hours. But that proved impossible.

I next tried my luck with the German border authority, who turned a deaf ear, and strictly warned me not to try to cross illegally as I could be arrested or even killed in the attempt. Dispirited, I went around and spoke with local people, asking those living near the border for help, but they mostly remained silent for fear of arrest.

Finally, after three days of searching in vain, I met a young woman whose job took her across the border each day. I told her about my effort to reach my husband, and this sympathetic soul revealed that there was a spot where the border was unguarded high in the Alps at a point known as "Das Steinerne Meer" - or the Sea of Rock. To get there, she continued, I would have to take a path up from the small village of St. Bartholomä, an isolated village on the Konigssee, a long, deep, narrow glacial lake surrounded by steep mountains. She told me how to get there, and also promised to visit Wolfram in Salzburg and relay my message that I would meet him at the pass in two days.

With our plan in place, there was no turning back: Without further thought, I traveled by train to the northern end of the lake and boarded a long, narrow rowboat across the Konigssee to the tiny village of St. Bartholomä. I was the only passenger and sat with the rower and rudder man dressed in their traditional Bavarian tracht. The water was crystal clear, deep and cold. Looking up at the beautiful snow-covered mountain peaks sticking out above a thin, swirling fog, I wondered how on earth I would be able to get across into Austria.

The village itself was nestled upon a small spit of flat land sticking out into the lake amidst a canyon of vertical rock faces covered with trees at their base. It consisted of no more than half-a-dozen houses and a picturesque church which stood right on the lake's edge. The end of the church facing the lake consisted of short

Above – the church in St. Bartholomä

white cylindrical chambers clustered together and connected by a central nave to the rest of the church. Each cylinder was topped with a reddish onion-shaped cupola and the church itself was crowned with two smaller cylindrical steeples topped with red mini-cupolas and a cross. It reminded me a little of a Russian church, and seemed a good omen.

When I asked people in St. Bartholomä where the path to the pass over "Das " was, the looked at me in wonderment. I certainly did not look like a mountain climber. I had no proper boots or kit of any kind and no backpack for supplies. All I had on was a silk skirt and a light blouse. My feet were in dainty shoes with relatively high heels. The only thing I had with me was a small leather suitcase. I had no idea about the conditions in the mountains and how difficult the trek would be.

The locals told me in no uncertain terms: "You will never be able to make it across the mountains like that, dear girl. You will certainly fall off the edge in the fog!"

But having come so far through so much adversity, there was no way I was turning back. "My husband needs his documents and I'm going to take them to him!"

With that I began my completely unconventional trek up the mountains. Spiritually alone, I pushed ever farther upwards. Only rarely did anyone pass me. They mostly looked at me as if I were crazy. In the first hours of the climb, I became terribly hot from the exertion. My heart raced and I was short of breath. But little by little I was able to regain my calm in the pure, light mountain air, and began to adjust to this new environment. Quickly and doggedly, I climbed further up the increasingly steep slope. I knew I had to reach a small mountain hut that lay along the way before nightfall, which locals had recommended I spend the night at.

And thank God, before the evening sun disappeared behind the mountains, and as the peaks were already beginning to glow in the setting sun, I caught site of the shelter. The hut lay in the midst of a magnificent mountain chain covered in various mountain flowers and plants of all different glorious colors. I looked out across the distance, and not a single human soul was to be seen far and wide. Longingly, I looked up to the top of the mountain. There, glowing in the sun's evening rays, lay the mountain pass, blanketed in white snow over which I had to cross the next day when the sun rose. When I lay down on a thin bed of straw on the hard floor of the hut, I wasn't able to shut my eyes the entire night. My feet were terribly sore, and I was very afraid that I might not be able to make it.

But as soon as the following day dawned, I continued my climb undeterred. By and by the last plant life disappeared from around me. Before me lay the large, dead "Steinerne Meer" – a harsh and imposing mountain range. Without looking back, I stove further upwards and soon came to an outstretched sea of snow, where the path was no longer visible.

With an anxious heart, I crossed myself three times over the chest in the Russian tradition and then went through the snow, at times sinking up to my knees. Still, I was always able to find my way back to the trail markings on the individual rock faces. Despite the streaming sunlight, it was quite cool at this elevation. My shoes and stockings were soon completely drenched and ripped and the high heels on my shoes were no longer visible. But my objective, the mountain cap, still lay off in the distance.

Above: The Steinerne Meer

A peculiar feeling came over me suddenly in the face of this barren and lonely sea of stone. I would have gladly run as fast as possible back down the mountain, but I knew, that my husband had been informed of my trek and was waiting for me on the other side of the pass. That gave me strength and courage for the last, most dangerous part of my journey, that seemed to grow ever more treacherous, and I was soon forced to tie my small leather suitcase to my belt so I could have both hands free to grab hold of the raw, damp rock face.

At one particularly difficult point near the edge of a cliff, I saw a large cross of Our Lord and Savior. I embraced this holy symbol with both arms and cried out to God. Then I gathered my last strength and as I calmly and surely continued my climb, it became so effortless and light, that I soon reached the final ridge. But before I stood at the top of the pass, I suddenly spotted a slender, rugged male figure in the distance rushing towards me, arms outstretched.

And then I found myself in the embrace of my beloved, who had come to meet my up the other side of the mountain. He picked me up and carried me across the pass like a treasure into Austria, until the path became wide and safe. Then he put me down on my feet and embraced me again. I knew at that moment, that I had not taken this difficult path in vain.

Love had united us, a Russian and a German, atop the serene mountains of the Alps.

Epilogue

As we walked through Salzburg to Wolfram's flat, clouds covered the sky and it started to drizzle with a little cold rain. We came to an old building halfway up a steep road, and into a small room that served as his living quarters.

A bed, a small music stand, and a coat rack occupied the entire space. On the nightstand stood a framed photograph. "He kept my picture!" I thought happily. But as I came closer, I noticed, to my horror another woman's likeness. I picked up the photo and sat down on the bed. It was a young brunette with big black eyes and a smiling face. There was no caption on the other side. "Isn't he faithful to me!" I thought, wincing with fear.

Unmoving, I sat on his bed and stared into this rival's face. The gray, bleak memories of the past two and a half years flashed through my mind. During that time, I thought about him day-and-night incessantly. Not one step was taken without thinking about how he would look at it. For his sake, I even sacrificed my love of the Russian language and spoke only German to Alexander. For his sake I stayed at home and paid no attention to the men who repeatedly showed interest in me. For his sake, I risked my life to cross the Alps alone. I loved him, loved him deeply and faithfully, as only a young Russian woman can love!

Time seemed to grind to a halt, and it felt like I was glued to his bed. I didn't want to think about anything else. The best thing would have been to freeze like this and remain motionless forever. "Maybe it's not so terrible, we should discuss it first," I thought, "But what if he does love that black-eyed stranger? Then it would have been better if I had fallen from the mountainside crossing the Alps! And little Alexander, who would replace his mother?"

"Who is this woman?" I finally asked Wolfram pointing at the picture of the stranger.

"That...? She's a singer!"

"Do you love her?"

"Nonsense! She's just a colleague of mine."

"And that's why she's at the head of your bed?"

Wolfram wasn't happy with that question:

"You have just gotten here and you're already getting jealous. My father was right when he told me that artists should not marry!"

"No, Wolfram! I was only asking!

This kind of woke Wolfram up, and he began to caress me. But how different these caresses were from those in Vienna. It seemed to me that Wolfram was not doing it of his own free will, but as if he were performing some unpleasant duty.

Wolfram's appearance had also changed greatly. Now, instead of his summer uniform, he was wearing a suit that was not tailored to his height and did not look good. The cloak and jacket had buttons missing, and the collar of his shirt was not looking fresh. He looked like a down-and-out slovenly bachelor and gave no impression of being an entertainer at all.

I took a picture of my chubby little son out of my purse and placed it over the top of the black-eyed woman. Alexander looked back at me with his innocent, laughing baby eyes.

At that moment I felt an unbearable longing for my son. "What is he doing there without his mother? I will come back to you soon, my dear little angel, and bring your daddy home. Your father must leave everything here for you, my child, and I am ready to forgive him the greatest crime for you."

I decided to tell Wolfram everything I had experienced and to persuade him to leave everything and return to Stuttgart. Calmed by this thought, I took out a small mirror and cleaned myself up.

I stood up and hugged him and kissed him hard on the lips. "Wolfram, my darling, dear! At last, I can hold you again!" I whispered, forgetting all fear at that moment. He stood motionless.

"Why won't you kiss me? You don't seem to be happy at all!" I said and dropped my hands in disappointment.

Suddenly his eyes opened wide, and he took the frame in his hands and began to examine Alexander's image.

"Is that our child?" he asked, smiling, "What a wonderful baby!"

I began to tell him all the details about life with Minimama, about our little boy, and about the relationship that his family and I had established during the time he had been away.

"Wolfram, you have a family that cannot live without you. I'll do everything for you and our son so we can be happy together!" I promised.

"I can't make up my mind to leave Austria so suddenly. If I go home now, I will never get out of there again. After all, we lost the war!"

But I disagreed with him and proved to him that the most important thing in life is to have a loving, caring friend, and drew him the most beautiful pictures of our future happiness. Finally, I managed to change his mind, and the next day we determined to sneak back across the border into Germany.

Afterword

I met Inna for the first time at the birthday party of her youngest daughter, Cornelia, in the little German village of Weissenbrunn. I'd met Cornelia in Nuremberg, near where I was stationed in the Army at the time, and she had been kind enough to invite me. I was the first to arrive, and was ushered in by Inna, who was preparing the birthday meal. In our short conversation before the other guests arrived, I learned the first details of the amazing story recorded in this book. I learned a great deal more about it over the years, as Inna eventually became my mother-in-law. As it happened, I didn't marry Cornelia, but her older sister, Sylvia. She had arrived with an inconvenient boyfriend, and Inna's husband, Wolfram, loved to tell the story of how I had asked him in my clumsy German, "Muss das sein?" *(Does that have to be?)* Of course, I'd been trying to come up with something more subtle to find out if they were going steady, but Wolfram never let me live it down.

A publicity still of Wulfram Zimmerman, in costume as Figaro.

When I met them, Inna and Wolfram were a sedate, middle-aged couple. He was a retired opera singer who still occasionally appeared on stage as a guest performer, and she had become successful voice teacher, numbering among her students some who performed at the Metropolitan Opera. They lived in a lovely house on the slope of Moritzberg (Moritz Mountain) overlooking Weissenbrunn. Their relationship had not always been so harmonious. After the dramatic reunion on the mountaintop described in the last chapter of the book, they had crossed back into Germany and returned to Stuttgart. Wolfram managed to secure a place as a lead singer for the Stuttgart opera and, as a handsome and charming star, had no difficulty attracting female admirers. The two eventually divorced, but somehow the bond between them endured. In time they reunited, renewed their marriage vows, and moved to Graz, Austria, where Wolfram accepted a role as lead singer. Sylvia has many fond memories of growing up in Graz. Eventually, they moved to Nuremberg, and built the house where I eventually met them in Weissenbrunn.

With the help of the Red Cross, Inna was finally able to reestablish relations with her family in the Soviet Union. These included the son of one of her cousins, Alexander Grinfeldt, and his wife, Marina. Both were successful scientists at an institute in St. Petersburg. However, with the fall of the Soviet Union, they were both out of a job, and with two daughters to support, their situation became increasingly desperate. Eventually, Inna managed to bring them to Germany, and provided shelter for them in her home until they were able to support themselves again.

After Sylvia and I were married in Weissenbrunn and moved to America, Inna visited us a couple of times. She was a wonderful mother-in-law, and she and Wolfram were fascinating playmates for their grandchildren. I found her to be very much the kind of person you'd expect after reading her book – strong, assertive, considerate, and kind. Her last years were free of the traumatic experiences of her early life, and she passed away quietly a few years after reaching her 90th birthday.

CPSIA information can be obtained
at www.ICGtesting.com
Printed in the USA
LVHW011623220622
721765LV00016B/1584

9 780578 291246